THIS IS MY
REAL NAME

THIS IS MY REAL NAME

A STRIPPER'S MEMOIR

CID V BRUNET

ARSENAL PULP PRESS
VANCOUVER

THIS IS MY REAL NAME
Copyright © 2021 by Cid V Brunet

ARSENAL PULP PRESS
Suite 202 – 211 East Georgia St.
Vancouver, BC V6A 1Z6
Canada
arsenalpulp.com

The publisher gratefully acknowledges the support of the Canada Council for the Arts and the British Columbia Arts Council for its publishing program, and the Government of Canada, and the Government of British Columbia (through the Book Publishing Tax Credit Program), for its publishing activities.

Arsenal Pulp Press acknowledges the xʷməθkʷəy̓əm (Musqueam), Sḵwx̱wú7mesh (Squamish), and səl̓ilwətaʔɬ (Tsleil-Waututh) Nations, custodians of the traditional, ancestral, and unceded territories where our office is located. We pay respect to their histories, traditions, and continuous living cultures and commit to accountability, respectful relations, and friendship.

Cover and text design by Jazmin Welch
Cover art by Jazmin Welch
Edited by Shirarose Wilensky
Proofread by Alison Strobel

Printed and bound in Canada

Library and Archives Canada Cataloguing in Publication:
Title: This is my real name : a stripper's memoir / Cid V Brunet.
Names: Brunet, Cid V, author.
Identifiers: Canadiana (print) 20210196661 | Canadiana (ebook) 2021019667X | ISBN 9781551528588 (softcover) | ISBN 9781551528595 (HTML)
Subjects: LCSH: Brunet, Cid V. | LCSH: Stripteasers—Canada—Biography. | LCSH: Sex workers—Canada—Biography. | LCSH: Prostitution—Canada. | LCGFT: Autobiographies.
Classification: LCC HQ148 .B78 2021 | DDC 306.74/2092—dc23

For every sex worker, in love and rage

CONTENTS

PROLOGUE

The VIP room is a dark maze of couches and loveseats closed off from the rest of the club. Pop music drowns out loud bass from the main-stage. Red, blue, green polka dots swirl from a disco ball, illuminating strippers performing moves I hope to copy. I lead my guy to a black leather couch in the back corner.

We sit side by side, thighs touching, while we wait for a new song.

"Is this really your first day?" he asks.

"First day, first dance."

The initial two guys I'd approached out on the floor were not inter-ested. So when this third one pulled out a chair and ordered me a drink, I ended up sitting with him for too long. I listened to him talk about his three kids, his job as a millwright, and his love of ice fishing, but I shied away from the big question. Like playground double Dutch, I was waiting for the right moment to jump in.

Finally, I said it: "Do-you-wanna-dance?"

"Thought you'd never ask."

The song switches to one by Rihanna, a favourite at queer dance parties. I stand and square my body in front of the guy, roll my hips around my spine, run my hands over my bra, knock the strap off one shoulder. In the other corner I see a dancer, like a bird of paradise. Effortlessly, she makes her round butt quiver and shake, a movement that seems cleft from the rest of her body. I try to copy her but don't understand what muscles to use. Instead, I take a handful of my ass and shake.

Tired of being teased, the guy grabs my hips and pulls me off balance and onto his lap. He wants friction. While he struggles with the clasp of my bra, I feel a flicker of fear. It closes my throat, flushes my cheeks. I want to stay in this before-moment and wildly hope that he never gets it open.

He drops my bra onto the carpet and begins fondling my breasts, his callused fingers roughly massaging my soft nipples. And it's too much. Too much sensation. I collapse slightly, trying to pull my chest inside my rib cage, out of reach. I hate the vague arousal stemming from my dumb body, the skin-to-skin contact that assumes I have a new lover. I suppress revulsion. Push it into the pit of my stomach and hold it there. This can be fine.

I grind my hips on the client's lap. Denim chafes the tender skin of my thighs, but I want this: sandpaper instead of silk. I squirm to avoid his zipper, button, and belt buckle as his erection stiffens. His hands travel freely over my skin, his breath quick and hungry. Passion weakens him and I am not afraid. I am a collection of helium balloons attached by ribbons to my spine. I float up, bobbing safely against the ceiling.

PART 1:
BABY STRIPPER

CHAPTER 1:
THE ROYAL

**THE ROYAL
SOUTHERN ONTARIO**

The Royal is a heritage mansion set against highways and overpasses. Boarded-up windows, black metal doors, a sign reading *Gentleman's Club*. My friend Izzy and I hold hands for courage, before walking past two statues of lions guarding the front door.

Inside, a neon pin-up swings her foot in time to the chorus of a song by the Weeknd, the one about trading bodies for fame. Metal chairs, round tables, abandoned beer bottles, and a stage with a single dancer, moving slowly. Under the black lights her pale outfit is a jellyfish pulsing through an aquarium. Lampposts topped by red globes bounce blood-shot light off mirrors covering every wall. The few patrons split their attention between the stage and the hockey game on TV.

The only other strip club I've ever been to was Café Cléopâtre in Montreal. The stripper who danced at my table had a blue diamond tattooed across her generously enhanced chest. Her perfection is burned into my memory. As I adjust to the dim interior of the Royal, every girl seems equally magnificent.

"You the girls who called?" A heavy-set, bald man juts his chin at us from behind the bar.

"Yes, we've heard good things about this place," I say.

"I'm Bruce, the manager." He doesn't shake our hands. "You danced before?" He has the body of an aged football player and tiny, closely spaced eyes.

"We took a pole fitness class," Izzy lies.

"You can give it a try, but listen, to make money you have to spend. Get your nails done and"—he glares at us—"fix your hair."

Women arrive wearing sweatpants and fuzzy boots, carrying bulging duffle bags. Some get a nod or a wave from the boss, others, the same cold gaze as us.

"Go see the DJ. He'll tell ya the rules."

Girls jostle around the DJ's booth, shouting their names to him. The set list reads like poetry: Aryanna, Gucci, Diamond, Katalina, Trixie, Caramel, Destiny. We try to introduce ourselves, but an amazon cuts in, folds cash into the DJ's palm, and hugs him, boobs pressed up under his chin. "Same songs as always," she says.

"Sign these," he says, finally noticing us. "And I'll need to see some ID." The rules he hands us are printed askew on the page from so much photocopying: no outside food or drink, no gang colours, stage fees paid before you begin your shift.

"No drinking?" Izzy asks about an all-caps rule. We just saw three girls buying each other tequila at the bar.

"Does it say that?" He looks amused. "What are your stage names?"

"Courtney," Izzy says. It reminds me of both Love and Kardashian, a perfect blend of punk rock and rich girl. I cast around frantically—why didn't I give this more thought? Who do I want to be?

"Michelle," I say, conjuring Michelle Tea's tough, street-smart protagonist in *Rent Girl.* I imagine her smoking a cigarette in a silk slip.

The DJ gives us a brief tour, assuming we've worked at other clubs before. "The VIP is back there," he says, indicating an ominous doorway winged with red velvet curtains. Izzy and I stay quiet.

"Tell me your three stage songs once you're dressed," he says and leaves us beside a descending staircase covered in carpet shredded by stilettos.

In the changing room, a mirror-backed counter hugs the wall, ending at a bank of coin lockers. The counter is crowded with girls, makeup, hair products, styling implements, and outfits. No one makes space for us, so Izzy and I check our reflections in full-length mirrors on the opposite wall. Frosted designs of Art Nouveau water bearers overlaid on the mirror make it difficult for us to see ourselves.

This is the first time since getting into anarchism, queerness, and punk that I've tried to pass as conventionally attractive. Izzy, despite her green mohawk and hand-poked tattoos, is far ahead of me. She remains invested in femininity, watching makeup tutorials, wearing perfume and lingerie.

We strip down. Nakedness feels better than the Limp Wrist T-shirt, now damp with nervous sweat, that I borrowed from my trans-masculine partner, Jace. I sort through the reusable shopping bag of supplies I brought just in case they hired us: a well-worn pink bra and thong, drugstore tinted lip balm, scuffed and chunky thrift store heels.

"What about my hair?" I ask.

"Go with it," Izzy says. "Dance to 'Body Work.'"

"Tegan and Sara are not going to make me look less gay."

"Men love gay women," she says.

"They only like them in threesomes. How do we get men to pay for an illusion when they could go out and buy the real thing?"

"I've never done this either," Izzy says. "But I think if they're at a strip club, they know they're paying for a fantasy."

"A fantasy that includes a girl with a mullet comb-over?"

She laughs. "You'll fix it once we get money."

Behind me, a dancer slices on eyeliner and pastes on lashes, long and delicate as moth wings. I want her skills, her confidence, her body. So attracted to her and the other dancers that I avert my eyes.

"Can I borrow some?" I ask about the golden bottle of perfume nesting in Izzy's gym bag.

"You can have it," she says.

I spritz myself with lychee and vanilla, masking my fear, and my desire.

Adrenalin shoots through both of us when we come upstairs in bras and G-strings for our first shift. Air conditioning brushes my lower back and rustles the soft hairs at the tops of my thighs. I hadn't shaved my legs or armpits in years, and sweat makes them burn. But it isn't my exposed skin that scares me; it's how ordinary I look compared to the other girls. Each is a complete package of excellence with her own unique style. I'm embarrassed that I had assumed stripping was simply showing up and getting naked.

Izzy and I stay away from the girls hugging and catching up at the bar, and the other ones standing apart, stiff backed, stonewalling an opposing clique. A client pulls out a chair for a dancer who was doing a slow lap of the floor. She alights, half-sitting on her tucked shin.

"Which table should we approach? What should we say?" Izzy asks.

"We need to chat them up until we convince them to go for a dance."

"But how?"

"Trial and error? Think how boring and stupid men are."

"You sound like Jace," Izzy says. Jace and I have started calling ourselves queer separatists. We feel entitled to take anything we want from the straight world.

"Men created patriarchy," I say. "They literally owe us. Besides, I'm less scared of the men than the girls."

"I know, why do they hate us?" Izzy, too, feels the heat radiating from the long judgmental stares of the other dancers.

We approach a table of two middle-aged beer drinkers with all the confidence we can muster. Surprisingly, my near nakedness didn't bother me. I am quite comfortable talking to strangers in my underwear.

"So, where are you from?" asks my guy, battling to maintain eye contact.

"The East Coast originally, but I came here for school and liked it so much I decided to stay."

"What did you study?" He sneaks a look at Izzy, engaged in an equally bland conversation with his buddy.

I heard it takes 100 milliseconds to decide if someone is attractive. I run my triangle-shaped pendant along its chain, drawing his attention to my neck and collarbone. "Actually, I have a university degree in art history." I chose this subject assuming I know more about it than him. I did enjoy it—before I dropped out.

"What can you do with a degree in that?"

The conversation is beginning to feel like a job interview, decidedly unsexy. Channelling ditzy girls in movies, I lean toward him, elbows on the table, and squeeze my boobs together. "It's tough, for sure. That's why I'm working here in the meantime."

"Do you girls know each other in real life?" asks Izzy's guy. Sunglasses tan, Budweiser baseball cap.

"We're friends," I reply.

"Best friends," Izzy corrects. Putting her arm around me, her sweat rubbing off on my shoulder, she asks *the* question: "Do you guys want to come for a double dance?"

I freeze, expecting laughter, rejection, but instead they squirm. "Actually, we're waiting for Caramel and Katalina."

We jump up and two angry dancers swoop in to replace us.

"That was rude," I complain to Izzy. "They should have told us right off they were waiting for other girls. There must be tricks to this, ways to know if we're wasting our time."

I've been romanticizing sex work for a long time, reading everything I could get by dominatrices, escorts, and massage providers. I drew inspiration from STAR to Stonewall, from queer history that was pioneered by trans women of colour. I thought my fascination with the industry would have given me more confidence and prevented this floundering. What would Michelle Tea do now? I imagine her shrugging; *Don't take rejection personally*, she would say from under a dark curtain of bangs, *keep going.*

I look around the room—no more tables of two.

"Let's split up," I suggest.

★ ★ ★

After my first lap dance the client shakes my hand formally, pays me, and leaves unceremoniously. I reverently tuck my cash into a borrowed purse as if I'm pressing rose petals. Using the wall, I steady my wobbling ankles to make it back to the main floor. Izzy gives me a thumbs-up on her way into the VIP, a hulking man in tow.

I sink onto a chair at the nearest table, massage cramped arches and wiggling blistered toes. I wonder if I'm a whore now. I don't feel any different, but there is a sense of having crossed over. Even out of breath and overwhelmed, I can taste power.

★ ★ ★

"So you're a lesbian?" The next guy I sit with says the word like it's dirty.

"I think some men are hot," I tell him.

He elbows me. "Sure you do. I see the way you watch the girls onstage like you're a dude."

He's not wrong. I can't tear my eyes away from the dancers spinning around the pole and crawling across the stage. It's nearing midnight and the club's sexual energy is amplified each time a new girl takes the stage.

The guy and I sit in silence for half a song, an irrecoverable lull. Can I just stand up and leave?

He turns to me. "You're too shy to work here," he says. "I'm in sales—you need to work on your pitch. Always be closing. You're fresh meat, so I'm going to help you out. Let's go in the back and I'll give you some tips on how to work a room, how to tell what guys have money."

In the VIP he won't let me dance. He wants me to sit on his lap, face to face, and take mental notes. "I would make a million dollars stripping if I was a girl," he says. "It would be easy."

I get in the occasional "Wow, that's a great idea," or "You're totally right," while, with each additional song, I recalculate the escalating cost he is willing to pay to have his ego stroked.

★ ★ ★

Behind the stage, vaguely reflected in the hallway mirror, I appear vampiric. Izzy already did her first stage show, and although she didn't do any of the pole tricks the other girls have mastered, her languid movements made her performance very sensual. She'd practised, and I wish I'd done the same.

My song begins with its familiar synthesized beats. I do a ten-second countdown before making my entrance. How many drinks have I had? Four? Men kept offering and I'm spinning. I teeter on my heels, catch the wall, hold myself in the doorway, and look out. All I can see is the reflective pole at centre stage, ringed by bright lights. I step out and the floor changes from carpet to linoleum. It feels like tiptoeing on ice. I latch onto the pole, which is warm from friction, slippery with body lotion. With no idea what to do next, I pose around the pole, killing time. I don't know how to spin, and I'm too afraid to try. Lyrics about angels crying. I might cry if not for this straight-up panic. I'm not flexible enough to do sexy deep bends and I can't shake my butt. Barely past the first chorus, I've done every move I can think of. It feels like when I was seven, awkward in a red-and-white tutu, laughed at by my classmates' parents. Unable to stay present, I switch into a completely placid mental state of zero gravity, floating out the remainder of my three songs in muted sounds and lights, as if from behind the thick windows of a spaceship.

When it's over Izzy finds me at the bar and touches my shoulder. My entire body shivers as I return to myself.

★ ★ ★

In the VIP, girls play with their hair, roll their hips, arch their backs. They trail fingers over their own faces and necks and touch their client's chests, flowing from one move to the next, concealing routine in steamy, primal seductiveness. My best is a choppy imitation. Between songs I am sweaty from overcompensating. My client must be wishing he'd taken the girl on the couch across from us instead; she moves like water. Still sitting on his lap, I down my vodka cranberry. Ice slides from the glass and rains onto my chest and stomach. The cold slap makes me realize how fast I'm going, how out of control.

"Do you want another song?" I ask.

"Keep going!"

★ ★ ★

Although Izzy and I originally intended to work arm in arm, we barely see each other in the final two hours. As it gets louder and busier, girls stop chatting and begin to hustle hard. I watch them approach tables fearlessly, a full-frontal attack of hair, tits, and ass, coupled with intimidating laughter and luxurious charm. Their energy casts a spell over the whole club that allows any guy who walks in off the street to become a client. Men are hypnotized, their wallets opening and closing like gills.

Following the examples around me, I refuse to continue talking after a lap dance is over, instead pushing myself to go sit with the next stranger. Surprisingly, most clients overlook my shortcomings, aroused by getting to "pop my cherry" as the new girl. It feels slutty, moving quickly from one sexual encounter to the next, constantly circling between the floor and the VIP, especially when I still feel the handprints from the last man, smell his cologne on my skin. But the next man doesn't mind.

When the bar closes, Izzy and I hail a cab and count our money in the back seat.

"The bakery pays above minimum wage and this is still more than I make in three days," she says.

I'd been looking for a way out of working exploitative, underpaid kitchen jobs when I found a roofing company hiring on Craigslist. The sketchy boss didn't think a girl without experience could do the job, but he was desperate. For two weeks, I woke at dawn and forced myself into a co-worker's dirty work truck, classic rock blaring.

At the site, I cut asphalt shingles with a hooked X-acto knife, stacked bundles of them on my shoulder, and carried the load up forty-foot ladders perched against the sides of half-finished mansions. It was dangerous, high-speed work with no breaks except for coffee, which, being the only woman, I fetched.

In the end, the boss said he didn't need me anymore and gave me a paycheque that covered all my expenses and a little extra. The cheque bounced.

I lean back in the cab and recount the cash in my hand. Shocked into silence by making my rent in five hours.

This changes everything.

"They said we can come back whenever we want," Izzy says. "Just sign in before nine."

The night's clients have already blurred into a collective of mostly white, middle-aged men. Creepy, rude, weird, normal, nice—all of it has ceased to matter. Memories of them wick off my skin into the night air whipping through the open windows.

"Okay," I say. "Tomorrow."

CHAPTER 2: PLEASERS

THE ROYAL
SOUTHERN ONTARIO

After we do a few shifts together, Izzy bails for the night, so I go to the Royal alone. A guy waves for me to come over to a table where he sits with his friend and a stripper I don't know. I hesitate, since this is dangerously close to breaking a cardinal rule: do not approach a table already occupied by another girl unless explicitly invited by her or an unoccupied man. Many unspoken codes of conduct are maintained by the threat of girl-on-girl violence. Girls who transgress against other girls get dressed in the manager's office at the end of the night, terrified to enter the changing room. I don't want to constantly look over my shoulder, so I scan social cues, afraid to break rules I don't know about.

I make the guy wave and point to me a few times, showing the other dancer that I've been summoned, that I'm not trying to poach from her table.

When I sit, she snaps, "You baby strippers, I swear. Where's your rag?"

"My what?"

She stands and picks up a bandana that she's placed between herself and her chair, waves it in my face. "You don't want to sit your naked self on these seats, or on some of these men. Not these guys, they're clean," she reassures the two at her table. "But you'll get nasty if you don't protect yourself."

Her guy laughs. "Cooties!"

"I'll get one tomorrow," I say, but the girl is already smoothing her handkerchief back onto the chair before refocusing on her client.

I don't wait long before bringing my guy to the VIP.

"These are perfect Cs," he says as soon as I've taken off my bra. "Not too big, not too small, exactly a handful."

Looking down at my breasts cupped in his hands, I realize I've never thought of them as an asset. As a young feminist I refused to wear bras under my hippie sundresses, yet I worried my breasts were too large to be uncontained, that their size made me immodest. Working on construction sites, I hid them under sports bras and baggy sweaters, not wanting to remind my male co-workers that I was a girl they could hit on. My breasts never fit into my ideal queer aesthetic either. I wanted to look bony, sulky, like Shane from *The L Word.* For special occasions I would bind them with a Tensor bandage, tightening it around my ribs, restricting my breathing until my T-shirt fell thrillingly flat down my chest.

"They're so perky and firm," the client continues. "You've got the best set of natural tits in this place."

"Isn't that subjective? I like all kinds," I say, and then immediately regret responding honestly, as he lectures me on subpar forms: from "bee stings" to "rock-hard fakes," defective shapes, inconsistent sizes, unattractive nipples.

"You're truly blessed," he concludes. "These puppies are your best feature."

★ ★ ★

I've been working a few weeks, and the other girls have stopped giving me death stares after realizing I'm not an especially good hustler and

I'm not trying to steal their customers. Sometimes curious or bored girls chat with me in terse, cautiously friendly exchanges, but most ignore me.

Girls who are good at the hustle take five minutes or less per table, and if they haven't hooked a man by then, they keep going. Meanwhile, I'm trying to figure out how to leave this drawn-out conversation with a prison guard.

"But *why* would you do this to yourself?" he asks again, dissatisfied with the stock response: "I'm stripping my way through school." He doesn't understand how any woman could debase herself so completely, sees me as subhuman.

I don't owe him shit, but he makes me nervous. "Money, obviously," I say.

"I guess it's okay to be greedy when you're young," he sneers.

I hate him and everything he stands for. Dancing for him would feel degrading, but I struggle to just get up and leave. Why do I care about having good table manners with a man who locks other human beings in cages? Then I realize it's because I'm afraid of being rude to a man.

But this is work, and he's not paying.

I channel all my contempt into a curt "Bye," but as I walk away, I fight the urge to shoulder-check.

★ ★ ★

The club always feels like midnight. Shifts run together indistinguishably. I begin a journal, without chronology or context. Just scraps of client dialogue like:

"Can I call you Annie? It's my brother's wife's name."

"You should be at home having babies. That's your real job."

"All men cheat."

★ ★ ★

This client is contaminating me. He's unwashed, sweaty, and he keeps licking his lips. I move his hands away as they repeatedly try to snake between my legs. And I have to push him back as he puckers, trying to catch a nipple in his mouth. He doesn't care that I've dropped my friendly persona, or that I've asked him to stop multiple times. He wants to get his money's worth.

Frank Ocean is singing about novocaine. I use the song's syllables to count time. I tell myself I have to make it one full song, or else this guy can claim I ripped him off, forcing me to fight for my twenty dollars and possibly involving the bouncer.

I used to be a dish pig at a fancy restaurant. One time, in peak summer, I was changing garbage cans and found the bottom of one lined with a slick, wriggling pile of maggots and the smell of rotting meat. I took the can to the parking lot and sprayed out the creatures with a hose. Then stuck my arm, pit-deep, into the can to scrub off the leftover slime. At least at the club I'm paid by the song and tipped in cash.

★ ★ ★

After following me to a couch in the VIP, a client says, "I don't know how you girls walk in heels that high."

"These are so much better than my last pair," I say, and cross my foot over my knee so we can both admire my new stilettos. "They fell apart after a couple nights, but these are Pleasers, basically the steel-toed boot for strippers."

I'd taken a stack of cash to the mall. Bought lipstick, nail polish, and mascara. I was repulsed by a rack of cheap clutches, garish and ugly. I chose a plastic alligator-skin wallet to carry on shift simply because it was the furthest away from my own taste. Then I walked around La Senza choosing lingerie based, for the first time, not on what was on sale but on what looked the fanciest. Picked some lacy push-ups and waited uncomfortably while the attendant wrapped them in pink paper. I wished she'd hurry up in case someone realized I'd balanced out the cost of the expensive bras by layering on as many thongs and G-strings as I could fit beneath my jeans.

On my way home I stopped at a sex shop with window ads of porn stars in Valentine's pyjamas. Another dancer told me sex shops were the only places that carried stripper shoes. I passed dildos and costumes, heading to the heels at the back. Wide platforms with strong stilettos. I examined each shoe like a sculpture.

I didn't want red ones because I flush easily and the colour makes me look drunk. I didn't want ones decorated with tacky stripes of neon plastic. I didn't have the dominant personality needed to fill the thigh-high, black, patent leather lace-ups, and I didn't think I could manage the clear, stiltlike nine-inch ones. So I asked to try on a pair of classic black four-inch platforms with dainty ankle straps.

Opening the box was like uncovering two ravens nesting in red tissue paper. Heels imbued with occult power to break ankles and shorten tendons, or to be weaponized when sex workers had to defend themselves.

I slipped my foot onto the elegant arch and buckled the strap. When I stood, my core engaged, calves tightened, butt lifted. On the balls of my feet, I rested comfortably, as if on the lip of a stair.

Now the client runs a finger down the shiny black heel, as if caressing the curves of a sports car. "Impressive."

★ ★ ★

Yasmine rules the Royal with a seven-days-a-week work ethic and a razor-sharp ponytail. She certainly has never considered my presence beyond noting another chubby white girl (the boss likes that type) who needs to get out of her way. She's all angles. Nine-inch heels and still shorter than everyone.

No one gives her the respect she deserves for her legendary stage shows, her high-power spins and flips. Once she pulled off a climactic ceiling-to-floor drop into the splits, but the friction from the pole burned the skin of her rib cage. No one noticed because her expression was stone. I only know it happened because the next day she showed up to work with a large bandage covering the wound.

★ ★ ★

"Why did you get into this kind of work?" he asks. A question that gets asked a lot.

I'm sitting on the client's lap in the VIP, facing him. Usually I would give the most bland and inoffensive response—school—but this time I decide to experiment with the truth. "Since we live under capitalism and I have to work for money, I want to make the most money with the least amount of time at work. Being a woman, sex work makes the most economic sense."

His tone turns sour. "You're a prostitute?"

"All of this"—I gesture vaguely—"is sex work. Stripping is sex work."

"Okay. Well, then you're saying you're lazy?"

"No, it's that all work is an economic exchange, right? If you take the moralistic judgment out of stripping, it's actually a pretty good job. I choose my own schedule, no nine-to-five, never have to wake up early. I have money and time to put into my political projects and collectives, and I can take time off whenever I want."

He narrows his eyes. "So you're some sort of a communist then?"

"Definitely not. I'm an anarchist, which means—"

"Never mind, sweetie. Just finish up the song."

Lesson learned: never talk politics at work.

★ ★ ★

I am onstage with another girl doing a "lesbian" show, egged on by two bachelor parties throwing fives. Their unnerving roar makes me dive between my companion's legs for a moment's peace. She smells like lemon meringue. I've never met this girl before, but like a pro wrestling match, the trick is to make it look real. So while I hold her hips and move my head like I'm eating her out, I maintain a professional inch of space between my lips and her pussy. Close but never touching.

"Give that back!" she yells, and I sit up. "That guy is stealing our money."

A man, swaying dumbly, is holding a fistful of swiped fives like a bouquet. Someone from the other bachelor party chivalrously pours beer over the thief, who tackles the saviour in return, and a brawl erupts. The girl and I help each other up and scurry to the back of the stage, backs against glass decorated with a stylized stripper: big tits, tiny feet. We watch the sea of fighting guys roil in front of us. The bouncers try dragging men out of the club, but they break free and rejoin the chaos.

"This is wild," I say to the girl.

"You must be new," she says.

★ ★ ★

Sasha doesn't look at the crowd during her stage shows. Her figure is Marilynesque; her smile burns like matches. She wears fuzzy leg warmers from below her knee to under her heel so her feet appear chunky as Clydesdale hooves, yet she moves like silk. Carries a fairy dusting of vulnerability that the other girls lack. I believe she could be hurt, but she dances to bold European techno. One song has a chorus of "pussy," repeated over and over, leaving nothing to hide behind.

★ ★ ★

He is sitting in the line of chairs closest to the stage, known as perverts' row, waiting for Chloe. She didn't come to work today, but he will go with no one else. He tells me Chloe is the architect behind the music. Did I listen to the lyrics of the last five songs? She picked them to remind him to be faithful. His dark eyes, magnified by thick glasses, search my face to see if I, too, understand the significance.

★ ★ ★

Wipers clear fog from my rear window, revealing a silver sedan idling among the cabs and designated drivers. I fiddle with music and heat so that the sedan can pull out before me, but it doesn't. I leave and it follows, cutting dangerously in front of a semi to shadow me.

I turn sharply with no blinker. He pursues. Another random turn and his headlights are still tailing. Terrified, I head for a fast-food parking lot, where at this hour there is a drive-through lineup of potential witnesses. Slam my car into park, roll down the window, and awkwardly lean halfway out. I don't know who is in his car, or how many. My phone is at the bottom of my too-full work bag. If I try to dash inside the McDonald's, he might grab me.

He pulls up beside me, window down. He is a guy I danced for in the last chaotic hour, unremarkable and quiet.

"Why the hell are you following me?" I demand. "What do you want?"

"Since you're off work now, I thought you'd give me your phone number?"

"Absolutely not. Would you have followed me to my doorstep to ask me that fucking question? You're a creep. A stalker."

"Oh, sorry, I didn't mean—" he puts his hands up.

"Get away from me. Drive away right now!"

As soon as he pulls out of the parking lot, I start to tremble. Dig out my phone and text Bruce. He responds, *Glad you are ok*. Although I'm not sure what I expected, his dismissiveness reminds me to never look to management for support.

I get in the drive-through lineup. Bright lights and a brief interaction with a real person as I order peppermint tea. I crank up the radio on the ride home. Concentrate hard on a documentary about the First World War featuring crackly recordings of veterans reminiscing about the jubilation at war's end.

★ ★ ★

"Mary is going to tear him apart," says Bambi, twisting a ringlet of her blond hair.

A grinning bachelor has flopped onto Mary's stage, and his friends have handed her a leather belt. Mary is a spitfire who dances to Metallica and wins bets with clients that her Irish/French heritage means she'll outdrink them.

Mary flips the bachelor onto his stomach and tugs his jeans down over his flat, furry butt. She does a theatrical countdown: three, two ...

The DJ pauses the music so that the crack of leather resonates across the bar to howls from the guy's friends and discomfort from everyone else. Other girls would give bachelors a few more playful slaps before flipping him onto his back and riding his hips, or putting their tits in his face, but Mary winds up again, and then again and again. He cries out and writhes in pain. Bambi and I cringe as she hits him so ferociously, he can no longer stand it and limps offstage holding up his pants.

★ ★ ★

Tiara returns to the changing room and furiously begins packing her things. Only minutes ago she arrived, dressed hurriedly, and went upstairs to check in.

"You're leaving?" I ask.

"I drove an hour and a half to get here, and they told me I can't work this weekend because they already have too many Black girls. Only in this goddamn industry."

"I'm so sorry," I say, dumbstruck.

"Fuck this club." The clang of metal reverberates as she slams her empty locker.

★ ★ ★

"I don't like her," says a guy as we watch Nikita's show from perverts' row.

"That's rude," I whisper. Even with the loud music, she's close enough to hear.

"She's the rude one. She's one of them Russians who won't take no for an answer."

Onstage Nikita steps out of her panties, revealing a tampon poking out between her legs. Not just the string but half the bloody affair. The client notices too and shades his eyes.

I stand up, trying to block her from the crowd. Gesture at the front of my underwear, then at her. I feel like I'm being sucked into a black hole of embarrassment. My panicked movements confuse her, so she backs up against the pole and looks between her legs. With a casual wrist flick she pushes the tampon back inside. Her stage smile doesn't falter as she continues her dance.

I sit down, mortified. "She handled that so well. I would die if that happened to me."

"She should have taken the day off. Hell, take the whole week off."

The scandalized man leaves in a huff, but I stay watching raptly. Trying to absorb Nikita's ability to not give a fuck.

★ ★ ★

Bored, I go downstairs to change my outfit. It's been slow and I haven't made much money.

"Why is it so cold?" I ask.

A girl wearing a pink, padded jacket over her bra and underwear is curling her eyelashes. "They turn off the heat down here when it's dead upstairs so we don't go on strike and hang out the whole shift," she says.

It's too cold to bother changing my outfit. I stomp back upstairs.

★ ★ ★

"Piece of advice—never, ever, tell a guy you have a boyfriend. It ruins it for us," the client says.

"Maybe you shouldn't ask a question you don't want the answer to," I suggest.

"It's not that I don't want an answer, I just don't want *that* answer."

★ ★ ★

A girl comes out of a bathroom stall while I'm applying lip gloss in the mirror above the sink. I move out of the way so she can wash her hands, but she says, "Hell, no. My hands are cleaner than that sink" and walks out on a cloud of bubblegum perfume.

★ ★ ★

"Who is that onstage?" I ask Izzy.

My attention gravitates to the girl with the brilliant smile and excellent posture as she bends from the waist like a Barbie doll. She radiates preppy-girl-gone-a-little-bit-bad vibes.

"That's Madison," Izzy says. "I heard she models."

Madison has a V-curve in her abs starting above her hip bones and dipping underneath turquoise panties, a ridge of muscle I'd like to follow with my tongue. She dances to a remix of "Summertime Sadness," a wildly popular song that already feels nostalgic.

"She is perfect," I say.

"Well, yeah," Izzy says, "if you like that blond, fake-tits kinda thing."

Does Izzy think there are many people here who don't like that aesthetic? I find myself applauding along with the men after Madison finishes her poised, flawless tricks.

"Careful," Izzy teases, "you're falling in stripper love."

★ ★ ★

Gerry's a softie with a job in IT who makes conversation easy. He comes prepared with a packet of mouthwash strips, and before I start dancing we both take one. Dry as a communion wafer, the strip dissolves on my tongue in a blast of peppermint that burns up my nose and down my throat.

He's my first regular client. Other girls talk about their regulars like possessions, property that can be stolen. A major unspoken rule is to keep track and stay away. I respect that, but possessiveness is not a part of my stripper game, and in real life I'm non-monogamous. I am relieved that Gerry has other favourites so I don't have to be his stripper everything.

The other girl Gerry really likes is Star. I want to say Star and I have become friends, but can someone be your friend if they only talk about themselves and know nothing about you? We are work friends, I guess.

Tonight, Gerry has taken us both to the back for double dances. Star is rambling, "You wouldn't believe this phone bill I got. I don't even know what happened. I need to call the company about it tomorrow because I can't pay. It's insane. Ger, can you drive me home tonight so I don't have to pay for a cab?"

"I live in the next city over," Gerry reminds her.

"Yeah, but you drive. I live downtown, it's real close."

"All right, I can do it this one time. Do you want a ride too, Michelle?"

At the end of the night, Gerry and I wait for Star.

"I have to work in the morning," he complains, "and you look like you're ready to hit the hay." Even though I like Gerry, this chit-chat is unpaid time. I slouch in the front seat. It's almost 2:30 when Star joins us, but Gerry acts cheerful when we finally leave.

"Go to the drive-through," Star commands. "I don't have any food at home and I'm starving." Gerry pulls into a line of after-hours cars, Star directing from the back, "Get four packets of barbecue sauce. Check the bag."

Gerry pays for her meal and a massive root beer. The cloying smell reminds me of my high school fast-food job. I want french fries so bad my stomach growls, but I've been restricting. After work, I'm always ravenous and I worry that if I start eating, I won't stop. So I crack open the window to air out my hunger.

Back on the road, Star says, "Rent's due, I need to go to the bank."

"Can't you go tomorrow?" I object.

"I'll be real quick, it's on the way."

I look to Gerry to back me up, but his lips are pursed. He's already switching lanes for the detour. I text Jace, *I'm so tired.* He responds, *Can't wait to see you! There are some people here. Come party.* I rest my head against the window.

The city's downtown is brightly lit, a bank on each corner. As I watch Star stumble in her Ugg boots to pull rent from the terminal, I realize I've found saving money easy. I haven't touched my bank account in months, keeping my money in cash, trusting the ebb and flow at the club to come out in my favour. I'm tired, sure, drinking a lot, definitely, but I've never made this much money. I've started squirrelling it away in envelopes marked: rent, phone, groceries, dog food for my husky mix, Mira. I paid a hefty cash deposit so I could get my first credit card and I bought a car. It's a beater but still, I bought a car.

I get a rush every time I add to the envelope for spending money. It gets thick with green bills, peppered with an occasional red or golden brown. Like I'm growing a garden of roses.

CHAPTER 3: INITIATION

THE ROYAL
SOUTHERN ONTARIO

Is it always this slow after Christmas?" Izzy wonders as we sit alone at a table. Tonight she didn't put up her mohawk, the ribbon of green hair brushed to the side and tucked behind her ear.

"Guys are all in credit card debt now," I guess.

The waitress comes by our table even though we'll have to pay for our own drinks. Izzy orders us another round. "Two tequila roses, please." She's switched from hard alcohol to curb her drinking at work. I am not making the same effort, but I like her choice of festive liqueur. It's like holiday candy, each sip a granular punch of sugar with a fiery aftertaste.

"You look sad," I say. "Did you break up with that guy you met here?" I pretend I don't remember his name to remind her that he's just one of hundreds we've met over the past nine months, many of whom say they want to be our boyfriend.

"We're in love and he wants me to quit," she says.

"But you met *here*. If he goes to strip clubs, he must understand that this is a job." She and I approached his table together. I danced for his friend while they hit it off. It was random that I went to the left side of the table and she to the right.

"He tells me he can't be serious with someone who works like this."

I roll my eyes. "Is he going to financially support you since he's forcing you to stop making money?"

"He says he'll help me find a new job. Or I guess I could ask for my old job back."

"His insecurities are not your problem. You're naturally good at this." Her sets showcase a smouldering exhibitionist side of her soft-spoken personality. She nods like she's considering my opinion, but I think she's already made the choice.

"Jace encourages me to work." My voice is shrill, defensive. "He knows I'm not here to meet someone to replace him. We get to spend more time together now that I don't have to work a shitty job every day, and he's happy I'm taking care of myself and making money."

I can't believe Izzy is thinking of quitting. I never want to quit. I like working in an atmosphere of low-key danger. It helps me empathize with the situations Jace has lived through: jail, addictions, parole. At twenty-one, he's a year younger than me and already been through so much. Plus, we both get off on the heist-like high when I come home flush with cash, hazard pay.

But the sentiment that good boyfriends don't let their women work in places like this has, through force of repetition, wormed its way inside Izzy's head, and even mine.

"It's not fair," I tell Izzy. "Why does some guy get to decide what's best for you?"

"I really love him, though, Michelle," Izzy says.

The waitress drops off our drinks. Pepto-Bismol pink in short-stemmed wineglasses. An ice cube island in the centre.

"This place will be lonely without you," I sulk.

★ ★ ★

Bobby flicks his tongue over the gummy hole where his two front teeth should be. "Want to go downstairs and make some extra money?"

"What's down there?"

"Don't play dumb." A grin splits his round face. "It's hush-hush, though. Only close personal friends of the owner allowed."

So the rumours are true.

"How much do you charge for a BJ?" Bobby whispers, though no one is close enough to overhear.

Sex work is work, whether it's lap dances, hand jobs, blow jobs, or full-service. No sexual act deserves more judgment or stigma than another. In trying to be a more opportunistic hustler, I memorized the price lists of local escorts who advertise under Craigslist's erotic services section. Bobby accepts my price and I follow him to the bar to speak with Bruce.

"Didn't peg you for a bad girl." Bruce smirks at me. Bobby slips him cash and receives a key.

I'm more worried about the opinions of the other girls than Bruce or Bobby. Some strippers who "only dance" think that girls who offer extras are stealing their business. They trash-talk them in the changing room, call them dirty prostitutes. Once, one of the only-dancers asked me what I thought about the "nasty whores" taking over our club. I said it was none of my business how other girls made money.

I scurry after Bobby down a staircase where vertical mirrored slats reflect red light like a carnival tunnel. One-third of the basement consists of the changing room, accessible only by the main stairs. We've come down a back way into a labyrinth of branching hallways, dead ends, and locked rooms. Music fades, replaced by the clicking of my heels on tile. Bobby opens room number four and locks us in. I see a bed against a gilded, smoked-glass wall. A black end table dusted with remnants of white powder. The acrid smell of an overflowing ashtray. From upstairs, I hear the muffled sound of my favourite Weeknd song, about meeting "the boys." Grim lyrics make me feel brave. I listen to this song on late-night dog walks beside the river. Big wind, silver ripples on water, alone in the dark, I dare the universe to show me its true ugly face. I take off my heels in case I need to run. The carpet is cold, as if laid directly over concrete.

"I'm going to call you Betty Boop," Bobby says. Instead of unbuttoning his plaid farmer's shirt, he hikes it up over his barrel belly. "You look exactly like her, big eyes, black hair." His belt buckle jingles as it falls to his ankles with his jeans. Bony legs, narrow hips, a nest of white pubic hair surrounding a mushroom tipped, stocky penis. He strokes it proudly, asks if I like what I see.

With shaking hands, I retrieve a condom from a pocket in my clutch. Since Jace and I got together two years ago I haven't needed them; our cocks are made of silicone. The sticky yellow rubber feels like a toy. Bobby protests, but I threaten to go back upstairs. Satisfied with asserting my boundary, I roll the condom on, kneel, and put his penis in my mouth.

Chemical banana and fungal sweat make me gag. I shut my eyes and begin counting the ins and outs. Try to rationalize—this is the same action I've done many times. But I was always attracted to the person. It's bittersweet to acknowledge I have never given head I didn't want to before this.

"I can't feel anything with the condom." Bobby locks his fingers into my hair, holds my head still, and begins thrusting hard.

How long has it been? My jaw is aching. I can't hear my song anymore, only my own sloppy choking. Rhythmically, his belly slaps my forehead and shoves my nose into his pubic hair. It's difficult to breathe. I hit his thighs to tap out, try to pull my head away, but he grips tighter. Vomit rises and I swallow it so I can continue taking desperate breaths through my nose. Panic. If I pass out, what might I wake up to? It's safer to surrender. I focus on snatching breaths until his pace quickens, his thighs shake, and his climax digs into the back of my throat.

On the edge of the bed, I fiddle with my shoes. Bobby ignores the snot and tears streaming down my face as he peels off the condom and lets it fall with a wet slap into a metal wastebasket. I don't need pity or an apology. Though it was awful, what happened felt unexceptional, just more proof of what men think passes for intimacy.

Bobby tosses money on the bed. "See you up there, Betty," he says. I will never speak to him again.

The walls and carpet suck fear and shock down into the building's foundation, send it deep into the earth, and the room resets, ready for the next trick. Reflected in the smoky mirror, my skin is ashen, bones made of charcoal. I dab off mascara, making a mental note to buy a waterproof kind, and rub banana-scented lubricant off my lips. I adjust my outfit in the mirror, smooth my dishevelled hair. I worry that someone upstairs will be able to tell that I've been crying, but I realize that no one is going to ask if I'm okay. There is comfort in knowing that I can endure and survive. Before my tears have dried I am calm. It could have been worse.

When I get to Jace's after my shift, he is pacing, worried about an upcoming trial date. It's a bullshit case for petty theft. One that is only making it to trial because he already has a record. To cheer him up I order the party special from our favourite pizza shop. Two mediums, honey-garlic wings, and cheesy bread.

I respect Jace's street smarts, knowing he'll understand as I tell him about my first trick. "He's a regular at the club, so I thought he'd be okay." I'm walking a fine line, trying to decide how to feel about it. "It was bad, but not that bad, you know? Anyway, I'm sure most tricks aren't rough like that."

Jace is wearing a shirt with the sleeves cut off to the rib cage. I love how, from the right angle, the armholes show off the keloid scars across his flat chest. You're my tough stripper-princess," he says. "A total badass."

Catlike, I arch toward his praise. "It's weird," I say. "I was scared in the moment, but as soon as it was over, I stopped feeling anything at all. I didn't tell anybody about it, went back to work like nothing happened."

Jace rubs my back, and his touch grounds me. "I took what I wanted from him, too," I say. "Like an initiation. I just wanted to get that first trick out of the way. Now I know it'll be what I always expect from cis men—you can't trust them."

I pay for the delivery and we dish up extravagant pizzas, laden with gooey cheese, salty pepperoni, and olives.

"All sex with cisgender men is rape," Jace says.

I don't agree, but this might be true for him. Besides, I'm not feeling benevolent right now.

"Fuck all men," I say, and with our shared can of Coke in two wine-glasses, we cheers like it's champagne.

★ ★ ★

My friend Lola has started stripping at the Royal. Sometimes we work tables together, and a few minutes into a conversation, she has her clients and me convinced that she used to be an Olympic swimmer, the child of famous seventies folk singers, or the rescuer of five children when a tourist boat capsized in an Amazonian river. The more outrageous the lie, the easier it is to believe.

When I was twenty and Lola was still a teenager, we lived in the same collective punk house for a summer, though she was always more punk than me. She tattooed ACAB on her knuckles and shaved her head. Drank forties of Olde English and pissed on the lawn of our suburban house.

Her head is still shaved, but she's styled more like Amber Rose now, with big hoop earrings and bright lipstick. In the VIP she moans loudly, fakes sex noises that make me blush.

Once, a man asked her, "What makes you cum?"

"Money," she replied.

★ ★ ★

When the shaved sides of my hair had grown into an awkward couple inches of fuzz, I made an appointment at a fancy salon. I told the hairdresser I'd been cutting my own hair for years.

"Obviously," she said, ruffling my black rat-tail and uneven fringe of bangs. "Anything I do will be an improvement."

Bleach fumes burned my nose as she stripped black box dye from my hair. It felt good to have someone massage my scalp. The bleach left my hair a patchy butternut squash, which she cut into a pixie. She suggested I get a wig because strippers can't have hair like mine.

"You know, my boyfriend says it's not cheating if I sleep with other girls," she flirted. More than once she told me that her boyfriend was away and she really wanted to party.

I was surprised she was hitting on me, since, with my head chopped off by a styling drape, I didn't look cute. Throughout my open relationship with Jace, he got hit on more often and more directly than me. In our small-city queer scene, I didn't begrudge him this. I was happy that in contrast to the straight world, the queer community loved him *because* he was transgender. On top of that, he was a charming bad boy, a punk, and a great dancer. The social capital he gained through his sex appeal sometimes led to threesomes and got us invited to all the parties. I loved having a hot boyfriend. But it was rare that I got hit on solo and rarer still that it was by a femme. I invited her to stop by my work.

When she shows up with a friend whom she introduces as her gay boyfriend I am surprised how drunk she is. They cackle loudly at the bar as if this is the funniest place they've ever been. In the VIP she keeps smacking my ass so hard that I can't turn my back to her. Tries to pinch my nipples and slaps at my pussy. She wasn't flirting with me; she just wanted access to a new party scene. I call the dance off early and spend the next few hours avoiding her and her friend, while they shriek with laughter and waste other girls' time questioning them about their outfits and hair.

"Maybe she likes it rough," I mention to Bambi. "Or she's used to letting her boyfriend treat her that way. But dancing for her was horrible."

"Straight women are worse than men," Bambi says. "They are so entitled and pushy, as if the rules don't apply to them. It's like they're trying to prove they're better than us because they're a waitress or a hairdresser or something."

"She's totally a hairdresser!" I'm surprised and disappointed by the confirmation.

"The worst is couples," Bambi says. "The woman shoots daggers the whole dance because her man is looking at you. Like what is he supposed to look at? The floor? Stay home and watch porn if you can't handle spicing up your vanilla sex life. Don't involve me in your drama."

"Are gay women any better?"

"I've only had one and she was nice, I guess. They don't really come into places like this." It *is* an aggressively heterosexual bar. My dream of a table of sexy queers showering me with money quickly faded. "The only lesbians I see here are that skinny, cracked-out dancer and her mannish pimp," Bambi says.

I cringe at the pejorative terms but know exactly who she means. The dancer flits bat-like around the club, while her partner, long hair pulled into a ponytail looped through a baseball cap, sits alone, quietly watching.

"Maybe one comes to protect the other if she needs it. Or maybe they share money. Lots of couples do, but it's just hyperstigamtized because one is a sex worker."

Bambi squints at me, tilts her head.

"How do you know she's her pimp?" I ask.

"I just know." At twenty, Bambi has been in the game a lot longer than me, having started stripping with a fake ID.

"Plus," Bambi adds, "the dancer calls the other one 'my man.' It's code."

I haven't learned how to tell if a dancer is pimped, as pimped girls exist in a secret society within our already marginalized one. Usually, girls warn each other: don't go over to that guy; he's a pimp. I keep my distance, scared by the "shark attack" metaphors of how pimps smell fresh blood, prey on the vulnerable, and actively "get" the friends of girls they already control. But the times when I've accidentally ended up sitting with a man wearing ostentatious brand-name athletic wear and thick gold chains, he will usually ask a recognizable series of questions: "Is your man taking care of you right?" "Do you want to quit this job and come party with me and my girls?" "Do you want to make some real money?"

Why would I ever, under threat of violence, want to give control of my money to a manipulative, parasitic man? It seems like an easy trap to sidestep, yet I'm aware that being pimped is a reality I don't understand, one I don't have to confront because of my privilege. I didn't grow up in communities that included sex workers, where intergenerational or survival sex work existed. I didn't have family members who were sex workers, and I never had to consider if pimping could be a job, not unlike sex work itself. I learned about pimps from pop culture, where they appear as one-dimensional, racialized, violent bogeymen. I don't have the relationships or the personal experience of violence that might lead me to want a strong-armed protector. Not that women aren't sexually exploited in the rural, white communities where I grew up. But it looks more like geographical isolation, domestic violence, alcoholism, and poverty.

The fact that some girls have pimps highlights how sex work, for me, is a choice, a chosen trade. The simple binary between exploited and empowered isn't enough. The industry is incredibly broad and diverse, with experiences that are not easy to categorize or compare. Over time, individual workers can move from choice to circumstance to coercion, and back again. Any understanding of sex work needs to make space for workers to feel all kinds of different ways about their work and to trust them to be the experts on their own experience.

I want to ask Bambi more, but in the club there is a general don't ask, don't tell vibe. I guess some girls are capital-P Pimped, but I am also curious about the grey area. What is the practical difference between a pimp and a deadbeat, abusive boyfriend who spends his girlfriend's money? Sex work offers the possibility of a single worker making enough money to support many others, and I don't think that's fundamentally bad.

Recently, Jace and I have been fighting about money. I told him I wasn't going to keep buying him cigarettes. "We'll never go hungry. I'll buy all the groceries," I said, trying to reassure him.

"Stupid to think I could trust someone who knows nothing about addictions," he muttered as he put on his bomber jacket to go out in search of butts. "Stuck-up girls from rich families don't know how to share."

Some months I don't know where he gets his half of the rent. Maybe it's borrowed from friends, or maybe it's part of a side hustle that he keeps from me. I can't bring myself to ask.

Bambi leaves to snatch up her regular and I slip deeper into thoughts of Jace. Money is an irritating factor in the main issue of our relationship. We had been dating just a few months when he began casually drinking again. Mutual friends warned me that I should try harder to help him maintain his hard-won sobriety, but I didn't see the need. Jace was a puppy dog and we were in love. A few weeks later, he was drinking like nothing I had ever seen before and I was scrambling to keep up.

One morning we woke hungover and sat outside around a smouldering firepit, filled with last night's empties melted into warped aluminum pucks. The yard sloped into the river, midsummer slow. We drank Rockstars, a vodka energy drink, as ducks waddled onto the lawn with clutches of fuzzy brown babies. I'd never been drunk in the morning, and it felt romantically self-destructive, a hedonistic novelty, until I realized Jace's intentions weren't to ride out the hangover this one time, go back to bed in the afternoon, and draw the curtains. He was gearing up to stop at the LCBO for a couple of six-packs.

A month later, we had our first really bad night. Jace blacked out, a state I didn't understand. I was sitting on our bed, so tired. I wanted to sleep, but he wouldn't let me drop whatever argument we were having.

"Hit me in the face," he commanded. "Just do it," His voice was eerily neutral.

The room revolved one way, then back the other, and I realized I was angry. It was such a stupid request. Didn't he know my fist was limp, unpractised? No one had ever hit me in the face, and I'd never hit any- one before. I couldn't hurt anyone. I rolled my eyes and tried to lie down, but he propped me up.

"Hit me," he urged.

I balled and raised my fist, connected my knuckles to his cheekbone. I thought it couldn't have hurt much, but then again, I couldn't feel my fingers, hand, arm, heart. He rubbed his face and I checked to see if it was red like in the movies, but it seemed like nothing had happened. I reached out to touch him, but he turned and punched the window. The pane shattered into dusty shards, ice flakes across our pillows.

Startled into tears, I retreated to the staircase. When Jace came to hold me, I said that we needed to break up, that it would only get worse.

"You don't deserve to be with someone who hits you," I sobbed.

"I don't care about that. I love you and I'm not going to lose you," he soothed. "Come to bed. We're not breaking up. We are not."

The ugly tension dissipated as we billowed the sheets, tucked the corners, turned the pillows cases inside out. We collapsed on the bed, leaving glass shards on the floorboards. As we were falling asleep, I said, "How did you put your fist through a window and not get cut? You are the most lucky and unlucky person I know."

★ ★ ★

Tim pushes my breasts out of his face. "Would it be all right if we concentrated on your feet instead?"

"Sure." I could use a break from regular dances, and I like to think of myself as kink-friendly. Once I walked into the bathroom to find a dancer washing her feet with the bubblegum-coloured liquid soap. "I hate freaks like that," she said. "They should go find a dominatrix and leave us normal girls alone." But as far as I can tell, most dancers don't find foot fetishes particularly offensive.

Tim makes room on the VIP couch and I cross my legs over his lap.

"What do you want me to do?" I ask.

"Just relax." He squeezes his hands down my legs until he arrives at my feet with a muted whimper. One at a time, he rubs my heels, twists his fingers between my toes, and rubs my arches. It's a relaxing foot rub.

He looks up and says, "You have beautiful feet."

"Really?" I've never considered them beyond utility.

"Exquisite." He returns his attention to touch. "Your arches have a natural curve and your toes are so dainty. Not too ticklish, I hope?"

It is courteous of him not to expect me to perform pleasure. I wish more clients would assume their actions don't arouse me.

"Can I lick them?" Tim asks.

Feeling generous, I stand on the cushions and draw a foot up his stomach and chest, onto his face. Am I doing this right? He cradles my foot, presses it over his mouth and nose, and inhales blissfully. His tongue bathes the bottom of my arch, darts between my toes. Okay, I'm not excited about having a stranger's spit on my body, but I don't pull away. Tim pops my big toe into his mouth like a Popsicle, then, excitedly, tries to wedge my whole foot into his cramped mouth. Imagining the way I would feel if someone's toenails were scraping my palate, coupled with Tim's suckling sounds and the decidedly non-erogenous sensations, I struggle not to get grossed out. I don't like my reaction. In queer scenes, sex-positive politics mean nothing is off limits if it's consensual. Nothing is gross because nothing is inherently wrong with bodies and sex.

When Jace and I got together I was enamoured by his crooked smile, pierced by the lip ring he bit and turned constantly, as well as his capacity for pain, revealed by the white-pink scars on his arm from self-inflicted cigarette burns. But we couldn't figure out how to have sex. So we were cautious, never wanting to hurt each other. Learning how to fuck was mechanical. We wrote and shared lists of what we liked and what we didn't. We clumsily asked, "Should I do this? Can I touch you there? Does this feel good?" Admitting ignorance made me humble and fed an eagerness to experiment.

Shame is our enemy. If I hadn't questioned and expanded the desires I was told to have, I wouldn't have discovered parts of my sexuality that I treasure. So, on an intellectual level, I applaud Tim for enacting his desires. But the strip club is not a safe space, not a queer scene. Tim is not my lover; he is a stranger giving me money to suck my feet.

Sex work is a master's course in endurance. By the time we wrap up, Tim is syrupy with dopamine. I use my bandana to dry my feet, and when I return to the floor they feel tight in some places, expanded in others.

★ ★ ★

"I'll have another," I order from Bruce, who's helping out at the under-staffed bar on a busy night.

"Fine, but I'm switching you to vodka sodas," he growls. "The whisky sours are making you fat."

★ ★ ★

"I like you," Madison says when it's just us in the changing room. She's applying fake lashes, "You're normal. I've already had negative experiences being too nice to a few of these girls. Some have serious issues— ouch!" Glue in her eye, she blinks away tears, daintily fanning herself.

No one has ever called me normal before. Tingling, I say, "I like you, too. Maybe we should hang out sometime. Outside of work?" I know she's a little bit gay, I can feel it, but she also reaps endless rewards for being a beautiful and available heterosexual. Dating a woman would be less personally advantageous to her.

"My boyfriend and I are going to an electronica show this weekend, you should come. It's an indoor rave. He's friends with the DJ, so we can skip the line."

Hanging out in a stadium-sized club on my day off with bros high on MDMA sounds like a nightmare. But she already knows from how eager I am to team up and work the floor that I'll follow her anywhere.

★ ★ ★

"So, what's your type?" I ask the client.

"Do people honestly have 'types'?" he asks. "I guess that's what happens when you grow up watching only one kind of porn."

"Come on," I tease, "no preference at all?"

"I guess, for me, I need to like how someone's face looks. Other than that, personality is the most important part."

★ ★ ★

"What's your type?" I ask him.

"Blondes with fake tits. You're only half of what I'm looking for."

★ ★ ★

In the changing room Crystal kills her cigarette and says, "I've always wanted a body exactly like yours."

I scoff, feeling bloated, and return to styling my hair. It's grown out enough that I can gather it into a bun, but it still feels like a work in progress. Freed from the elastic, it bushes into chaos. Each strand, split from bleaching, creates a teased look, lending an unwarranted bubbliness to my appearance. My straightener, turned to max, sizzles as I close it over a puff and drag it down.

"Girl, don't laugh," Crystal continues. "Your body is perfect." She pulls a thong strap up over her hip bone, which protrudes from under her skin. "I only date girls with curves. You are so totally my type."

Her flirtatious chats annoy me. I have those with men, for money. I grit my teeth and smile when clients compliment me on what they call my baby fat, round tummy, or child-bearing hips, but Crystal should know better.

My eating disorders began in high school and persisted for years before I entered this industry that demands thinness. Those self-destructive behaviours are ubiquitous and encouraged here. I've met strippers who eat only Skittles and laxatives, those who only allow themselves one meal post-shift per day, and those who use substances like pre-workout supplements or cocaine to control their hunger. Others punish themselves at the gym daily or spend thousands on cosmetic surgery.

"Honestly, I'm jealous," Crystal says. "I've always been so skinny. I eat three thousand calories a day, but my metabolism is too high. It all melts off."

"Must be a lot of calories in cigarettes and Red Bull," I deadpan.

I confided in a friend who isn't a sex worker that I am considered chubby at my club. Unimpressed, she told me that I was participating in fatphobia, that I just needed to accept and love myself. But she also said that I wasn't actually chubby, as if that word means something objective. I can't tell what is true about bodies. Even after obsessively comparing every aspect of mine to that of other strippers, I can't grasp its size or shape, almost like there is an ethereal quality to a body. As if, by living inside of one, I can't perceive my own clearly. All I know is that mine is not good enough. That I need to work harder and push myself further. But no matter how many meals I skip or throw up, I've never been able to attain the physical changes I want.

★ ★ ★

Sparkle pulls up a chair to the table where I'm sitting beside a client. She interrupts the guy to say, "I brought these for your puppy," and hands me a bag of Milk-Bones.

"Thanks, Sparkle." I'm touched. "How are your little guys doing?" She shows off the newest reel of a Chihuahua and a Lhasa apso snarling at the camera and ripping apart cat toys.

"Don't get me wrong," she says, "I love my kids and grandchildren, but honestly, I think I love my dogs more."

★ ★ ★

"This gentleman would like to order three tequila shots and a white wine," Rosa tells the waitress.

"No tequila for me," I say.

I am driving Rosa home later. She was one of the first girls to be nice to me when I started. We often team up, and she's an incredible hustler, better at pushing my assets than I am. We used to take turns staying sober, but one night when I wasn't at the club, she got wasted and drove her car into a telephone pole. A week after the accident I picked her up for work. She pulled her turquoise sundress up to reveal bruises like lakes from knee to armpit. "I tell the men my ex beat me up," she said. "They give me more money because they feel guilty." The bartenders aren't supposed to serve her anymore, but they do.

Tonight she's very drunk, rolling across the table like thunder. The client drinks from his bottle of water and leaves the shot she made him buy untouched. We do our "lesbian show" in the VIP and Rosa is all over me, with wet lips and sharp bites. The guy doesn't deserve a show this real, so I keep moving her head away, fingers locked into her curls, trying to whisper no softly enough that he won't hear. I'm relieved when he ends it.

"Two songs?" He tries to hand her the money.

"No, it was four," Rosa says.

"I'm pretty sure that was only two, little lady."

"No, it was four. You don't believe me, go talk to the bouncer, he will tell you."

He drops the money and storms out.

"It was four songs. Men are stupid. He can go talk to the bouncer, see if I care. We did two songs each, then we switched, right? Did two more."

"No, it was only two songs," I say meekly. We walk out of the VIP with her leaning on my arm. I can feel her whole body sweating against mine.

"They tried to rip me off!" our client yells at the bouncer.

"You owe us for another two songs, you cheap, horrible man!" Rosa stomps and her wine leaps out of its glass and runs down both our bare legs.

"Everyone calm down! What happened?" asks the bouncer.

"Let's just walk away. This is not worth it," I whisper in her ear.

"No. No! This man did not pay us the correct amount." Turning to the bouncer, Rosa says, "My girl was there with me. She will tell you. This man owes us."

I am allowed to remain silent only because everyone else is yelling. Two minutes ago, the client was dumbstruck by the communion of our bodies, and now he's launching insults and threatening to call the owner, whom he's known since high school, to get us fired.

"I've never had a problem with this girl before," the bouncer says about me. "She wouldn't lie to me, would you, Michelle?"

As soon as the bouncer breaks eye contact, the guy lunges toward Rosa. He puffs out his chest and raises a clenched fist. He's not a huge man, but she's only five five in heels. His aggression startles us both and I stumble back, but she falls and crab-crawls away, feet trapped in the straps of her high heels. The man puts his arms up and allows himself to be escorted out.

Avoiding the broken wineglass, I help Rosa up. She tenses her body and stamps her feet. A thin scream escapes her.

★ ★ ★

Madison dances to sad house music. It reminds me of a four a.m., no-sleep comedown when you start to hear birds before dawn breaks. I kissed her once behind the entrance to the stage, the only place clients can't see. I know we have something special. Even the staff call me Madison's little friend. Still, I felt her hesitancy in the barely-there pressure between our varnished lips.

We approach tables together. Whoever she chooses sits up straight and his friends look at him with jealousy. I've become bolder so I can work by her side.

This group of guys is no different. We step up into a clunky horseshoe-shaped table made for dancing and lean into the men across a small divide. Some man puts his money on the table. I'm thrilled every time I get paid to dance with Madison. With my stomach pressed against her butt, I unclasp her bra. I move her hair and let my lips graze her neck. The muscles of her legs are wonderfully thick, her skin taut and warm. She touches me soft and gentle, a little conservative, like we are secret lovers in a Renaissance painting.

After the song, her guy pulls her away from me, into him. "You are the prettiest one in this whole place."

His friends look at me to see if I feel insulted, but I speak directly to her. "It's true, you are the most beautiful one." But her eyes only light up when she hears this from men.

Cocaine gives us a reason to be alone together. She always asks me to credit-card crush it. Makes me feel like the boy. The private basement bathroom we've locked ourselves in smells of mould from the shower drain and cigarette butts in the toilet. She, however, smells like intoxicating citrus. I've spent my whole night watching her take her clothes off over and over; it never gets boring. I want to press her against this countertop. Help her cheat on her boyfriend, the one who makes her watch golf and chooses to believe she's a bartender.

I'm embarrassed to be another one of her friends who's fallen in love with her. I'm sure it happens all the time. I suspect it's something she cultivates in all her friendships, regardless of gender. She feeds on other people's infatuation.

After one of the raves we went to she asked if I wanted to stay over. I watched her remove her wig, sigh with relief as she shook out much shorter hair that matched her dark eyes. She talked to me from the shower, leaning out to hear my answers. The clear plastic curtain stuck to her body, daring me to come closer, but I was paralyzed by the fear of being a creep. In her king-size bed I should have kissed her. Instead, I watched dawn creep through the blinds and admired how her hair curled naturally as it dried.

In the basement we pass a rolled bill without touching. Inhale swiftly. Cocaine smells like a hospital. My heart speeds up and I fixate on her belly button ring. The diamond glints like a lure at the bottom of a lake.

"I wish you'd kissed me that night," she says. "Back when I had a little crush on you."

No, I think, *you don't.*

PART 2:
STATUES OF LIONS

CHAPTER 4:
PAPER DARTS

**LAKESIDE TAVERN
SARNIA, ONTARIO**

E ntering the LakeSide at high noon makes the windowless, chilly tavern feel cavelike. As my eyes adjust to the gloom, I notice five dancers already dressed and waiting for the lunch-break clients to come in. They wear skimpy dresses paired with wedge heels. They look like women, not girls. With stern faces, they take me in and break me down. As non-threatening as I'd like to be, I'm invading someone else's turf. I straighten my spine to look confident, or at least, unafraid.

Nadia and I drove past windmill farms and horse-drawn carriages, over an unbroken stretch of highway so long we needed to pull onto the shoulder to pee. All with no guarantee, other than Nadia's confidence, that I would be hired at her home club.

She marches us directly to the Greek-style white-and-blue-tiled bar. A television tucked beside the till shows a soccer game, volume up. The boss greets Nadia with a hug. "I saved the biggest room for you," he says.

"Aw, that's sweet, thanks." She runs a hand through her straight sepia hair, already performing. "This is my friend Michelle."

I give a dainty wave, but the boss sweeps me into a bear hug, smothering me in aggressive cologne.

"Any friend of Nadia's is a friend of mine," he says and dangles a key, returning to Nadia. "Beautiful girls like you should stay a week, not just the weekend."

Nadia promises to come for longer next time. She shows me the code on the door behind the bar, the four digits erased over the years: four, three, two, one. It beeps us into a wooden stairway, the walls coated in primer, red outdoor carpet stapled to whitewashed steps. The second floor is a haphazard series of shoddily constructed rooms, careless angles, and wavy wall-to-ceiling lines, but it's bright with sunlight. A sickly palm is the only decoration.

"This is the washroom," Nadia says, showing me a room almost entirely filled by a tiled jacuzzi. "Don't use that, though. It's broken." Instead, she points to a coffin-sized shower wedged into the back corner beside the toilet. "Our room is nice. Some of the others are pretty cramped."

Our spacious lemon-coloured room has mirrors behind a makeup counter, a microwave, a mini-fridge, and a doorless closet. Two large windows, held open by chunks of two-by-four, coax a breeze from the Saint Clair River.

"It feels European," I say, dropping my bags on one of three twin mattresses.

"Sort of," Nadia replies. She routinely goes to Europe to visit family and is less impressed. Beneath our feet, the volume of the music rises and the day shift begins.

I feel brand new again by the time we descend into the loud darkness of the night shift. Most of the women in dresses have gone, replaced by younger, sexier girls. They, too, size me up, as I do them. I imagine they wonder if I have anything to offer that they don't, or if I will cause problems.

The DJ is surrounded by wires, soundboards, a bulky desktop computer. He peers from his booth through a shaft, not unlike food tray slots in prison. "Names?"

"Michelle and Nadia."

"Oh, Nadia, it's you." He puts down his clipboard with the set list. "I've still got your songs saved somewhere. Make sure you tell your girl the rules. Remember, it's your responsibility to get your money, but you're not allowed to ask for it up front."

"Do the clients know that policy?" I ask Nadia as we walk away. "Isn't it like telling them it's okay to rip us off, that no one's going to lift a finger to help us?"

"Some clients know," she says. "And if you ask for it all up front, the guys will complain about you. I usually ask for the first three songs at the beginning, just so I know they've got the cash. At this club, if they say they're going to the ATM after a dance, they're not coming back." She shows me the layout and we survey the mostly empty club.

"How do you want to do this?" I try to sound casual. "Should we work together, or do you usually work alone?"

"I'm easy."

Nadia only started stripping six months ago, while I've been doing this for nearly two years now. Her comfort must stem from a deep-seated self-confidence, the kind that eludes me. I suggest we try a few tables together to see how it goes. We approach two men who look like they just got off shift from one of the chemical factories in the valley. While I ask permission to sit and formally shake hands with my guy, Nadia swoops in and forces her guy to meet her eyes by running her hand from arm to neck to scratch the stubble on his jaw. She rises, the sun in his universe. I try to ask my guy questions about his work, but Nadia's flirtatious voice is distracting. Within a few minutes she has whisked her guy into the back room.

"Do you want to follow your friend?" I ask.

"No ... I'm going to stay here a bit longer, enjoy my beer."

Dejected, I take a seat at an empty table. I'd been anticipating that my seniority would give me an advantage. I thought I'd get to share my hard-earned tips and techniques, but it's apparent that Nadia doesn't need me to teach her anything.

A girl sits beside me. "I'm Keesha. Are you Nadia's friend?"

I try to guess her age, but there's no way she can be as young as she looks. I nod. "Nadia's in the back."

"Obviously," Keesha replies. "They love their white girls in this city." She smiles and the elastics on her braces are bioluminescent green.

"When does it pick up?" I ask. "Nadia told me it's always busy."

"My girls and I rolled in from Toronto around noon, nothing all day, and I doubt it'll get busy until after midnight."

"You're working a fourteen-hour shift?"

"Every day this week." She smiles ruefully. "There's nothing else to do in this town, so if I'm just sitting around, I might as well be working."

We watch the stage as a tall dancer comes on. It's cramped up there because the platform is high and a bulkhead blocks a square around the stage ceiling. The dancer's face and neck disappear behind it. It's eerie watching a headless woman dance sexily.

"Hey," Keesha says as she fiddles with the zipper on her clutch, "can I give you a piece of advice?"

"Please do."

"Don't linger in the bathrooms or the hallways upstairs. Girls can get mean when money's tight like this."

Threat or warning, it's good advice.

My first cash of the night comes in the form of a one-dollar bill slapped onto my ass as I'm walking by a business-casual table. They roar with laughter as I bend to pick it up.

"I'm going to take that as an invitation," I say and sit, focusing my attention on the Slapper, the oldest and roundest man. He is wearing a cowboy hat and has a stack of ones beside him, half as tall as his Corona.

I try to estimate the total amount, but it doesn't really matter. The display is enough.

"You must be the boss," I say.

"Damn right." He peels off another bill and tucks it into the front of my bra. "I told my employees here that if they've never been to a Canadian strip club, they've never been to a strip club at all."

A girl approaches from behind, wraps her arms around the neck of a man across the table, and starts whispering in his ear.

"Don't ask me," the man says to the girl. "Ask him."

"Daddy, can I take your boy for a dance?" she asks the Slapper. He interlaces his hands across his stomach and leans back. She comes around the table, taking bouncy baby steps, leaning over me to run a finger down the strained buttons on the Slapper's chest. "He says you're the man with the plan."

"You promise you'll show him a good time?"

"Oh yes, the very best."

The Slapper retrieves the real money, a fat roll of twenties, from his pocket.

"All right, princess, as long as I have your word." He sends them off with his paternal blessing and whistles rudely for the waitress. "Another round," he orders.

"And for the lady?" the waitress asks about me.

"No, darlin', just for us," he says and shoos her away. A bad sign. I squeeze his meaty leg above the knee and try my pitch. "If you're not going to buy me a drink, you at least need to take me for a dance."

"I think you're right, little lady." He surprises me. "Lead the way." As I wrangle him toward the back, he drawls, "We came over 'cause they don't letcha touch, south of the border."

"Well, you can't touch south of *my* border here, either," I say.

Stapled to the doorway of the VIP is a rule addressed to dancers: *Keep One Leg On The Floor At All Times*. I imagine herons, flamingos. Inside, the room is very dark and packed full of couches, leaving just enough space to perform. The Slapper pours himself contentedly onto a strained couch, springs creaking beneath him.

"You girls crack me up," he says. His shirt is damp and I try not to touch him. Periodically during the dance he reaches out and places both hands lightly on my bare chest and giggles, then pulls away.

I spend most of the night keeping my head down, working the edges of the room and avoiding the regular girls with the biggest personalities. Even though this tavern is seedier than the Royal, the work is essentially the same.

"These guys are here every weekend," Nadia says when I join her at a table. "They were just telling me how they own lofts. In *Sarnia*."

The men are too busy shooting tequila to notice her jab. The most obnoxious of the four is wearing a fedora and yelling about the type of boats he wants to buy. Pleasure crafts, he calls them. I end up talking to Fedora's mild-mannered friend, Carson. His black-framed glasses and curly blond hair remind me of a guy I went on a date with once, then avoided his calls. Carson buys me a drink and slips me a twenty for hanging out.

"What do you buy with all the money you make?" he asks, assuming all strippers are rich and we don't spend our money like everyone else, on rent, debt, phone bills, groceries, car repairs.

"Purses?" I say, knowing they can be a status symbol. I still carry my water bottle, library poetry books, wallet, journal, and pens in a backpack like a student. Though, lately, I've started to envy the boastful, bitchy aesthetic of women with large Louis Vuitton bags who sport full-face makeup when they're out running errands.

"I love girls with good taste," Carson says. "You should let me take you shopping. What are you doing tomorrow before work?"

"I don't know ... I usually don't see people from here on the outside."

"It'll be fun. I know this great store with all the brands."

Just because I can't justify spending my own money on a purse doesn't mean I couldn't accept one as a gift. I take his number, thinking of Keesha—what else is there to do in this town?

Fedora climbs onto a half-wall divider between seating sections, crushing plastic ferns, to attract the group's attention. "Let's see how quick they kick me out tonight."

A bouncer shuffles over. "Come on, Mike. You know you can't be up there. Get down."

Launching off the ledge, Fedora takes a swing at the bouncer, who dodges easily. The momentum of the drunk punch lands Fedora on the floor, where he stays.

"Get him out of here," the bouncer sighs to the table.

"Every time." Carson shakes his head. "We'd better get him home."

I'm used to relying on the spectre of a strip club bouncer to keep clients in check. The fact that this hired muscle is acting so tolerant makes me think it must be club policy. He must be ordered to let clients do whatever they want, instead of dealing with this shit like they do in other clubs—with violence. If even the bouncers aren't allowed to put clients in their place, then I am completely on my own here.

Carson helps his friend off the floor. On his way out he says, "Text me tomorrow and we'll get you something nice."

★ ★ ★

"You were busy tonight," I say to Nadia as we follow a procession of fifteen girls to the rooms upstairs at closing time.

"It was all right," she replies modestly.

From the street below patrons call to us. Nadia leans out the window to whoops and cheers. She calls back, "Any of you have a cigarette?" Men crush beneath our window, but the paper darts they throw don't reach her and she gives up, leaving to bum one from another room. I keep clear of the windows; anyone with basic climbing skills or drunk determination could figure out how to get up to the second floor.

My night's total is around the same as a shift at the Royal. Factoring in travelling expenses, as well as this club's rougher clientele, discourages me. I will have to work harder, smarter, tomorrow to make this trip worth it. I snuggle into my sleeping bag and listen through the thin walls to the sounds of girls going over the night with friends, playing chill songs in their rooms, smoking weed and cigarettes in the halls.

I text Jace, *Can you get me drugs when I get back?*

He replies, *What are you talking about?*

For work, the other girls don't get tired like I do.

Does Nadia get high?

Omg no, I look over at her eating a protein bar and scrolling, supernaturally calm. *She doesn't even drink.*

Before I started working at the Royal, if I did drugs, I did them with Jace. He has the connections; he decides what and how much we use and when we are done. I was fine with that because he's the expert, but it's become frustrating. I don't even wait for him to respond before sending *Just because you got addicted in the past doesn't mean that will happen to me.* I realize how arrogant I sound and try to tone it down. *I just want something to take the edge off at work.*

That's not entirely true. I want to experiment on my own, without him. I want to feel everything in the world just to be able to say I felt it.

I won't be responsible for introducing you to the hard stuff, he says, *some things are so good it's best to never try them.*

I toss my phone into my bag without saying I love you. I don't like being controlled, even if he is trying to protect me. It's hard to know how many girls are high or drinking each shift. It's easier to point out the sober ones, like Nadia. It's not just that using drugs, especially cocaine, is widely accepted; it's that there is one girl on every shift who is there as much to sell as to dance, and there is always someone's boyfriend who can be called in. I don't need to go through Jace anymore.

Below our window, the crowd disperses and the street quiets down. Nadia and I talk our night to death and slip into silence, windows open to the cool air.

★ ★ ★

"I can't believe a vegan café exists here," I say, as Nadia and I sit down for lunch the next afternoon. "Everything on this street is either boarded up, a pawn shop, or an art gallery."

"It's like they started to gentrify but gave up," Nadia agrees.

I contemplate my green bowl of massaged kale, sunflower sprouts, fried tempeh, and tahini dressing. "Do you think I should contact that Carson guy?" I ask. "He said he'd buy me a purse."

"What kind of purse?" Nadia asks.

"I don't know. What kind should I get?"

Nadia lists a bunch of brands from an alternate reality.

"How will I know if they're pretty? They all look the same to me." I pour a liberal amount of soy milk into my tea to make up for the lack of cream.

"It doesn't matter if they're pretty," she says. "Take whatever he'll get you, and if it's ugly, you can resell it."

I take out my phone but hesitate. "It's a lot of extra work to hang out with this guy all afternoon." Nadia shrugs and picks at a pink pickled turnip in her falafel pita. Not wanting to disappoint her, I text him. He writes back immediately, *When should I pick you up? You should invite your pretty friend too.*

I spin my phone on the table and sunlight glints off the screen. "How do I confirm this isn't for fun? He must know I don't actually want to spend time with him for free?"

Nadia takes my phone and types, *You know this is our time off so you'll make sure to compensate us right?*

He responds, *absolutely.*

The mall Carson drives us to features dollar stores, cheap teen clothing, low ceilings, fluorescent light, and empty hallways. He takes us directly to a store he thinks we'll like filled with obscenely priced leather purses. Not the kind strippers like. These are for suburban soccer moms—too much practical natural leather. I pick up one by the handles and try to put it over my shoulder, but it doesn't fit. Maybe it's only for holding and swinging like a lunch box? I feel like the opposite of a kid in a candy store. I look at Nadia, who pinches her nose. The strong leather smell offends her.

"These are really nice," I say, as Carson follows me around, getting me to check out different items in the mirror, while providing a running commentary in a voice like pudding. I pretend to be excited about a brown bag, even though I can't imagine incorporating it into my look. The cashier rings it up and we wait. Seconds tick by until a realization dawns on all of us simultaneously.

"You didn't think I was going to pay for it, did you?" Carson asks.

"Yes, actually, I did." I want to crawl under a rock, or smash that rock on his kneecap.

"I don't think we're close enough friends for that yet. Sorry you got the wrong impression."

Smoothly, Nadia interjects, "Wow, this is really embarrassing for you, Carson. You should probably take us home now."

She directs him to a liquor store parking lot, where he lets us out.

"I'm so sorry," I tell Nadia, nauseated with embarrassment.

"He's a classic time waster." She waves the experience away. "All those purses were off-brand." She's confused by how humiliated I am and tries to cheer me up. "Let's go back to the café on our walk home. They have these raw almond butter Nanaimo bars I want to try."

★ ★ ★

By the time we get on the floor that night, I feel like I've been working all day. The failure with Carson was an unpaid shift. I pray he doesn't come in tonight. Nadia's off almost immediately with a regular, and I get called to do my show.

Facing a new stage is intimidating, but I've found that my simple, comfortable routine is easily transferable. Plus, with a nightly rotation of three shows, where each show is three songs, I've had a lot of time to practise.

The stage is a square, tiled with red linoleum. The bulkhead cuts off my view of the bar, so I can only see the tables closest to the stage. The pole is too short for tricks, so I don't feel bad about knowing only the few rudimentary spins I've picked up from watching other girls. I wipe down the pole with the bandana we all carry like a tail feather tucked into the strap of our thongs. I rub the cloth up and down the pole like I'm jerking it off, but it remains greasy as the handrails in a subway. For my first song I've picked a raunchy Nicki Minaj track called "Truffle Butter," which has a mesmerizing looped beat. I twirl under my raised arm. Plant my heels and bend at the waist, showing the sparse crowd my butt. I've been watching twerking videos, but my technique isn't good enough to attempt it up here. Instead, I do an easier version, clicking my heels together while keeping my legs straight and relaxed, making the fat in my ass and thighs quiver.

★ ★ ★

"What are those?" I ask Nadia as she passes me with a handful of glossy papers.

"Coupons. Do you want them? I get my regular to save them for me. They're all from burger and fast-food places."

"But you're vegan," I say.

"He wants to feel special," she says, throwing the stack into a garbage can beside the bar.

★ ★ ★

Tonight is better. Fewer noes, more easy yeses. Knowing that I've already made good money relaxes me, makes me nicer, and that in turn gets me more clients. The VIP is consistently busy, and with that, girl-on-girl tension evaporates.

It's almost the end of the night when I get stuck talking to a guy who says he's a border guard. "Usually they haven't made up their minds yet and we can get them down," he says. "Or at least keep them talking until one of our guys can sneak up behind and grab them. But this one guy parked his car in the middle of the bridge, ran to the railing, and threw himself off. At that height water is—"

"Thicker than concrete—yeah, I've heard." I'm trying to come up with a way to extricate myself from this non-lucrative conversation.

"He had no hesitation at all," the border cop says.

He began talking about the bridge after telling the story of a woman who was so intent on getting into Canada that she murdered her elderly mother and left the body behind a Walmart. The "depravity" of people is why he says he went on leave. I wonder what he gets from recounting these stories to strangers. Is he haunted by the trauma he helps the border enforce? Or does he crave pity and admiration from positioning himself as a hero? He certainly loves the institutions behind his job and bragged earlier about his special police combat training.

Other girls have mastered apathy. They would easily follow up his revelations with, "Aw, that sucks. Let's do a shot, then go for a dance to get your mind off it." But I can't get past his first story about the twelve-year-old boy who tried to sail to Sarnia on an inflatable raft. I imagine the squeaky plastic of the raft, a toy for a lakeside vacation. A stick for a paddle. An unknowable country ahead, guarded by people who will lock him up before turning him away.

★ ★ ★

Unable to sleep, I wiggle out of my sleeping bag and look out the window. In the shrubs across the road, before the land dips underwater and is reborn as Michigan, a stray dog bounds after a rabbit. In and out of tall grass, a silent but ferocious chase ensues. The rabbit makes an unexpected turn and leap to safety while the dog continues jumping hopelessly through the scrub.

★ ★ ★

"I'm not sure I liked that club," I say to Nadia on our Sunday morning drive home. "But it was good to try someplace different. Half my money came from being a new girl. Would you ever come work with me at the Royal?"

"I have family in that city. I wouldn't want my uncles to walk in."

"Fair," I say, one hand on the steering wheel, sunglasses not dark enough to keep my headache at bay.

"Excited to go home?" she asks. Her question grabs my guts and twists.

CHAPTER 5: LOVE JAIL

THE ROYAL
SOUTHERN ONTARIO

Nine months after my trip with Nadia I'm still working regularly at the Royal. Tonight is slow, so I'm making conversation with Star on high stools along the bar.

"I have a crush on my friend Luke," I tell her. His name has become my new favourite word.

Star is half listening, scanning the room. "Don't you already have a boyfriend?" she says.

"Yes, but we've always been in an open relationship, and he moved to Montreal six months ago. Long distance has been really hard."

On my monthly visits I find Jace half a six-pack in, his mood like curdled milk. He rages against my politics, my friends, and my small city. I fight back with bitter jealousy about his cool new queer friends and dates, and criticize his constant partying. When he feels judged he brings up the privileges I have that he doesn't, and then he accuses me of not loving him anymore. After hours of arguing we can almost get back to softness.

Star wrinkles her nose.

"He's even dating someone else." I try to sound nonchalant. The non-binary person he's dating is aloof, heavily tattooed, and plays in an industrial noise band. Thinking about them together gives me a sick feeling, like being snubbed by the popular kids.

Star rolls her eyes. "Open relationships don't work."

"Maybe not for you, but I could never be monogamous again. Monogamy reinforces jealousy and control." I spin it like a fairy tale. "Makes you miss beautiful opportunities with interesting people. It forces you to pretend you're only attracted to one person. It's crazy."

I cling to the tenets that make polyamory sound reasonable and romantic. Double down because there's no other way to justify the situation where I'm infatuated with Luke but refusing to give up on my relationship with Jace. Constantly stressed, I reread *The Ethical Slut* like gospel. It seems obvious to me that most humans crave variety, and I think it's possible to have new sexual and romantic experiences without compromising love and commitments. I'm constantly told that polyamory is wrong, while all around me monogamous people cheat, lie, and pay for sex.

Star drums rhinestone-studded nails on the rail. "You just want to cheat on your boyfriend."

"It's not cheating when everyone consents. It can get pretty messy ... but so can serial monogamy. The point of polyamory is to honestly communicate your deepest desires and make your intentions clear. It's actually the opposite of cheating if you—"

"If my man ever fucked another bitch, I would murder him," she says. Then, "Look, that table at the back opened up." Money hungry, she drags me out of my seat so we can try our two-blondes-with-tattoos hustle.

Star bends me forward over a chair at the guy's table, leans across my back from behind and weighs my breasts, packaged in a sparkling bra, for him, as if judging grapefruits. "Want to see how wild we'll get in the back?" she asks him.

He stirs his rum and Coke with a pinky and says, "I date girls as hot as you all the time. I never have to pay for pussy."

To me, this signals a rude but clear pass. Star, however, doesn't like to hear no. She climbs onto his lap, forces him into an argument. "Why are you here then?"

While I wait out the battle of wills, I think about the dance party my collective house hosted a few nights ago. We moved all the furniture against the walls of the living room and lit one lamp, a scarf draped over the shade for ambience. Luke danced by himself, comfortable without attention or reassurance.

Luke is new to this city after doing three months in jail on political charges. In 2010, most anarchist communities across Canada, including mine, were involved in organizing against the Olympics in Vancouver and the G20 summit in Toronto. We were hit hard with a wave of repression led by undercover police who had infiltrated our groups and homes, leading to charges that saw many friends spend time in jail.

Readjusting to his freedom, Luke takes daily long walks by the river. He often stops by on his way to pick up my dog, Mira. I'll hear him open the screen door and ask her if she wants to come. Her nails click as she taps with excitement. She always returns muddy and happy-tired.

At the dance party I joined him. He smiled when I put my hand on his chest. It felt good to touch him, easy. I was tired of feeling like being with me was the hardest thing in the world. I leaned into the chemistry that, in the comfort of my living room, felt safe to explore. By three a.m. I was emptying the dregs of a sixty of vodka into his mouth while we rolled around on the floor, making out.

I woke up with a shameover, having broken my "no cis men ever again" rule. I was glad I hadn't invited him to sleep with me, because sex would have taken away the control I feel at being able to maintain intimate distance from men.

I walked into the kitchen to find that my housemates had kept the party going by inviting everyone back for brunch. As usual, no one else had gotten as drunk as me, so they weren't hungover as they trickled back in, offering a stick of butter, garden kale, or a dozen eggs from backyard chickens. Luke arrived with a bag of whole coffee beans. He asked me where we kept the electric grinder and I handed it to him wordlessly. Friends buzzed around preparing omelettes and serving each other cups of syrupy coffee in chipped mugs. Luke's presence was calm but magnetic. I avoided him until he sat directly across from me at the table. Then I lifted my eyes to his.

★ ★ ★

"I'm in love," I admit to my friend Maddy a week later. I am boxed into their kitchen table between shelves of pots and pans and cookbooks. It smells of their salt-brined pickles fermenting in a large ceramic crock. "Luke and I spent the night together for the first time and we didn't even fuck. We cuddled the whole time, like, entwined."

Maddy applies a slab of butter to a steaming piece of cornbread baked in a cast iron skillet. "You're obsessed. You told me last week you were only going to hook up with him. Don't you think it's a little dramatic to be diving into something intense? Luke's still unpacking everything around jail. Plus, your relationship with Jace is ... what, exactly?"

"Complicated," I concede. "Especially when we phone-fight for hours every day."

Maddy shakes their head. They've been growing out their hair, a thin braid pulled to the front of their shoulder. "I bet Jace hates Luke," they say.

"Luke is cis, so of course Jace hates everything about him."

"What happened to you being a queer separatist?"

I blush. "But have you seen Luke's eyelashes? And his muscles are so big after jail."

"Gross." Maddy pushes cornbread toward me. "Eat."

I decline. I'll be leaving soon.

Maddy doesn't let up. "When Jace moved away I hoped your drinking would slow down, but it hasn't."

"Habits are hard to break." I try to shrug it off, but I'm aware that most nights I either work and therefore party, or sleep all day then mix a bubble pack of cold medicine with a bottle of wine. Seek out my small clique of friends to drink with, or, if no one is available, bring the bottle to bed, draw a black curtain, and watch *Trailer Park Boys* alone.

"You and I have been friends for a long time," Maddy says, "and I've known Luke for a few years, too. I'm worried you're both too self-destructive right now. That you're going to crash and burn."

"I hear you," I say, "but I need to be near him. It's chemical."

I'm coming, I text as I hurry toward Luke's house down the quiet streets of the historically Italian neighbourhood where many of our friends live. I pass Faithful Heart Church, kitty-corner to an inactive chemical plant. Raspberry bushes in a community garden wilted from frost. Hood up, Luke approaches in the dusk. We hold each other. His jacket smells like laundry soap and campfire.

"I know it sounds crazy," he says, "but I missed you since this morning."

"This doesn't feel like the casual thing we talked about," I agree.

"Have you checked in with Jace today?" Luke asks.

"We fought for hours. He called me a sellout queer. Says I'm bad at polyamory and just going to fall in love with you and leave him. I can't support him full time like I used to. It's impossible long distance. Plus, I know he's drunk every time we talk. Friends say he's getting worse."

"I'm sorry you're both going through that," Luke says. "It makes me feel guilty that I've been enjoying the time we're spending together."

"Me too," I gush. "So much."

"But maybe you need us to pause until he feels better?"

"Jace will never be okay with us," I realize.

When we get to Luke's place, I sit on the kitchen counter and guide him in front of me. Everything else moves to the background. My legs hold his hips, feet linked behind his back.

"What is happening to us?" I ask.

"I don't know," Luke says. We touch foreheads, breathe together.

★ ★ ★

A week after I started dating Luke against Jace's wishes, some friends and I drive to Montreal to support Jace for one of his court dates, a potential sentencing. I hoped the presence of old friends might defuse the tension, but when I arrive the night before court, still buzzing with new-relationship energy, Jace immediately shut me in his bedroom to process our relationship. His eyes are dark wells. I know he's in there, but he's far away.

The next day, Jace's sentencing is postponed again. I thought this would make him happy, but it doesn't. At what could have been a cele-bratory lunch he picks at his runny eggs, ignores friends from away, and leaves to party with new friends.

When he comes back to the apartment late that night, he walks straight past me and into his bedroom and begins smashing everything. Glass bursts, plastic snaps under his heel, objects smash against the wall like clams on rocks. I imagine the room, its shell cracked, meat exposed.

With each thud, I try to remind myself that the things Jace has lived through justify his rage. That putting off a jail sentence is not the same as beating the case. His anger is appropriate. Then I ask myself if dating Luke makes me a traitor, puts me on the side of the enemies. I shrink around that thought, jump with every crash. Jace's cat hides under the bookshelf, tail twitching, eyes wide. I tell her not to worry about a neighbour calling the cops, or about what could happen next. Tell her to stay still, wait for it to pass. And it does stop, for a moment, and in the silence I hear Jace call my name.

His room looks like a car accident. He throws me atop a pile of dirty clothes inside his closet. The paint is robin's egg blue, a clear sky. I stand up and say, "It's over, I'm done."

"No," he says, "you're not."

He pins me on the bed by my wrists and we struggle. I must have hit him because his lip is bleeding. When I make a break for the front door, he catches me by the arm and whips me into a brick wall. I crumple onto a pile of shoes and coats.

★ ★ ★

Friends and I drive back to Southern Ontario in a hellish blizzard, pushing the safe speed at sixty, passing transport trucks in ditches. They drop me off at Luke's.

Through the window, I see him at the piano, in the knitted vest with anchors his sister made. Luke knows what happened because I called him after escaping Jace's apartment. I kept repeating, "He has never gone this far," as I stumbled to a friend's house, oblivious to my slush-filled flats, my feet iced a violent pink.

Luke helps with my bags, which contain almost all I own.

"I'm glad you're safe," he says as we crawl into bed. "I'm trying to contain my toxic masculine impulses, but if you want someone to beat him up ..." It's nice to hear, and it feels more like a gesture.

"A while ago Maddy told me I was digging a hole that wasn't going anywhere," I say. Friends have spent hours, years, helping me work through my relationship with Jace, and now things are finally clear. "It's time to stop digging."

★ ★ ★

From the parking lot, Luke and I can hear the club's bass.

"You don't have to go back to work yet. It's only been a month since Montreal," he says, as we sit in his car.

The Royal has no set schedule; dancers show up when they want. But it feels difficult to go inside. The lights, noise, touch, and social interactions guarantee that I will feel overwhelmed after taking some time off.

"I'm happy to support you financially for a while," Luke says. "Designing electronic motors isn't hard like your job." He works for a green tech company, building engines.

"I have to go," I say. "I need to make enough for groceries, dog food. You can't keep paying for everything." All I want to do is lie in bed with him, memorize his freckles, exchange stories, enjoy the rise and fall of our bodies, open like books. Sex so good that orgasm makes me cry. It is painful to be separated from him.

His face is grim. "I want to support you in whatever work you choose. This offer is for if you need more time to figure out what's best for you."

I bite the skin beside my nail so hard it bleeds. "It's only five hours." But the fortress exterior of the building reminds me how strong I have to be.

Some of our mutual friends do sex work and Luke had heard me talk about my job before we got together, but I worry that our new intimacy has changed how he feels.

"Is it weird for you?" I can't help but ask. "To have a girlfriend who does this kind of work?"

"I don't want you to have to manage my emotions about your job," he says. "It doesn't feel easy for me, but I never want my man-hurt to be something you feel responsible for. I can work on my masculinity so you can come home and I can care for you, instead of you having to care for yet another man. What you do for work isn't up to me. What is up to me is how I respond. I want to be with you, and I don't want to be another shitty dude in your life, so I have to be something better."

Luke and I didn't decide to become partners—it is simply what we are. All in, all at once. I'm moved that he's willing to dive so deeply with me as I'm going through a rough time. I've been depressed before, but this is different. I see the wrong colours, panic at night about being murdered, feel high without drugs, and sometimes I detach from reality, watch my life like a movie. Luke is a lifeline for me, even more so now that I know he's had his own struggles with mental health.

This past week I'd taken Mira on a walk along the rail line toward the place punks called the Woodsquat. I was trying to walk off the nebulous stress and fear that had intensified since I cut off contact with Jace. The mental energy I no longer expended worrying about him redirected itself inward for the first time in years. *We are not okay*, it kept panicking, *we are going crazy*.

Walking usually helped, but on that day the cold air and sparkling snow tripped my brain and suddenly everything was too beautiful. Vivid colours, patterns, soft fractals in the snow and sky. I stopped to marvel at Queen Anne's lace crowned with snow and rabbit tracks shaped like small lakes. The world radiated. I saw creation vibrating in all things.

Mira and I made it to the bottom of the reformatory quarry, rounded like a curved hand by prisoners who dug out the cliffside, milling the stones to build their own prison. Smashed beer bottles shimmered sharp as the shattered shale across the rock bed.

Four or five years ago, we punks had hung a bedsheet banner from the top lip of the quarry to be read from the nearby highway: *Evict the City*. That was after the police destroyed the shack houses and tents we'd erected in the forest, encircled by a scout camp, slaughterhouse, and encroaching suburbs. The largest of the squats had one wall built out of a piano soundboard with strings attached. We thought we could spend our lives singing around a campfire in the red pine grove, reentering the city only to Dumpster-dive and take an occasional hot shower.

I touched the base of the cliff and shivered. The sandstone held grief. On the way home I balanced on the iron tracks while Mira wove in and out of the sumac chasing squirrels. The beauty of the world threatened to grind me into stardust.

Despite the encroaching dusk, I decided to stop at a convenience store. I didn't know that navigating blaring car radios, blasting exhausts, and other people would be too jarring. I searched the candy aisle for a chocolate bar at what my brain was telling me was the end of the world. And then the ground dropped like a missed step and began to shake. I shrieked and cowered as the candy shelves convulsed and the fluorescent lights rattled in a terrifying riot of colour and noise. The earthquake lasted maybe five seconds. It took another ten for me to realize that nothing was out of place and the cashier was staring. Embarrassed and scared, I hurried home and sat at the kitchen table until Luke arrived. "I am losing my fucking mind," I told him.

Luke sat across from me, coat still on, and together we made a list of resources to get me help.

"How do you know so much about this process?" I asked. I had no idea there were hotlines, crisis intervention teams, emergency psychiatric care wait lists.

"I was institutionalized in a psych ward two days after my twenty-first birthday."

All the noise in my head quieted so I could listen.

"It was worse than prison. At least in jail I knew who I was, what my principles were. The psych ward was exactly what you'd expect," Luke said. "They strapped me down and injected me with drugs without my consent. I lost myself, couldn't tell my own story." He picked at a drop of purple paint staining the table. "I was there almost a month and hated every second of it. But it saved my life. Before I went in, I was talking to God, directly. I could see the whole expanse of time and space. I understood everything. I also began to believe my family were possessed by demons. I saw black smoke coming out of their eyes and believed I was trapped in hell. Attacking the demons was the only way back to reality, but I chose to stay trapped in hell rather than hurt the people I love. If my mom hadn't gotten me to the hospital when she did, I would have died."

It was hard to believe that horror had happened to the gentle, patient man in front of me.

"Even though I haven't had another episode, I take my pills every night because I never want to put anyone in that position again."

"I had no idea," I whispered.

Luke smiled ruefully. "I don't mean to draw parallels. Craziness is different in everyone. I'll call my mom tomorrow—she's a nurse. Then I'll call my doctor to see if we can get you an emergency appointment. Have you eaten? Let's make food." He gave me carrots to chop, slow and careful, while he made the rest of a simple coconut curry.

Now that I've seen Luke's doctor and I'm waiting for a follow-up appointment with a psychiatrist, I want to get in one night of work, to keep myself afloat financially for another week. It's getting colder in the car, humidity from our breath frosting the windows.

"If you change your mind, I'll come get you," Luke says. "I know you're strong, but be careful with yourself. I love—" We haven't said the word yet, but it has been there since the beginning. Still, he's embarrassed, trying to balance how much he cares for me with how much he wants to support my choices. "Sorry, sorry. Call me if you need anything."

I walk under the pink neon into the club, glowing.

★ ★ ★

In the spring Luke and I move to his hometown, into a house we rented from his older sister. My parents gave us their old pots and pans, and we bought a couch from the Mennonite thrift store. After much debate, we left the chameleon walls, which colour-shifted throughout the day, though we disagreed about whether they were fundamentally yellow or green. When Luke was at work, I spent hours watching the light move through our bedroom, gathering enough energy to walk Mira along the Iron Horse Trail.

Luke and I are so focused on each other, we stop seeing our friends. Love jail, they call it. We stop organizing. We stop drinking together, and we stop drinking alone.

As spring melts into summer, I work sporadically in moments of wellness for financial subsistence. A psychiatrist diagnoses me bipolar, but it doesn't quite fit. Doesn't frame what had happened, doesn't make sense of the exquisite joys and terrors that had made up that frenetic

CHAPTER 6:
REAL NAME

**THE ROYAL
SOUTHERN ONTARIO**

I "I haven't seen you around much lately. You been out on the circuit?" asks Sean, a regular. He's referring to the work loop west to London and Windsor, back through the clubs in and around Toronto, north to Barrie and Sudbury, east to Montreal, and back.

"Travelling a bit, working here and there," I say. "Mostly, I work here. Money is consistent and I like this club." At the Royal I fly under the radar. Management trusts me enough to leave me alone. I come and go as I please.

"Don't take that away, it's not finished!" Sean yells when Bruce reaches for his glass. "There are alcoholics starving to death in Poland, for God's sake! Pour me another double—I'm dehydrated."

Despite a volatile temper from years of being a bouncer, Bruce extends endless tolerance to Sean. Perhaps it's the sheer volume of alcohol regularly purchased by Sean and his buddies, Harry and the Bus Driver. The other two must already be downstairs.

"What are you having, Michelle?" asks Bruce.

"A bottle of water. I'm driving tonight." Bruce wipes sweat off his forehead, bar towel over his shoulder. He considers me for a long moment with uncharacteristic softness. "When I hired you, I knew I was saving you from a life of homelessness and drug addiction. Look at you now. You've really made something of yourself."

"Wow," I say, because I have to respond.

I worked—I am working—so hard to cut down on drinking, to pass up free drugs at work. I go to the gym, and I'm rebuilding some of the friendships I lost while Luke and I were nesting. I'm taking a poetry course, which has me writing every day, and I still call my mom, even though my lies about what I do for work have created distance between us. I've made choice after choice that forces me to be healthier. Yet Bruce feels he deserves the credit for saving me?

"Michelle, meet me downstairs. The old booger sugar is calling." Sean taps his nose, lurches off his bar stool, and heads down the back hallway. Sean never goes for VIP dances, but he will give me money to hang out with him and his buddies in the basement.

Despite my bad experience with Bobby, I continued to experiment with other clients who wanted extras. Bobby was the exception. The vast majority of men who paid for hand jobs or blow jobs were predictable and harmless, nice enough and easy to forget. These days, I rarely bother to go downstairs, except with clients like Sean whom I've known for years. Tricks carry more risk, and therefore more stress, compared to straightforward lap dances. Not that police raids are common, but cops in uniform do sometimes swagger in to look around, and being caught in one of the basement's private rooms could lead to a prostitution or drug-related charge.

In 2014, the federal government made it a crime to pay for sex work but not to be a sex worker. These laws don't protect sex workers from being vulnerable to having their human rights violated. Especially Black, Indigenous, trans, and migrant sex workers, and sex workers who use drugs. That's why many pro–sex worker organizations advocate for full decriminalization of sex work, to combat violence, stigma, and exploitation.

Sex work is everywhere, not just in the margins, outside of normal society. Because it has so many forms and expressions, sex work can't be erased through legislation, stamped out through criminalization, or regimented through legalization. From my privileged status as a stripper who works indoors and chooses, or refuses, to offer extras, I'm rarely in a position where I could be arrested, but every time I go downstairs I'm taking a calculated risk and fear hangs over me.

Downstairs, grey light from scattered fluorescents obscures the hallways. Behind a metal door, I hear a man grunting and the theatrical pleasure of a woman. Someone making money on a slow night. The next door is propped open by a trash can. I slip inside and see a naked girl standing on the bed, storytelling to a captivated audience of Harry, the Bus Driver, and Sean. She hops off to hug me and rests her chin on my shoulder as if we're sisters. "I'm Lydia," she says.

"Do you work here?" I have never seen her before.

"Harry brought me from outside." She winks. "Don't you love these guys? They really know how to party." Her cavalier nudity suggests that I should do the same, but no one has offered to pay me to get naked yet. The strap of my burgundy bra digs into my shoulder as Lydia guides me to the bed.

"She's so pretty." Lydia touches my hair. It's grown out thick and nearly reaches my shoulders. "Set me up with a line off her," she tells Harry. Sean is slumped in a chair, his shirt buttons undone, displaying patchy white chest hair.

I become a slab of marble. Harry taps enough powder onto my sternum to show no one is playing around tonight. I hate looking up at him, his nose hairs, the dirt under his fingernails. Harry is cheap and handsy, always testing to see how much I'll let him hug and touch me before I pull away. Lydia cat-crawls around me with anticipation. Her skin is inked with pincushion hearts and bat wings, designs dated enough to suggest she's a year or two older than me, maybe twenty-six. She inhales the line without a straw and cleans the crumbs with her tongue, giving me goosebumps.

Lydia resumes telling the story I interrupted. "After that, things got too intense for me in Toronto. I came out here to slow down, take in the countryside." She spreads her arms as if she's walking through a meadow. I picture fat bumblebees wrestling nectar out of purple clover.

While the men take turns doing rails off my chest, I zone out. Stare at the mirror on the wall, framed by yellow triangles, the spikes of a wooden sun.

"Sean, looks like you're going to pass out," Lydia says. "Don't give up on me now. We've got the whole night ahead of us." She pulls on a strapless dress, zips up salt-stained suede boots, and pulls Harry with her upstairs to get drinks.

"That girl is too much," says the Bus Driver. He is bug-eyed, sitting on a chair shaped like a red velvet high heel, like an oversized fairground toy. He removes his baseball cap, smoothes back his long hair, collected in a ponytail at the nape of his neck, and repositions the cap so the brim faces backward.

"She is too wild for me," Sean agrees. "We found her on Backpage last night and she came right over. Didn't even bat an eyelash showing up to Harry's apartment where three strange men were on day four of a bender. First thing Crazy does? She pulls out a bag of mushrooms! She's lucky it was us—could have been anyone."

★ ★ ★

"Child welfare keeps calling because my mom lies about me to the government," Haylee says, sipping from her triple-triple and leaving a lipstick print that matches her grown-out acrylic nails.

She flips through a slide show of toddler pictures, a blue baby shirt, a toothy smile celebrating unwrapping Christmas gifts. Casual as washing her hands, she says her boyfriend broke her ribs while she was pregnant, causing her son's sister to come out dead. She carried the tiny casket to the cemetery and hasn't had a chance to visit the grave since.

"But no one will take my son from me," she says with a depth of conviction I've never felt. "No one."

★ ★ ★

"The only reason I took you back here was to see for myself if they're fake or not."

"Why would I lie? They're natural," I say.

"I'm not an idiot. I know fake when I feel it," he says.

★ ★ ★

"Do you like applesauce?" a client interrupts the lap dance to ask. "Sit down. I'll give you my special recipe. First you turn your oven to three seventy-five, then you bake chunks of apples in orange juice ..."

★ ★ ★

"What does my hair smell like?" Pleasure asks, leaning in, her curls a tropical beach.

"Like mangoes and sunshine," I report.

"Good. I worry I still smell like burger grease from my day job at McDonald's," she whispers.

"I didn't know you worked two jobs. That's badass."

She rolls her eyes.

★ ★ ★

I ask a client for birthday wisdom on his seventy-fifth and he tells me, "I was dating a girl once and she wanted to get married. I said no because I was waiting for someone better. Eventually, she smartened up and left me, found a husband, had a bunch of kids. She's dead now, but she had a good life. Me, I kept waiting and waiting. I don't have many regrets, but

I never did find anyone to love. My advice to you is to find someone you get along with and love them with all your heart. If it doesn't work out, that's fine, but at least you gave yourself the chance to try."

★ ★ ★

"I feel bad that you have to dance for freaks like that." The bouncer nods toward George.

"He's always been nice to me," I say. George is wearing his signature leather jacket, branded by the insignia of a motorcycle he could never afford.

"That Santa Claus beard of his is probably full of cow brains. Did he tell you he works at the slaughtering plant? He's the trigger man. You can't kill animals, day in and day out, without that affecting you."

"Don't you eat meat?" I ask.

"Sure, but it's not the same as—"

"Dime!" George shouts, recognizing me from across the bar. He runs over and picks me up. Spins me in a circle. His beard smells like decades of cigarettes. Setting me down, he asks the bouncer, "Know why I call her Dime? 'Cause of this tattoo right here." He points at my ribs. "Looks like the *Bluenose*."

George doesn't have much money left after blowing most of his paycheque on girls and drinks, but it's the lull during supper hour, so I take him up on his offer to massage my back as I perch on a high stool. With most clients who give massages it's about their pleasure and usually leads to a reach-around, but George makes it medicinal. He told me his grandfather was an energy healer, and I can feel his pride in this magical lineage as his fingers press energy in, draw pain out. Midway up my spine he pulls his thumbs away as if my vertebrae shocked him. "You're bent all out of shape. Who hurt you?"

I forget to lie. "My ex." Memories rush in like cold air through the windows that Jace broke that final night.

George comes around and looks me in the eyes, his wiry chest proud. "You tell him if he ever hurts you again, I'll kill him."

"Thanks, Georgie." I smile. "But I'm okay now."

★ ★ ★

I hate when the randomized VIP playlist lands on "Meet Virginia." I'm trying to play a hypersexual woman-girl without a history, without relationships or family, and this song's country twang drags me back to the passenger seat of the family minivan with Dad driving me home from a piano lesson, or, later, basketball practice.

The stars were so bright in rural New Brunswick that I imagined wherever Virginia was, their brilliance overwhelmed her too, as she sat on a curb, drank her midnight coffee. Virginia might have been the first woman I loved in my imagination. *Don't fight yourself*, I told her in my fantasies. *Your contradictions make you beautiful.*

★ ★ ★

"Great, Cindy is here," Star complains. "I don't know why they let her work. She's certifiable."

Cindy is wearing a sparkly corset and top hat, a Playboy bunny type of costume. Maybe she started working when there were still feature girls who danced with fire or snakes and had to wear full costumes: nurses, construction workers. But that isn't an Ontario thing anymore. Cindy swaggers to a table of two guys and begins to rap at them, a song different from the one on the speakers.

"She told me her husband is Michael Jackson," says Star.

I squirm, watching the men figure out Cindy's not joking. She builds up to the chorus, fist pumping. One guy chugs his beer, the other puts on his coat, and they duck out around her.

Cindy spots us and walks over. "I'm not dealing with this." Star bails, heading for the changing room.

"My son is coming to pick me up soon. Isn't he handsome?" Cindy says in a dreamy voice, showing me pictures of Eminem. Red blush spots her cheeks, and lyrics multiply in her speech until she's shouting the words to "8 Mile Road." I don't feel threatened, but she is a lot bigger than me and her tone is angry.

She stops rapping and says, "God is on TV, come." Taking my wrist, she pulls me behind the bar into the brightly lit office cramped with staff jackets, bulk olives, tropical drink mixes, boxes of liquor, and four old security monitors on a messy desk. She taps the glass of an inactive screen. "He's in here," she says.

Bruce steps in behind us with the bouncer. Cindy squats and bends, knocking me back against the men. The bouncer is whispering to Bruce, but she shushes them. "Can't you hear God?" Cindy asks.

"He's not here," the bouncer says, "but he told me he'll meet you in the bottle service lounge. He says you should go wait for him." Cindy thanks the bouncer and marches to the lounge to sit, resolute and out of sight. The bouncer laughs. "What a psycho."

I feel the need to say something. "Does she have medication, or is there a doctor we could call?"

Bruce rubs his temples. "How should I know? Once she was having a fit, screaming on the floor, so I used her phone to call her husband or boyfriend or whatever. When he showed up, I gave him the number of a mental health line, but he acted confused, said she gets like this when she's drunk."

"She's always like this," the bouncer says. "Girls get pissed 'cause she scares away clients, and every time she comes in we have to convince her to go downstairs to sleep, or get her out in a taxi."

Sex work can be an accessible job for people who struggle with their mental health. Because of the high pay and the flexible schedule it is the most forgiving job I've ever had. When Luke and I first moved to his hometown I also worked at a shelter for people experiencing home-lessness. I liked the parts of the job that let me offer direct care and resources to at-risk people, but the mandatory overnights, the limited time off, the pressure to get a degree in social work, and the dangerously understaffed work environment meant I was extremely stressed at work and spent my time off dreading going back. And the fact that it paid a dollar above minimum wage meant I couldn't cover my rent. I burnt out, as I do with most jobs, around the six-month mark. But even if stripping helps me balance a need to make money with my fragile mental health, I know it doesn't work for everyone.

I feel like I should know what to do for Cindy, but I don't. "Why do they let her work when she's in active psychosis?" I ask.

"They make her pay a double stage fee up front," Bruce says. "Owner doesn't care if we have to kick her out, long as they get their cut."

★ ★ ★

"I save the final bump for the very end of my night when I get home. I can do it and go right to sleep," says one girl.

"I save the last for first thing in the morning," her friend replies. "I don't get to sleep 'til four and my kids wake me up at seven. I'd be a zombie without it."

★ ★ ★

"I screwed up," I say as I crawl miserably into bed.

"What happened?" Luke turns on a lamp. It's warm under the sheets, but I can't stop shivering.

"You remember Jersey?"

"Is she the one you've been working with a lot lately?"

"Yes. I told you last week she introduced me to her boyfriend, who came to visit her. He was older, soft spoken. He seemed nice, but I think he might be her pimp. I asked her and she said he's not."

Luke props himself up on an elbow, takes a drink of water. "Someone in that position might not be able to call it what it is," he says.

"Tonight she wasn't working, but her boyfriend came in and asked me to go for dances. I feel like I'm not allowed to refuse when someone asks me directly, but I knew I should have found a way out of it. He spent the whole time talking about how he wants to bring me out with him and his girls, to go work in Mississauga. I barely touched him, I just stayed up against the wall, but within the hour Jersey had texted me a million times like, *How dare you dance for my man?* I feel so stupid because I knew it was a mistake." I twist into the fetal position.

"All the rules you talk about," Luke says, "it sounds a little like prison, where people get jumped for wearing shoes in the shower or flushing a toilet at night."

"Maybe I should quit," I say.

Luke rubs my arms. "That is always an option."

Mira clicks upstairs and spins three times before curling into a sleeping ball on her dog bed.

"But I've been there longer than Jersey and there's nowhere else to work around here. It's my club. What do I do?"

Luke clears sleep from his throat. "You said Jersey hasn't had it easy."

"She once told me her boyfriend cracked his ex's head off a car in the parking lot because she disrespected him. She said he made her watch, and the girl's head was bleeding."

"Do you want me to come in the next time you work?"

I try to imagine Luke sitting in a corner of the club next to one of the Roman statues of naked women. On guard, ready to fight. Him witnessing me working a room and picking up men would be so much worse than him theoretically accepting my job description. And if Jersey's boyfriend did come in, I could see it ending in blood, concrete, cops.

"I don't want that," I say.

Luke folds himself around me, his warm breath on the back of my neck as I run through scenarios.

"This situation is pretty bad but not impossible. I'll need to find a way to apologize to Jersey without losing too much face. Let her know

I'm not trying to steal her boyfriend. And I swear I'll never speak to that man again."

"That's reasonable," Luke says. "But I'd like to drive you to work and pick you up. I'll wait in the city so you can call me if you need to."

I lie awake trying to figure out who angers me the most: Jersey, her man, or myself.

The next day I show up at the Royal, and even though I'm scared to the point of trembling, I beeline to a table where Jersey is with a client. We developed a working friendship, so it's been okay for me to approach her table uninvited. I sit, pretending that's still acceptable.

Using the client's presence as a buffer, I put on my most cheerful dumb bitch persona. "How are you doing today?"

She stiffly refuses to look at me. "Fine."

"Sorry about that mix-up. I didn't mean to get in the middle of anything. It won't happen again." I slide this casual admission of wrong-doing toward her, hoping she'll accept my lighter tone, instead of the one she was using well into the early hours as she continued to send vaguely threatening texts.

The oblivious client, excited he has two girls at his table, calls over the waitress.

"Let me buy us some shots?" I offer our favourite blend of red and blue liqueurs. "Pornstars?"

Jersey's jaw is clenched. Her naturally red hair is so thin it won't grow past her shoulders without breaking.

"How's your friend Jada?" I ask. Jersey had been mentoring a new girl recently, the cousin of a friend of hers. I bring it up as a reminder that I've been helping out by taking Jada to tables with me while Jersey is in the back.

Jersey glares at me. It doesn't look like she got much sleep. I can't tell if she's going to hit me or start crying.

Boldly, I reach out and rub her shoulder. Her skin is chilled because they keep it so cold in here, but she doesn't flinch or pull away. The gentle contact melts some of the tension. We let the fight end, along with any future friendship.

★ ★ ★

"I thought of you at this hardcore festival on the weekend," Tom says. "They had death metal–style T-shirts, but the graphic was of Céline Dion."

"I cannot believe you didn't get me that. I would have given you at least ten free dances," I joke.

Tom is part hipster, part metalhead, pure nerd. He also lives in in the same city I do, which is a high-tech hub, employing a cohort of young computer engineering grads like him, who make more money than they know what to do with. Tom pours his money into a house he bought in the same subdivision as his parents, where he lives alone. He leaves the blue light of his massive gaming system on when loneliness becomes too strong.

"I could barely tell what renovations you're working on from the pictures you sent," I say. "Everything looks demolished." He's had my phone number for at least a year. He doesn't abuse it, texts me sparingly, usually professional, *I'll be in tonight if you're working,* or pictures of his home renovations: splintered studs and cracked tiles, a floodlit beached bathtub.

"Oh God, the washroom." He scratches his beard, eyes wide.

"It's going that well, eh?"

"It's impossible."

I reach out and hold his hand. I mean it when I tell him, "You're smart, you'll figure it out."

He adjusts his thick-framed glasses. "I'm going to have a barbecue next week. I don't know if any of my friends will come because—who am I kidding?—I don't really have any friends, but I want you to come. I'll cook something nice. Actually, I'll probably buy something because I don't know how to cook. Maybe my mom will make some potato salad."

"You're really selling it," I say.

"I'm serious."

A selfish part of me wants to go and be adored as a goddess. Shower him with affection in front of his Dungeons & Dragons teammates. Have them whispering to each other, "How did *he* get someone like *her*?"

"Okay, I'll go," I kid, "but only if I get to wear a Budweiser bikini and squeeze an entire bottle of barbecue sauce on my tits."

"That's not exactly what I had in mind." Smile gone, he stares at the floor.

★ ★ ★

I stand to hug Mr Bigshot, Bruce's rich and famous friend, but he greets me instead with a firm handshake.

"Very businesslike," I tease.

"Work hard, play hard." His smile is straight and white. He shoves a discreet dispenser up one nostril, inhales sharply. Flakes of snow have yet to melt from the shoulders of his peacoat.

"Never tried this stuff before my forty-second birthday, but I've been high on blow every single day—three hundred and eighty-seven of them—since then. Let me tell you, my life has improved a thousand percent. My company doubled in value. My sex drive is insatiable. Every day I wake up and grab life by the balls." He beams and tugs, trying to loosen his striped scarf.

★ ★ ★

"Hey, do you know if that guy over there has money?" A dancer I've never met points with her chin toward a bullfrog of a man. It's Bobby, tucked away at his regular back table, far from the lights of the stage. Shoulders hunched, dinner-plate face, he waits for a woman who doesn't know him.

"He has some money," I say, "but he's a creep."

The dancer looks at me quizzically, but I just shrug. I don't know her. I worry if I tell her what happened, she might blame me for going downstairs with him in the first place.

She bows her head, raises a hand. "All right, thanks, girl," she says, and goes to a busy table instead.

★ ★ ★

A client asks if strippers sleep at the club. I tell him that after the bar closes we turn into the gargoyles lining the castle-like roof. We become daughters, mothers, partners, secrets. We transform into the statues of lions guarding the door.

★ ★ ★

"It's hotter than a bloated camel rotting in the desert down here." Sean unbuttons his pink dress shirt and tosses it over a chair.

"I'm freezing," I say.

"You're always cold. You got an icicle up your butt?" It's like he saves up the outrageous things he can't say in front of his wife and two daughters.

Our shoulders touch as we sit on the lower level of a bunk bed, a nightstand in front of us, in the smallest of the downstairs rooms. The room doubles as storage for broken chairs, particleboard shelves, and other assorted refuse from the club, including a stack of foot-high stools that look like drums, similar to the ones elephants are forced to balance on in the circus. Girls used to use them for table dances, but they've fallen out of fashion.

"This one's for you, Nefertiti," Sean says, separating out a third line for the oddest item in the room, the bust of an ancient Egyptian queen, perched on an Ionic column, painted garish primary colours.

Sean always has coke dick, so sometimes I rub his back, or we cuddle, but mostly he pays me to keep him company while he gets high. As he shifts the powder with his credit card, I'm reminded of being a kid, opening a sugar packet on the table of a diner. Sculpting the grains into snakes, spirals, my crush's initials. Sean has to move his huge belly aside to get low enough to the table. He snorts like a boar, animality that gives me a vicarious rush. He sits up, pupils stones of obsidian, and says, "Your turn."

"Are you trying to kill me? That is way too much. You know how I get." My guts are shivering, begging me to consider six a.m., sketched out, jumping at shadows, but the desire to feel immediately different is strong.

When I do blow at work, I can barely approach new tables. Once the warm, rolling high inevitably gives way to anxiety, I find myself standing at the back of the room, near panic, needing to go back to whatever client was giving it to me for free. I don't do coke with any of the other girls anymore, and I rarely seek it out on my days off. It isn't difficult for me not to do coke regularly, but it feels impossible to think about never doing it again. I party outside work much less than I used to, but I always keep a baggie squirrelled away in case I'm overtaken by a self-destructive wave of boredom, one of my least tolerable emotions.

Maybe if I only have a little bit, it will be okay. Scooping with my long acrylic pinky nail, I tap a fraction into my tilted-back nose, inhale sharply.

What if the police show up right now? What if Sean loses his mind and holds me down, his weight restricting my breath. I'm always worried about rape, even if it's with people I think I trust. It's already hard to breathe. What if someone follows me home, waits under the lilac tree by the front window until I'm asleep? Goosebumps tingle across my body.

I rub powder into my gums to distract myself. It tastes like antifreeze spread over snow, so cold it burns. "I like forming words while I can't feel my tongue," I say. "The numb is more fun than the high."

Sean cocks his head. "Cocaine is the wrong drug for you."

"I know. I hate it." I want to flat-out run.

"Ever tried opiates? You'd like 'em." Sean's phone rings, his wife for the hundredth time. He turns it off and ploughs through another line.

Softly, I say, "You're going to have a heart attack."

He laughs. "Tell them I died doing what I love."

I am buried alive in this basement. I need to get out, get home, but there are hours left of this shift. This has to be the last time.

I'm worried Sean can tell I'm freaking out, but he's entranced by the emotionless statue. "Nefertiti, you've been through it all," he says. "Must've seen some pretty nasty stuff down here. This is no place for a princess."

★ ★ ★

"Did you see the fire on the news? That was my barn," a client says. "Nearly sixty thoroughbreds all burnt to hell. If insurance doesn't come through, I'm ruined. Do you know how much a single racehorse costs?"

The steroid-swollen muscles in his neck flex as he grinds his teeth. He keeps talking, but I'm fixated on panicked whinnying and a roaring avalanche of flames.

★ ★ ★

"Is Bambi working tonight?" I ask Bruce. "I haven't seen her in a while."

"I told her she can only work half-price nights. No one wants to pay full price for that."

★ ★ ★

Nick shows me his niece's glossy grade one photo. Strawberry blond braids, a self-conscious smile covering buckteeth. I can almost smell the plastic of the pull-down backdrop, printed like bookshelves, and feel the static cling of a picture-day sweater.

"My sister's an alcoholic," Nick says. "It's why she named her daughter Lexi, a whore's name."

"You could call her Alex," I suggest, but he's not trying to think of her another way.

"What future could she possibly have with a name like that?" he asks. "Disappointing—she's smart as a whip. She'd be better off living with me." Nick never makes eye contact, but when I look away, he stares at me, his dark eyes heat lamps. He leans in, whispers, "I brought some elastics. If we put your hair in pigtails, you'd kind of look like her. Let's go downstairs, play some games."

What was I doing in grade one? I remember playing a mouse in *The Nutcracker*. I looked up to the older girls, dancing as sugar plum fairies with pink blush on their cheeks and flower crowns. I was a tomboy, exploring old barns, taming feral kittens on my best friend's farm. Everything was a dare, from tightrope-walking beams between haylofts to crossing frozen streams.

Around that same time, I was also getting molested by two boys. Whenever we were left alone, they'd force me to play "doctor," a game where I was examined between my legs as the patient and, in the role of doctor, was instructed to touch the boys in the same way. I remember thinking it seemed like an odd place for there to be so much sickness. One day, bored of the game, I tried to refuse and the older of the two boys got angry. He called his penis a jackknife, said if I didn't play, he would stab me with it. When he was done examining me, he sneered and said that I shouldn't have let them touch me, and because I was a girl, if I told anybody, I would be the one the adults punished. He said I was dirty down there, and a new sensation—shame—began to burn between my legs.

"No," I say. I don't want to hear things I can't unhear, touch and be touched in Nick's fantasy of abuse. Even if I were to tell myself it is only role-play, I couldn't unsee the girl's face, freckled like a bag of spilled pennies.

Nick shuffles away, looking for someone else to convince. I shudder and hope that he found that little girl's picture, lost, in the pages of a second-hand bookstore.

I wish I had leaned in, cute and demure, and whispered that I would love nothing more than to castrate him. To literally cut his dick off. I would love to look into his eyes and curse him: you will die alone, a broken person. Lexi will grow up powerful, and she will destroy you with the magnitude and the wholeness with which she lives her life.

★ ★ ★

"Didn't the military test Agent Orange at Gagetown?" I ask Asim.

"In the sixties. Only for one year."

"When do you go back?"

"Basic training starts again next month. It's so far away, it's like another world. At least I've gotten to see you a few times while I'm trying not to think about it."

A shy person, Asim has to work to flirt and I appreciate the effort. The chemistry I feel when we make eye contact means I have to work as well, at maintaining boundaries, not slipping into something more intimate.

"What I know about military training is from boot camp montages in movies," I say. "Crawling through mud under barbed wire and struggling to get over walls. Is it like that?"

"Sort of. Plus firearms."

I have driven past his military base in Oromocto, New Brunswick. The no trespassing signs on the deer fence off the highway warn of live fire drills in progress. Even though I abhor his job, I recognize a good heart in this man.

"I spent time in New Brunswick growing up," I say. "Racism is so strong there. Do people give you a hard time?"

"Most of the people I work with couldn't find Egypt on a map. But they're okay unless they're drunk."

During the lap dances I forgo my bouncy routine, exposing my slower, more natural sensuality. He touches me so sparingly and softly that I almost want more. I lean into him willingly. Trail fingers down his neck, muscular shoulders, the soft skin of his forearms and wrists. Fingers to fingers, hands to hands. Neither of us breaks the spell by mentioning that this is as real as it gets at a strip club. I hug him when he leaves and wish him good luck.

★ ★ ★

A man holds my hips still in front of him and touches the scar tissue above my belly button, twice pierced and twice rejected.

"Has anyone ever told you these look like the big dipper?" he asks as he traces the light years between the largest freckles on my stomach.

I contain galaxies.

★ ★ ★

I usually avoid best friends Chris and John, but there is no one else in the bar and at least they will buy me a drink. I regret my decision as soon as I sit and hear Chris calling the girl onstage a slutty teapot.

"And she has an ass like a shovel," John adds.

As soon as my drink arrives I remove the straw. The tonic water glows a ghostly blue under the black lights. I swallow half in a gulp.

Chris turns his attention to me. "I like your hair all grown out. Now you don't look like such a dyke. Never once did you convince me that you actually enjoyed the company of men." He strokes an air erection. "But no, really, you're a good girl now. I remember the stuff I used to be able to get you to do and you don't do that anymore."

"Nope, that was a different time." I crunch an ice cube and try not to remember the new-car smell of his Mercedes as he drove us down gravel roads in the dark countryside, looking for a place to park.

A girl approaches, arms crossed. "Oh my God, it's you guys. Didn't you get enough on Saturday?" She addresses me, "I was wearing a one-piece and these goofs told me I looked like André the Giant."

Chris and John burst into the childish laughter of grade school bullies.

"You gotta admit," Gary says, "that outfit was a little ghetto."

The girl cocks her head. "You'd better be careful, buddy. Maybe I'm ghetto enough to come and pop one off into your face." She makes her hand into a gun and presses her nail into the skin between his eyes. "Pow." She pulls the trigger and walks away.

"That girl is fat and has bad teeth. You have to choose one," Chris says. "You can't have both here."

★ ★ ★

"Do you have a boyfriend?"

"Of course not," I reassure him.

"Didn't think so. No real man would let you do this."

★ ★ ★

"Is Michelle your real name?" He asks the question I hear more frequently than all others.

"Doesn't it sound like a real name?"

"Yeah. But is it yours?"

"Of course."

★ ★ ★

"Where's Izzy these days?" demands Grover.

"She hasn't worked in years. I tell you every time I see you, she quit and is doing the family thing now." Izzy is still with the man she met at this club. She doesn't post much online besides a few pictures of their son hitting mud with sticks or playing dress-up.

"I miss her so much." Grover has wandering eyes. He can't help himself. Even when he is talking to me, he's following other bodies. "Izzy was always my favourite. I never met such a sweet girl." I know exactly what he's going to say next—it's why I call him a Muppet's name in my mind.

"Once she wore a Cookie Monster sweater. How odd is that? She didn't care that you're not supposed to wear those kinds of clothes here. It was so cute."

Izzy was exceedingly nice to everyone, and it worked for Grover, a client with some level of intellectual disability, who rarely spends money but is here almost every day. He would take her for dances because she didn't hustle him. I don't know if I've ever seen him take anyone else.

Grover's vision of her almost replaces my own—Izzy with a cartoon-printed, blue hoodie draped over her skinny frame. Fuchsia hair gathered into two twisted buns on top of the shaved sides of her head. A Tank Girl look for a slow Tuesday. I have yet to meet her son, but I hope one day she'll introduce me.

★ ★ ★

About a year after Luke and I moved to his hometown, he suggests we host a get-together of his old crew as a belated housewarming party. And to reignite the flame of small-town anarchy that was smothered after the G20. His friends come wearing patches of screen-printed vegetables saying, *squash the state* and *beet the system*. They talk about fixing bikes and the best stores to buy bulk organic almonds. And they bring gifts for our new home: a ficus cutting in a repurposed honey jar, apples from the farmers' market, a vegan gluten-free loaf. Someone gives us a card showing two crows building a nest. The housewarming has the makings of a tender and sweet evening.

I can't deal.

I rail coke off the back of our toilet, then hurtle myself back into the small group, where I dominate the conversation by boasting about outrageous nights at work, and the wild parties Luke and I have attended. Drugs, girls, clients, cash. Don't they realize anarchy is over? The real goal is getting money.

I take a bite of vegan loaf. Dry zucchini and cinnamon crumble in my mouth. I put it back on the coffee table, not even concealing my distaste.

"Let's *do* something," I say to the group.

"We *are*," Luke replies in a rare cutting tone.

I know I am annoying him, but I don't care. I want to get wrecked, destroyed. Leaning back in my chair I say, "I'm fucking bored."

Silence. No one meets my gaze. I feel the same frustration I get at work in a room of broke clients.

"I'm going to call my stripper friends. Maybe *they* want to party." I go back to the bathroom.

After Luke's friends leave, I mix myself a strong drink.

"What the hell was that?" Luke says, his voice devoid of its usual warmth. "You're high, aren't you?"

"Who cares? That party sucked."

"It wasn't a party. It was six people drinking tea. You were rude to my friends."

I want to fight, but not with him.

"I hate cocaine," Luke says. "I've seen what it did to friends of mine. I don't want it in my life. Don't do that in this house again."

It hurts to hear a hard boundary coming from someone I thought had endless patience for me. I want to say I hate it too, but the gap between my feelings and actions is too wide.

Luke goes to bed and I am left trying to be quiet in a quiet house. I check my phone, but none of my stripper friends have texted me back.

PART 3:
THE CIRCUIT

CHAPTER 7:
LITTLE WINDMILL

CLUB GOLDMINE
SUDBURY, ONTARIO

TUESDAY

A sound like bones knocking on hollow wood wakes me from a shallow sleep. A large raven stares at us through the window, it's throat rattling.

"That has to be a bad omen," Bailey says from the air mattress.

"Violet," I call to our other friend. "Come see this."

The bird clicks around, repositioning itself on the aluminum sill, then jabs its open beak into the screen and twists.

"Great, now it's trying to get inside?" Bailey pulls up her sheet protectively. She is so beautiful. Sometimes I can still see her as she was when we met four years ago, baking pies so the oven would warm her unheated punk house. A rat, rescued from the humane society, perched on her shoulder, shrouded by her hoodie.

"Maybe it's looking for shelter," Violet says, her half-straightened hair the same bottomless black as the bird. "I saw some of them panting earlier because of the heat wave."

The raven croaks, then rotates its head upside down.

"Enough. That's creepy." I throw off my blanket and the bird takes flight over a courtyard boxed in by brick dormitories, like our own off-season university apartment. "We have to start getting ready—it's six o'clock."

Bailey's stripping off her clothes. "I'm going to puke. Only two hours to get to the club before the cut-off?" She runs to the shower. "What should I wear?"

A half-hour nap wasn't enough to sleep off our boiling-hot drive in an overpacked car with a broken air conditioner. We crawled through Toronto traffic, financially and emotionally committed to a week together. I'm the link between my two friends who hardly know each other. Also, I'm the only one who's been to Club Goldmine before, so I feel responsible. Not to mention this is Bailey's first time stripping, ever.

I unzip my suitcase and remove a plastic bag stuffed with outfits. Nylon ties wrapped around knee-high socks, lace underwear, jewelled bras tangled like a ball of mating snakes. I tug loose a white bikini with a green, purple, and pink leopard print, something snow bunny Barbie would wear in a hot tub. I pack it in my work bag, along with pink heels, magenta lipstick, glitter body spray, deodorant, bandana, baby wipes, combination lock, and a Percocet disguised inside a bottle of Tylenol. Percocet makes me feel impenetrable, physically numb, and they make people tolerable. Even annoying, boring clients become temporarily interesting when I'm high.

From the shower, Bailey yells, "What if they don't hire me?"

"They will definitely hire you," I answer for probably the fiftieth time. "You're a blonde with big tits, you're golden."

Violet sits in the kitchenette in front of a full-length mirror she moved from the bedroom, straightening her hair. She has been working one year to my four and is seemingly unfazed by the prospect of a new club. The table is covered in the palest foundation, black eyeliner, and a gothic selection of pomegranate, slate, and charcoal nail polishes.

"I showered while you guys were sleeping," Violet says. "The water wasn't going down, so I had to pull a huge clump of hair out of the drain."

"That's revolting," I say. The unwelcome image produces a slimy soap taste.

"The hair was so long it must have been pieces of someone's extensions. I bet it's exclusively strippers who stay here while school's out."

"Other than having to touch other people's hair—" I shudder "—this apartment is a good deal. The building is spooky, though." Cavernous echoes followed our rolling luggage up metal stairways and down empty concrete halls, stopping at our heavy metal door like a barricade.

"Dorms, prisons, hospitals—they're designed to be alienating spaces," Violet says.

The first time I saw Violet she was giving a workshop on women in the Paris Commune of 1871 at an anarchist book fair. I feel like we are as much comrades as friends.

"Can I have one of your energy drinks?" I ask. "I need caffeine."

"Of course. Do you want me to mix you a drink?" She puts down her straightener and pulls a bottle of vodka out of the freezer.

"I brought cups." I grab the bag of dollar store plastic plates, children's coloured cups, and a handful of forks and spoons wrapped in a tea towel. Temporary homemaking is fun, and work justifies my party-girl alter ego.

Violet upturns the bottle and spikes a glass of cherry energy drink. The vodka is so strong it tastes like high school. She pours another for herself and calls, "Can I make you a drink, Bailey?"

"Obviously, bitch!"

"She's just nervous." I hope Violet finds Bailey's crassness endearing.

"No worries." Violet smiles. "I remember my first day. It can be very stressful." I'm relieved Violet is prepared to take care of herself.

"You're going to hold my hand, right?" Bailey asks when I deliver her drink. "Like, literally?" Wanting to be included, she's left the shower curtain open and soaked the floor.

"Of course. We'll do everything together. Tables, dances. We can tell guys we're cousins if you want. They love shit like that, and we sort of look alike."

I try not to stare as she lathers herself with almond-scented soap. I remember running my hands across her rib cage, tracing her spine down to the dimples on her lower back.

"I always wanted to be a stripper," she says.

"Really? I never thought about it until I decided to apply at the Royal. It just seemed like the only way to make good money."

"In high school I loved the idea of dancing in front of men. I had this scene stuck in my head from *Flashdance*. Have you seen it? It's a dancer with a chair and water gets poured on her and she flips her wet hair all sexy-like."

"Stripping is nothing like that," I say.

"Call it daddy issues, but I've always needed men to want me."

"I can't relate to that at all." I draw a heart with my finger in the steam on the mirror. "I have five or so spots open in my life for 'good men' who I love and invest in. The rest are trash."

Bailey leaves my blanket statement unchallenged. "When Casey and I were dating we'd sometimes go to the strip clubs in Ottawa and I'd be so jealous—not over him but of the girls. I wanted to look like them and move like that. But Maria didn't want me to do it," she says of her most recent partner.

"Why not?"

"I'm not sure. She never told me no, but I could tell she wasn't excited about it, so I never pursued it. We're officially broken up now, so there's no one holding me back." She turns off the water and gulps down her drink.

"You're going to do so well," I say, and then reassure her again that gambling a week off her call centre job will be worth it.

"Seriously, though, what should I wear?" She stands on the soaked bath mat, smearing herself head to toe with coconut oil from Costco.

"Wear the shiny pink outfit that makes your tits look like disco balls," I decide.

Before this trip I took Bailey to a stripper tailor in Hamilton to buy outfits and shoes. I offered to front the money she needed, as her credit cards were maxed out. In contrast to the two Yorkshire terriers that darted out snarling from behind display mannequins, the tailor was friendly, smiling, waving us in to explore her sunny store. We browsed aisles created by stacks of black and red shoeboxes, crowned with the heels they contained.

"Can't I wear my bar-bitch heels?" Bailey asked, after checking a few price tags.

"The shoes are essential, believe me. Regular heels will break your toes after a few hours. Besides, no one wears regular heels." I wanted her to fit in on her first day.

The tailor beckoned us to the counter and laid out piles of hand-sewn, clingy, spandex creations. Bikinis, one-pieces, and wraps in camo, stars, holographic, animal print, lace, Lycra, and mesh, all available in an endless combination of colours.

"What size are you?" she asked Bailey.

"I don't know, medium?"

"Try small. You want tight, not loose." She shooed us into a closet with a curtain tacked over the doorframe.

"Is it really supposed to fit like this?" Bailey was checking out the bikini in the mirror, unsure if she hated or loved it.

"It's not like regular lingerie. Let me fix it." My touch sent goose-bumps across her skin as I retied the knots at the sides of the string bikini bottoms and moved them farther up her hips, in a more pleasing V. I scrunched together the iridescent fabric holding up her breasts, exposing formidable amounts of side boob.

"It's seamless, you already look the part," I pronounced.

★ ★ ★

We pull into a dust bowl of a parking lot, the building a squat warehouse, eaves hanging dejectedly off the roof. The only way to know it's a strip club is the sign: *Cold Beers — Hot Girls*.

"Is it even open?" I ask.

"Oh, it's always open," says the cabbie who drops us off in the back of the building in front of an unadorned metal door.

"Moment of truth," I say. "Allen, the owner, told me to come on the phone, but you never really know until you show up. He could say there are already too many girls if he doesn't like us." I rein in my worry. "But that is not going to happen. He told me to come back and bring my friends."

"What's he like?" Bailey asks.

"When Nadia and I were here a few weeks ago, I tried ignoring him and he started throwing ice cubes at me from across the room to see if he could 'get my nipples hard.'"

"Charming," Violet says.

Inside, three doors split off into the changing room, the DJ booth, and the stage. The main club is a factory floor. Black spray foam clings to the high industrial ceiling, but dim lighting creates an oppressive atmosphere. Chin up, I lead us through an expanse of tables to the bar, where Allen, wearing a faded Pink Floyd shirt, is serving drinks to his buddies.

"Remember me?" I say with a wave. "I came back because I missed you."

"And you brought friends. Who are these lovely ladies?" The bar's backdrop is a tropical beach where women in eighties bikinis drink out of coconuts under palm trees.

Allen kisses each of us on both cheeks. "So, I'll put you all on schedule. That means two day shifts each. We pay you but not if you show up late. Day shift means on the floor, ready to go at noon." I wasn't expecting this—Nadia and I hadn't been asked to do day shifts—but we all agree.

"Don't just sit around," he says, before we're allowed to go change. "If you want to make money, you need to work for it. And *smile*, ladies."

He extends his palm from his chest like a Shakespearean actor and says, "Project energy and fun. Let me tell you, if you aren't making a thousand dollars here every day, then you are a fucking idiot."

"We're all very hard workers," Bailey says. Then he makes us each a drink "on the house," because he is, as he states, the world's best boss.

Once we've signed in with the DJ and I've taken Bailey on a tour of the club, there's nothing left to do but start working. Violet is already at a table solo.

"Are you ready?" I hoped the easy hire would give Bailey confidence, but it hasn't. She's picking at her nail polish, mute. "How about we try to get a double out of that old guy in the plaid shirt?"

"I'd rather try the two younger ones who came in a few minutes ago," she says. "I think I'll find them easier to relate to." Generally, I avoid young guys until all other options are exhausted. The power dynamic doesn't feel as weighted in my favour. Young guys don't have as much desperation, and sometimes they're there just to show off to friends, or to feel superior because they think they're hotshots. Plus, they intimidate me. I don't like to play games or feel rejected. But for Bailey, I lead us to the two badly sunburned boys in polo shirts.

"You have to be nice to her, it's her first day," I say.

"Naw, she looks way too good. You girls want a drink?"

We pair off. I hope Bailey doesn't feel like I am abandoning her as I let my guy tell me about the highway extension he's helping build between Sudbury and Barrie. I keep sneaking glances at Bailey's long legs and the reflective wrapping around her platforms that make her look like she's floating. More relaxed now, she bats her lashes and playfully slaps her guy's chest: *oh you, behave.*

"She's so skinny," he says to his friend about Bailey, as if he just can't believe it. The skin dips between her hip bones like a sheet stretched to dry over the backs of two kitchen chairs. I can't help feeling jealous that Bailey stopped eating a few days ago. A nauseating combination of fear and preparation for this job intensified previous disordered eating behaviours.

"And mine is an alternative pin-up girl," my guy says. "Look at this hourglass." He draws my shape in the air, his hands starting wide, dipping in almost to touch, and then flaring back out, reminding me that I am classified as "not skinny."

Allowing men to project their own eroticized stereotypes onto me is part of what I think of as my job, and even though I try to let their comments affect me as little as possible, direct comparisons between my friends' bodies and mine are extra difficult. I already compare my body with everyone else's, especially other sex workers, and I'm constantly battling internalized fatphobia and an eating disorder that leave me with a distorted view of my own body. Comments like this remind me that men judge me in the same ways I judge myself.

The polo shirt boys likely have sunstroke after a day playing golf. It's Bailey's guy who suggests, without need of convincing, that we all go to the VIP. I had forgotten until I saw it again how much I hate it. Instead of being a private, cavelike room, this VIP is an open platform to the right of the stage. The whole bar can see in. Two rows of ten oversized red vinyl chairs are corralled inside wooden railings like a cattle feeding station. The rows are separated down the middle by a three-foot dividing wall over which the clients face one another whenever they look over their girl's shoulder. It's a horrible set-up where clients see themselves reflected in the men across from them or are made uncomfortable by the experience of accidentally looking at another man while turned on. Unless dancers can fully keep their clients' attention, this man-on-man closeness can make clients want to prematurely end an awkward experience. The narrow space is prohibitively small for dancing, and the bulky armrests on the tacky chairs prevent many up-close moves. After my last stint here I had sore hips and bruised shins and knees.

To keep an eye on Bailey I autopilot my lap dance: make my ass jiggle, get up on the arms of the chair so my pussy is at his face level, slide down his body collecting tension in my back muscles. A chair away, Bailey laughs with her guy. Whispers in his ear and tries out some moves that aren't just riding his lap. Like most people socialized as women, she can fake a good time for the benefit of men, so despite how convincing she looks I'm still anxious to find out how she feels.

"This is as much as I would make in a five-hour shift at my other job," she says once the dances are over and the boys have gone back to the bar. .

"It's easy, right?"

"It's good. It's awesome, I guess." She's got that stunned look, eyebrows frozen in surprise. Bailey is one of the most emotionally articulate people I know, so it's disconcerting to see her overwhelmed, unable to check in with herself.

"I don't know if I can do it," Bailey says about her imminent stage show. The three of us are reunited, sitting at a table with stools so tall our heels don't touch the carpet.

"It's not like dancing," I say. "It's like fake, sexy, whatever. Once you're up there, you can count how many guys are here to watch you. It's still early, so there's less than ten. They're not even going to care."

"Or you can look at us," says Violet. "We'll be right here cheering for you. You've been practising and you're going to do really well."

Wow, that was much more reassuring than what I said. I should do something, rub Bailey's back, but I hesitate, not wanting to draw attention. The DJ announces, "Onstage after this song, the brand new, ultra-sexy Bailey!"

"Why did you tell him it's my first day?" She is miserable.

"You only get to be new for real once. Guys love it. They'll be lining up to take you for dances."

She stares intently at the floor, almost hyperventilating, and when I touch her forearm it's burning up. "Listen, you're sexy as hell. You're going to be fine."

"What if I fall?"

"Laugh it off and do some floorwork," Violet says.

"What if they boo me?"

"I've never seen a girl get booed onstage," I say. "Ever. If guys want to say something mean about you, they'll do it behind your back."

She grimaces. While I'm trying to think of something nicer to say, the DJ calls her name. Bailey sets her shoulders and paces to the stage as if she's walking the plank.

The multicoloured Christmas lights looped above mirrors at the back of the stage illuminate Bailey's skin with possibilities. She begins her first stage show, as I did mine, anchored to the pole. Unlike at other clubs, this pole isn't attached to the ceiling. It rises seven feet and is capped by a sphere of brass. The screws securing it to the stage are loose so the pole wobbles. I can see Bailey figuring that out, leaning only a portion of her weight on it in case it gives out. She's braver than me, and in the second song she ventures out along the T-shaped catwalk. Gets on her knees and prowls. When she tries to get up her heel won't hold on the wax-slicked stage and she slips. My heart leaps and I grab Violet's arm. We watch Bailey laugh, take a knee, and carefully stand. For her final song she dances to "Toxic." Bailey's persona mirrors Britney Spears, and the patrons are loving her.

"Give me a bill so I can go up with her," I order the nearest man. Tucking his money into the front of my bikini, I crawl onto the stage and lie on my back.

"I'm so proud of you," I say, as she slides up between my legs and settles onto my pelvis. When she arches her spine, it is as if I'm inside her and the heat between us melts the time between now and two weeks ago. Her mattress on the floor, tarot cards propped on shelves like saints honoured with altars of seashells and dried wildflowers. Between my legs the tight bands of the strap-on harness caused both annoyance and arousal. The taste of her, bold as the flickering beeswax candles, was fresh on my tongue. We flipped so she was beneath me. Often in sex I receive, so it was a gift to be able to give, to fuck. Bailey's breasts heaved as she twisted the cotton sheets, while decals of monarch butterflies on her window migrated in the moonlight.

Onstage she whispers as she sweeps her body forward, "Did you see? I almost fell." Hair shrouds our faces.

"Really? I didn't notice."

Bailey leaves the stage to an enthusiastic round of applause from the small but vocal audience, including Violet, who can do a very loud dog whistle. Bailey pulls me into the women's washroom, used by both dancers and female customers. Her underwear around her ankles, she pees with the stall door open, counting the money she's made so far.

"You did so good up there!" I congratulate her.

"I've already made more than a hundred dollars," she says.

Bailey is constantly hiding cash in marked envelopes and freezing her credit cards in blocks of ice. It's not just a love of shopping that gets her in trouble—she thinks of her access to money as a privilege that should be shared. Once she put a friend's entire gender-confirming top surgery on a credit card and was never reimbursed. The hundred dollars she's made so far tonight is a drop in the bucket of her debt. It is groceries and gas. It will be passed off to a landlord, or a credit card company, or the phone bill.

"Wait 'til the end of the night," I say.

"The flirting part is easier than I thought, and the stage show, not that I was good at it, but it was fun. *Bailey*," she refers to herself in the third person using her working name, "loves this shit!"

"I knew you'd be great." I sound like a boastful coach, as if my belief in her did half the work. In the mirror, cover-up is making the dry skin on my forehead flaky and set against purple lipstick my teeth appear yellow.

I check my texts from Luke. *Did you guys get checked in okay?* Followed by a picture of Mira sleeping on her back in what we call her dropped-from-an-airplane position. Followed by, *Hope it goes really well for you tonight! How's Bailey doing?*

I respond, *She's a little drunk but she's doing well. How are you?*

He writes back almost right away, *glad she's okay. I'm in bed but call me in the morning.*

I send a series of sparkling heart emojis and shove my phone back into my clutch.

"Let's go," Bailey takes my hands. She is clammy, sweating but cold.

As the night speeds up, Bailey and I lose each other for periods. We go into the VIP together but leave at different times and pick up new guys and disappear again. It's steadier than the Royal and the clients don't need much convincing. I keep a running tally of exactly how much money I've made—tonight will be a good night. When I get a free minute I see Bailey entertaining a table of five guys.

"These gentlemen had a hard day golfing and now they're here to have fun with us," she greets me. This is ..." She proceeds to name all of them correctly, and we applaud her sharp memory.

"Now," says the loudest of the bunch, "Michelle and Bailey, are those your real names?" His tone suggests he doesn't like being lied to.

"My real name is Victoria Secret," I say. "Hers is Diamond Princess."

They laugh and let it go. One guy whistles loudly. The lone waitress leaning against the bar jumps at the sound. She might have been a dancer once with the way her sassy high ponytail swings as she approaches.

"What?" she demands.

The guy with the money orders another round by wordlessly throwing a fifty on her drink tray. To us, he says, "You girls are both very pretty, but I gotta tell you, I'm a breast man. So you know I'm not lying when I say, Bailey, your breasts are incredible. Best I've ever seen." He kisses his fingers like she is a pizza. "Michelle, your breasts are nice. They've got that good perky shape, but they're just not as big and round as Bailey's. No offence."

I start an internal stopwatch: by the time the waitress returns we have to convince them to take us to the VIP or we're leaving.

"That's not a very nice thing to say," Bailey scolds him like he's a naughty child.

"He's right, your tits are sooo sexy." I lean onto her to jiggle them, weightless and warm. Her sternum is flushed.

The loudmouth slams the table. "Show me a nipple!"

"You can see everything you want in the back. Let's go right now." I extend my hand, but he waves it away.

"No, I'm teasing. You girls like golf?"

I turn my whole body away to scan the room. More than a few men have empty seats beside them. It's worth it to move on. Violet is in the VIP corral again. Her pale skin makes her look like a strip of steam, ethereal against the dingy backdrop of a faded old man.

"Your friend is rude. She in a bad mood? You're so much nicer than her," says the guy closest to Bailey. He is younger than his friends, late twenties, tanned, muscular, reeking of Old Spice. On his right bicep the tail of a tribal dragon tattoo pokes out of his golf shirt.

"Don't be mean." Bailey pets him.

"Last chance, boys," I say, as I stand up and remove my drink from the waitress's returning tray. I hope Bailey will follow, but she stays.

When I find Bailey again later, she's with a scruffy-looking biker. "Look what Daddy made for me. I'm his stripper wife." She holds out her hand for me to examine. On her ring finger is a wedge of brown glass, the lip of a broken beer bottle. She wiggles it off her knuckle, away from the delicate webbing between her fingers, and places the trinket in my palm. Her skin has warmed the cool glass. I run my thumb over the sharp edge, "I'll keep this safe for you. For later. Do you want to come do some tables with me, or is he going to take you for dances?"

The biker addresses me. "Bailey and I have an understanding. She knows I ain't going for dances, but anytime she needs a drink, she's to come see me."

I pull Bailey up, spin us off together. "You're too nice to them," I warn her.

"He's harmless. His wife died and he needs someone to talk to."

"Fine, but he needs to pay you for talking." I sit us down at the nearest open table.

By the end of the night the VIP is a sloppy, tightly packed party. Bailey is working hard. She holds her hair up and lets it fall onto her sweaty, naked back. Leans back onto their chests and puts her arm up behind her to touch their necks. The guy I've ended up with is perfectly lazy. He doesn't want to go home yet, and doesn't want to bother finding another girl, so I keep dancing, winding down the clock.

At exactly two a.m., hanging tubes of fluorescent lights switch on. The song ends and silence takes its place. The echoes of the party reverberate through the warehouse and brightness exposes the dark corners, like kicking the top off an ant colony. The men who exceeded their cash flow line up at the ATM, the girls they owe sticking close. The waitress rushes to spray sticky tabletops and collect bottles. Allen has long since gotten drunk and probably driven himself home.

Violet and I collapse at a table, waiting for Bailey to finish talking to her final client. "We should have driven," Violet says. "They told me I'm on schedule for noon tomorrow, so I stopped drinking hours ago."

"That's too soon."

"I know. I'm going to get four hours of sleep." Her mascara is smudged and her black cherry lipstick runs thin.

"Look at this," Bailey says as she joins us waving a handful of bills.

"Put that away," I urge. "Never let girls see your money. We don't want to stick around, so put your clothes on fast."

The changing room is a congested mob of girls. Some talk to their boyfriends, or call cabs, while others try to figure out which client they're going to party with.

"Do you girls need any green?" asks a stripper whose thick foundation covers deep pockmarks.

"No, thank you, we're fine." Violet is ever polite.

I'm waiting in sweatpants and a crop top while Bailey sits checking her phone. "Come on, let's do that later," I push. She stands and a girl throwing a gym bag over her shoulder knocks into her. The girl doesn't apologize, but Bailey doesn't notice.

"You girls aren't from around here," a girl with box braids says.

"We're only here for a week." I like to let girls know they only have to suffer our presence for a limited time.

"You all worked hard today. I like that." She shakes our hands. "I'm Ruby. If you need anything, let me know." I find her friendliness suspicious. What does she get out of being nice to us? Another girl snorted with laughter when Ruby complimented us, but she was looking at her phone, so I can't tell if she was laughing at us. Have I become that jaded?

The oldest stripper at the end of the packed row is picking through a takeout container, mumbling to no one in particular. Her thin hair is pumped with hairspray, clip-in extensions visible. She has the kind of tits that make people uncomfortable: round, hard, and too high on the chest. They stand wrinkle free while the rest of her tanned skin sags. I know her name is Kitty because I've watched her stage show and heard men say awful things about her.

"My drink and my bandana were sitting with my client, right at his table, and that girl sits down while I was away for a minute and steals him. I'm going to kill that little bitch." Kitty slams the counter. The girls around her don't react.

"I'm going to kill her!" Kitty shouts. "I'm going to steal that bitch's beauty! Take some keys and cut up her pretty little face! Nobody likes a girl with scars."

"Kitty, calm down, darling," says our new acquaintance. "It's not a big deal. There are enough clients to share."

"Maybe there's lots of clients for you, Ruby, but I needed him. He was mine. The next time I see that fuckin' girl ..." She stabs a forkful of poutine.

When we enter our apartment it doesn't feel like coming home, but it is a relief. We forgot to turn down the AC when we left, so it's freezing and, somehow, still humid. I put on a pair of slippers and eat the rest of the rice crackers I brought to snack on in the car.

"I've got to wake up so early to get ready, I'm going to bed." Violet disappears into her bedroom.

Bailey counts her money on the floor, wearing only a pair of baggy grey sweatpants and a serious expression. She sorts it by colour: red, green, blue. Presses the wrinkles out of the bills and flips them all the same way so their faces stare at the ceiling.

"This is more than I make in a week," she says, then fetches a pen and leather-bound agenda from one of her many bags and opens it to a page titled *Expenses*.

"Here is everything I borrowed for outfits, the hotel, and gas." She places the majority of her first night's money in front of me.

"It's all profit from here," I say, as I set the bills on my purse. They feel hot, as if I've stolen them from her.

When Nadia and I were here we waited until our first day off to count our week's take. After sleeping until two on that Monday we stacked piles of hundreds on our polyester bedspreads until they looked like a checkerboard. I thought, *This is so much and not nearly enough.*

★ ★ ★

WEDNESDAY

Violet checks the microwave clock. "I can't believe it's eleven thirty. Can you call me a cab? I'm going to be late for my stupid day shift."

"I'll drive you," I suggest.

"Are you sure?"

"I need to get tea anyway. Let me put on some clothes."

I change quietly in the room where Bailey is passed out. She is wearing a sleep mask with an embroidered weed leaf over each eye, like coins for the dead.

The first breath of outside air is crushing. Sweat instantly beads, stinging my recently shaved skin. We open the car doors and fan them like gills to move some broiling air. I turn on the car and mash the buttons to open all the windows, but only the driver's side moves. I try pressing buttons nicely and individually, then turning the car off and on, but three windows stay sealed tight. "We are going to die on the drive home," I say, panicking as I imagine us stuck in Toronto traffic with one working window and no air conditioner.

The drive-through line at Tim Hortons seems like the entrance to hell. My thighs are liquid against each other, underarms sweating clean through last night's deodorant.

"Can you call Bailey and ask what kind of coffee she wants?" I ask Violet. "I should know, but I can't remember, can't even think."

"I'm so hungover. Don't talk to me about coffee ever again," Bailey answers and hangs up.

"I don't want to do this," Violet says as we pull up to the club at 11:55. The parking lot contains two cars, most likely belonging to Allen and Gordie, the bouncer who doubles as a daytime DJ.

"Call if you need anything. We'll come in early if you want company," I promise.

Violet wrestles herself out of the car, juggling her coffee and her overstuffed work bag. "I'm assuming I'll be hungry by nine. Can you guys bring me an energy drink?" she asks. "Red flavour."

Bailey hears me struggling to get the key into the lock while balancing our drinks and opens the door. Forehead furrowed, cheeks ashen, she squints against the light.

"How are you doing, buddy?" I step inside.

"I will puke if I drink that coffee," she says. "I may puke anyway. Check it out, it looks like my pussy got attacked by sandpaper." She opens her fluffy blue robe. Bending down to take a closer look, I see her skin is swollen and red.

"It's because I got a Brazilian yesterday morning, right before we got into the car."

"Let's put some ice on it. It might help the swelling."

"Ice and a Percocet, as soon as I'm sure I won't throw it back up. Oh God, it's day two and I'm already broken."

Other than the bottle of vodka, the freezer contains one blue lunch-box ice pack. I wrap it in a clean work bandana. Bailey holds it against herself and says, "As long as I don't make zero every other night, this trip will have been worth it." She smiles for a second before lurching to the bathroom.

In the courtyard of our dormitory is a lone gazebo. Lying beside Bailey on the wooden floor, I see graffiti and crushed beer cans nailed to the ceiling.

"Who is texting you so much?" I ask as Bailey's phone beeps again.

"Matt."

"Who?"

"That bro with the dragon tattoo from last night."

"You gave him your number? Why?"

"I don't know. Want to see a picture of his dick?" We take a moment to stare at the photo, sent from his bathroom at 3:45 that morning.

"Did he even take you for dances?"

"No, but—"

"Bailey, delete his number right now. He just wants to brag to his friends that he can get a stripper for free."

"Maybe I want to have sex with him," she says.

Nothing moves except the ravens who sail in and out of view. "Boring," I groan. "I met him for two seconds and he's so grossly normal."

She sets down her phone and lights another cigarette, her blue acrylics the same colour as the packaging. "I didn't say I wanted to date him.

Honestly, I'm embarrassed, but right now I need dudes to like me. I want a trophy fuck to remind me I'm hot."

"You're hot!" I exclaim as she shakes her head. "He doesn't even respect you enough to pay you while you're working."

"He is a total garbage person. I know that."

"Then why?"

"We can't all be lucky enough to have ourselves a Luke," she says.

"Oh no, I forgot to call him. I'm a terrible girlfriend."

"You're not the easiest one to date," she teases.

"I'm too high to call Luke now," I say, pleasantly adrift on painkillers. "I'm working, he'll understand."

"He will. He's a good man."

I nod.

She picks up her phone and starts texting again. "So you really think this thing with Matt is a bad idea?"

"It's a terrible idea. If you can get him to give you money, it's different, but if he's not paying you, he's playing you."

"Nice rhyme, loser."

★ ★ ★

Club Goldmine is as dead as Violet warned it would be. She follows Bailey and me into the changing room and sits while we get ready. The heels she's wearing are my favourites, stilettos shaped like guns, their black platforms studded with a mini belt of bullets.

"None of the girls spoke to me today. I am a pariah," Violet says. "I ended up getting a lot of notation done for my thesis, though, so that's good."

"Here, have these." I hand her an energy drink and a protein bar.

"I can't believe it's only eight. I feel like I've been here forever." She allows her spine to round, sighs before eating slowly.

My style tonight is trashy: underwear that look like jean shorts, paired with knee-high white socks printed with red and blue weed leaves. I don't even like weed—it makes me unhinged and anxious—but I get attention from placid stoners, who make tame clients.

Violet takes a picture of a sign that says, *Photography is Forbidden*, then we crowd in for a selfie under another that reads, *The Prettiest Face is the One with a Smile.*

★ ★ ★

"Be careful onstage," Ruby warns. "It's slippery up there because they keep waxing the stage even though we tell them to stop. A lot of girls slip and fall if they wear heels. But if you take your heels off, watch out for the broken flooring. Sometimes sharp chunks of vinyl stick up. I cut my foot open so bad I had to get stitches."

I no longer find her friendliness suspicious; she's just nice. While she talks she bends her wrist all the way back until her fingers touch her forearm. Catching me staring she explains, "I'm a double-jointed contortionist."

Her stage show features a series of brutal-looking positions, including tucking her knees behind her skull and performing splits so deep her knees bend the wrong way. I can't stop watching; it's probably the most unique stage show I've seen. For the climax, she stands, then bends backward and over until her chest touches the ground, until her body looks like a wagon wheel.

★ ★ ★

The client is holding Bailey's hand. "She is so perfect I may have to kidnap her. Throw her in the back of my truck, take her home to have my way with her."

Jokes like this are common, but there's something especially sickening about the way he looks at her, with infatuation, as if he thought this would charm her, maybe boost her self-esteem, now that she knows he thinks she is good enough to abduct and rape.

★ ★ ★

Usually I avoid men I find attractive. Hormones and charm can trip me up, make me forget why I'm here, but I can't resist sitting with this guy with his long dark hair pulled into a single braid, rocking black athletic shorts patterned with bright fishing lures.

"Great shorts," I say.

"I know." He tips his chair back, arms crossed. So he's a quiet type, too—again, not my strong point. It's easier for me when they like to talk about themselves. Reaching for something to say, I tell him the automatic windows on my car are all stuck closed.

"It's the fuses. If you're around later this week, I'll come take a look." He says this with the mild annoyance of a teenager agreeing to help his grandma with her computer.

"That would be really great, thank you."

"Are we going for a dance then?" He jerks a thumb toward the VIP.

"Absolutely, yes, let's go."

★ ★ ★

"This club isn't that bad," Violet says between clients.

"Are you kidding? The ceiling leaks everywhere." I point to multiple five-litre buckets scattered like forest mushrooms around the club. "Those are full of water and it hasn't rained in months. The stage is dangerous and the half-demolished shower stall makes the washroom a construction site."

Violet shrugs. "When I waitressed at the strip club in Hamilton I had to start putting my clothes and purse in a garbage bag when I got to work because I was bringing home cockroaches. I made sure clients couldn't see them crawling on drink trays, but sometimes they'd fall into their drinks and I'd have to make them a new one."

"You win," I say.

"How is Bailey doing?" she asks.

"I can't tell. She's pretty drunk again." I can hear her cackling from across the bar. I consider explaining how a recent breakup has made Bailey a little less balanced, a bit more out of control than normal but then realize that I have no idea what is happening in Violet's world. "How are you?" I ask.

"I'm fine," she says, and it seems like she's talking through the crack of a locked door.

I join Bailey at her table. Her eyes are dry ice as she closes the distance between us and begins to kiss me, mouth wet from shots of vodka. I let myself sink into the softness for a moment before pulling back. "Not for free," I whisper to her, but she windmills her arms and grabs my hips, kneels and pretends to go down on me. With my legs clamped together I bend to push her away and the table of guys hollers, egging her on.

"We'll be right back," I promise, dragging her into the bathroom, where I hold her shoulders. "You need to chill and drink some water. You can't kiss me like that here."

"I kissed you?"

"You don't remember two seconds ago?"

"You're sexy."

"Other girls will see that and think you're giving more away than they are. That's bad."

"I'll be good, I'll be good." She wants to return to the action.

At the end of the night Bailey is taking too long to get dressed. Violet had agreed to drive us home as I have a day shift in the morning.

"Where did you put the car keys, Bailey?" Violet asks, searching her purse.

"I don't know, bitch. Check your purse," Bailey says playfully. She's sitting on the ground struggling to undo the tiny buckle on the strap of her heel with nails like claws.

The only other dancer left besides us is a tough-looking white girl with 905 tattooed on the back of her neck. She's casually reapplying mascara, which I assume means she's waiting to be picked up for a booty call or end-of-the-night trick. I'm fully dressed and leaning against the lockers, arms crossed, compiling a mental list of things Bailey did tonight that I need to talk to her about tomorrow.

"Dig for the keys, you slut!" Bailey shrieks at Violet, who is elbow deep in her purse.

"Get your pants on," I tell her. I can't wait to crawl into bed. Even though it's a flimsy twin mattress on a hard wooden frame, I want to be quiet and alone.

"Whoa, whoa, relax. Don't be such a whore," Bailey says.

Incensed, 905 turns to Bailey. "You should feel blessed that you have these girls to help your drunk ass. Don't talk to them that way after they carried you around all night."

"We're not offended," Violet says. "She's just kidding."

"Personally, I think she's being a little bitch. I wouldn't put up with that if I was you. You're trying to be her friend and she does you like that? I would knock her ass out."

I force a short, calm response. "There's no problem. We're good."

She turns back to the mirror, completely unconcerned that it would be three of us against her if she started a fight. "Y'all wanna be careful. The two of you taking care of that drunk bitch, not standing up for yourselves ... Someone might think they could jump you, easy."

Thankfully, Bailey remains quiet. Concentrating hard, she bypasses the clasp by ripping her shoes off her feet and struggling into shorts.

Keys in hand, Violet moves Bailey ahead of her and out the door.

"Have a good night," I say to the girl. She doesn't respond or break her eye contact with the mirror.

A bloodless moon floats above the empty parking lot. As I lock the doors behind us and ram the car into drive, Violet turns to Bailey in the back seat and says, "That was really harsh."

"Why did she have to be so mean?" Bailey begins to cry.

"Sometimes girls act like that because they're upset. Maybe she didn't make much money tonight. I doubt it was about you," Violet says.

"But doesn't she know that I know how blessed I am to have you guys? I wasn't being rude, was I?"

"Well, yes, but not extraordinarily rude." I keep checking the rear-view. "Guys, I think she was considering robbing us." I can't tell if I'm being paranoid or not. "If that had broken out into a fight, we might have had to leave town." I worry that 905 will be there again tomorrow, that she might bring friends.

"She didn't scare me," Violet says. "I'm small, but I know how to fight."

We wait at red lights with no other cars in sight. Fog in the ditches and frost-carved dips in the asphalt. Head down, Bailey cries in the back. I would fight, even unskilled and terrified, to defend her.

Once we get into the dorm room I begin to calm down. Bailey, however, collapses onto the kitchen floor, crying so hard she can't breathe.

"She's just drunk and overwhelmed," I say to Violet.

"Maybe." Violet pulls a package of baby cucumbers out of the fridge and perches on a kitchen chair. It's so humid in here the concrete walls are almost in tears. I boil water for tea.

"Why did she hate me?" Bailey asks.

Violet responds, "Three new girls at once is a lot in smaller clubs. Plus you're pretty and young, and you know how these places encourage competition through insecurity and scarcity."

It's a good answer, but Bailey is responding to an internal dialogue. "Doesn't she know I mean 'whore' as a compliment? I love strippers. I used to be a camgirl. I love escorts, all sex workers."

The kettle clicks off. I pour valerian tea for myself and place a plastic mug of tap water in front of Bailey. "Drink this."

"Water is gross," she says.

I sit beside her. "Drink it all at once."

She downs it, then throws the cup at the opposite wall and yells, "I didn't want him to touch me like that, but he wouldn't stop."

A chill floods over me as if she'd thrown the water in my face.

"Who wouldn't stop?" Violet asks.

"Sheldon. He was that bald engineer I was with for so long."

I shake my head, unable to keep track of all the people we met.

Bailey continues, "He works for the city, total slime bag. He was squeezing my tits so hard, and he kept putting his fingers inside me. I told him no, like you guys said, gently, like, oh, haha, don't do that, honey, but he kept doing it anyways."

"Where? When?" I rewind the night, trying to remember.

"In the VIP, near the end. I even moved his hands away a bunch of times, but he wouldn't stop. I told him the dances were over, but he kept giving me money and I didn't know if I could refuse. I didn't know what to do."

"It seems like you got a really bad guy," I say. "It's not always like that and we can work on your boundaries. That happens so rarely—"

Violet cuts me off, saying what I should have said. "Bailey, what happened is an assault. It's not your fault."

"I need sleep." Bailey picks herself up, runs her hand along the wall to guide herself to the bedroom. When she collapses, the air mattress exhales as if punched.

I turn to Violet. "We were back there together and I was watching her, but I didn't see it."

"This is awful," says Violet.

"I feel sick," I say. "She's so good at acting I couldn't tell anything was wrong. Do you think she'll want to go home?"

Violet pushes away her package of cucumbers. "I'm sure she'll let us know in the morning what's best for her."

★ ★ ★

THURSDAY

I want to bring Bailey coffee and coax her out of bed. Watch her tie her cotton candy hair up with a bandana and go sit with her under the gazebo again to see if we can get back to laughing. I want to know so badly if she will want to leave, but she is still sleeping when I leave for my day shift.

The club is going through the motions of being open, but no one expects any clients this early. Seven other girls are spread throughout the club, absorbed in the blue of their phones. Gordie plays a stream of dusty songs geared to middle-aged nostalgia. I am wondering how many times I've been forced to listen to "Enter Sandman," when Keesha sits at my table.

"I didn't know you worked here." I'm happy to see a familiar face.

"I come up here a week on, a week off," she says. "It's good in the summer. Actually, it's good in the winter, too. All the dudes come in on their Ski-Doos. It's way better than the city." She means Toronto. "Everyone in the city clubs wants to be a baller, wants to be seen. Up here it's more honest. If a guy comes in, he's buying a dance, not trying to pop bottles and take you to his condo for an after-party."

"I can't believe they force us to work this early, though," I complain. "If I was a guy, I wouldn't want to be in a dank strip club on a day like today. It's gorgeous out."

"Yeah, but we're gorgeous, too," she teases. "And it only takes that one client to make it worth it." She's wearing a gold necklace with a four-leaf-clover pendant. "Guys up here are starving for new girls, so it's easy to snag regulars. I got one Tuna coming in for me tonight. I get a stack off him every time."

Like a wasp to the honey of human voices, Gordie lumbers over. "You girls remember Sugar?" he gossips. "She was old and batshit crazy?"

I shake my head, but Keesha nods.

"She overdosed in the bathroom a week ago."

"Did she die?" Keesha asks.

"Don't think so." He shrugs. "But that's super low-down. If you can't work without smashing a bag of heroin, that's pretty bad." He chugs the rest of his second extra-large energy drink.

"You know they have Narcan now, right? It's like an EpiPen for opiates. You could keep some behind the bar," I say.

"You think Allen's gonna spring for that?"

"You can get it for free," I press, but Gordie is moving on.

I'd read that people only have a set number of words they can speak per day. As an introvert, I have a word count that is lower than most people's. In this profession, every unnecessary sentence is a waste and Gordie, with his incessant chatter, is depleting me.

"Nadia is the best one of yous I've ever seen," Gordie reminisces. "One time she had a competition with her friend. They bet to see who could make the most money over twelve hours, and do you know how much Nadia pulled in?" The number shocks me. I've never made that much in a day.

Nadia is blessed by the river. It flows for her in a perpetual springtime of cold, swift waters. Men drown in her ability to appear genuinely attracted to them, interested as much in their jobs as their rehashed stories of heroism. The way she touches their arms and chests stimulates memories of the slimmer, more muscular bodies of their youth. Running her fingers through her hair, she coaxes them into her current.

"She's a natural." My throat is dry.

"What's she doing now?" Gordie asks.

Her social media is splashed with photos from a recent European vacation, sunbathing beside an aquamarine ocean, skin banded in the shade of palm fronds.

"She retired." I slash my word count. Stripping my sentences down to their skeletons. Saving my charm for someone who pays me.

Gordie is shaking his head. "Believe me, girls like that don't quit."

Marching in from a smoke break Allen stops, swoops down, and kisses me on the mouth, reeking of cigarettes and garlic bread.

"Well, he's drunk already," Gordie says when Allen's gone.

"Oh my God, ew," Keesha says.

I rub my lips, getting lipstick on the back of my hand. "How does he get away with stuff like that?"

"He's the owner." Gordie shrugs.

I excuse myself to go for a smoke break. Put on clothes and sit on the concrete slab behind the club. Press myself up against the sliver of shade from the building, pick at rocks and pieces of glass. The clouds are an oil painting. I call Luke.

"My love," he says, followed by my real name. Hearing that name is vexing. As if it shouldn't be uttered while I am full-time Michelle.

"This is awful," I say.

"Not as good as last time?"

"The nights have been good, the money is good, but day shift is a scam and I have to do two of them. I'm wasting all my energy being mad and cold. This place is dead. Like not one single person in here. And the DJ won't stop talking to me. I don't hate the work itself. What I hate is sitting around doing nothing."

"Especially when you're supposed to have enough energy to pull a double," he says, then adds cheerily, "You should see this stuffed baby-doll toy that Mira found in the park on our walk. She carried it all the way home, so proud. It was too cute, I couldn't take it away from her, and now she's ripping it apart on her bed."

"That is disgusting and wonderful." I lean my head back against the steel blue of the hot metal siding. I miss sweeping our wood floors while sunlight moves through the rooms, how even the dust motes sparkle.

"What are you doing now?" Luke asks.

"Pretending to smoke. They make you ask permission for smoke breaks here. They treat us like children and expect us to act like sex objects."

"Misogyny is bullshit," Luke says.

"I wouldn't have a job without it," I answer. I hear him getting off the couch and the sound of Mira's nails clicking as she follows him through the kitchen and out the glass doors to the back porch.

"What did you mean when you texted me to say Bailey had a bad night?" he asks.

It seems impossible to explain, as if the drama is years old. "Basically, she got too drunk and another girl got mad at her."

"Is there going to be a fight?" Luke is usually very good at controlling his reactions, but I pick up serious concern.

"I don't know. That girl isn't here today, so maybe she won't come in. I'm not a fighter."

"You are very tough in other ways," he says.

I hesitate before continuing, knowing the heart of the matter is much more upsetting. "And Bailey got sexually assaulted last night."

After I provide brief context Luke asks if he should come get us. "I could be there in six hours if I borrow a car."

"No," I say slowly, "I don't think we need that. I haven't talked to Bailey today, but we'll see how tonight goes."

The door swings open and Gordie sticks his head out. "Almost done, Michelle?"

"Why? Are there men in there now?"

"You only get five minutes for break, so hurry up. I've got to get you onstage."

"There is literally no one here!"

"Boss's orders. He wants girls onstage periodically in case a guy happens to wander in."

"I'll be there in a minute." I turn away from him until he closes the door. "Apparently I have to go."

"What happened to Bailey is fucked. If there's anything I can do ..."

I feel close to tears but choke out, "I love you so much, but I'm handling it."

I send Bailey the text I've been putting off: *Do you think you're going to come in tonight?* Ants crawl across cigarette butts stained with lipstick and pieces of gum flattened into the cement. Last night I could have leaned over the divider in the VIP, yelled at her client, publicly shamed him in front of the men, and absolved Bailey in front of the girls. "What do you think you're doing?" I could have screamed. "She told you to stop, you rapist fuck. Give her her money and get out of here!" Instead, my rage remains bottled up with no place to go.

I refuse to dance to my high-energy nighttime mix and choose bratty high school pop punk: Blink-182. First I clean the pole using my bandana, then spend until after the first chorus fixing my outfit in the mirror. I walk instead of sway. Step around the pole instead of spin. Let my clothes fall to the floor unceremoniously. Not one time does Allen or his buddies look up from their huddle at the bar.

I'm feeling like death, Bailey responds to my text. *Violet wants to know if we should come in early?*

No! Do not come in early. I haven't made any money in five hours. Getting ready with my friends is my favourite part and I'm bitter I'm missing it. But at least now I know that Bailey is neither taking a day off nor packing it in and driving south.

★ ★ ★

Kitty has been giving me death stares all day, but now she is waving me over to a table with the two boys she pounced on the second they walked in.

"He won't go without a girl for his friend," she tells me and resumes negotiating with her guy by whispering in his ear. The boy I sit beside won't make eye contact, let alone carry on a conversation. He has a huge silly grin and glasses as thick as a slice of bread. So we sit in silence until Kitty says, "We're ready now," and herds us into the VIP.

The boys call it quits after two dances. Kitty goes directly to the changing room, but the boys stick with me.

"That was the weirdest hand job I ever got," her guy says.

Glasses says, "Gross, dude. You let her jerk you off?" He spent his whole dance happily stunned. It had been enough for him to softly hold my hips with sweaty palms while I moved through my bends and jiggles. He didn't even notice the service his friend received a few seats over.

"Yeah, but I told her I only had a twenty," the friend snickers, opening his wallet to prove he still has multiple bills.

"That's so rude." My voice is shrill. "You're supposed to pay her *extra*."

"Yeah, but did you see her? She's like my friggin' grandmother."

★ ★ ★

Bailey and Violet show up right before the cut-off. "We drove here," Bailey says. "It'll give me a reason to stay sober tonight."

The skin around her eyes is puffy and the lines on her forehead more pronounced. As much as I spent the whole day hoping she'd decide to come in, I now wonder if it might have been better for her to take the night off.

A client jokes, "You girls should pay me to dance for you."

I laugh extra loud to cover the fact that Bailey just can't.

Being a good conversationalist is an essential part of my hustle, but constantly smiling, listening, validating, flirting, and complimenting becomes a grind in itself. It's draining to be both interested and interesting while having similar conversations over and over.

"You girls want shots?" he asks.

"No." Bailey looks sick.

The client begins casting around for the more fun girls, hoping Bailey and I will move on. Bailey has been making clients uncomfortable all night. Her presence forces them to confront the fact that this isn't a party and some of us are trying to make it through a long shift sober, after a rough night.

★ ★ ★

Violet catches me, her eyes wild.

"What's up?" I ask.

"First, a client's girlfriend cornered me in the bathroom and yelled at me for disrespecting myself."

"Wait, what?"

"And then some guy took me for dances explicitly because I'm the skinniest girl working. I was like, it's fine that he likes smaller girls, people have fetishes, but then he was just horrible." She is holding her forehead as if she can't quite believe it. "The whole time he kept pinching my hips, saying, 'Normally I don't take girls as fat as you. I like my girls to be under ninety pounds.'"

"Which guy was it?"

Violet points to an obese man across the bar.

"The hypocrisy," I say flatly. "Ninety pounds puts people in the hospital."

"I know, right? Or he just hates women. Clearly, he enjoys humiliating and demeaning us." She pauses, maybe searching for more than an intellectual analysis. "But why did he say that to *me*?"

"Fuck him. He was trying to hurt you."

Despite trying to teach myself to not care what men think of me, despite the fact I *know* fat is beautiful, sexy, and normal, and the shapes of our bodies don't determine our human worth, that interaction would have hurt me too. I imagine Violet is navigating similarly complicated feelings, an unsafe thing to do in this hostile environment.

"Whatever," she says. "I'm done working tonight. I'm not asking management to go home, but I'm not taking any more clients. Not even if they ask me. I'm going to sit, and drink, and that's it." Violet is nodding along with her decision; her black hair trembles and seethes.

After work Bailey drives us around town searching for an elusive twenty-four-hour convenience store.

"This place is well stocked!" she says when we find one, admiring the variety of chips lining wire racks like party balloons.

Days of restricting food have me attracted to every salty temptation. "I can't choose."

"Let's get everything," Violet says.

On the drive home we open bacon, all dressed, poutine, ketchup, jalapeno, and dill pickle flavours. Pungent sweet vinegar mixes with our perfumes. Then we start to scream about all the things we hate, one on top of the other. Together, we hate almost everything.

★ ★ ★

FRIDAY

Moonbeam is the name of the park, a belt of sand leading into Ramsey Lake. The radio warned us not to go swimming because of an outbreak of a rash-causing bacteria, but the locals don't seem to care. A few of them are throwing sticks for dogs or splashing with toddlers in sun hats. Violet and I coat ourselves in sunscreen, while Bailey sheds her layers, using a sports bra as a top.

Solemnly dedicated to some leisure time, we try walking along the sand, but it's covered in goose droppings. So is the closely cropped, soggy grass, so we wade into the lake. Seaweed swirls around my ankles. The wind is loud enough to mask me sighing out my sourness. At the end of the beach, boulders rise into a hill. We climb a ridge beside hardy trees growing in cracks, up to a sloped flat ledge where we spread our towels. The rocks are warm and ribboned with sparkling pink quartz.

As a kid, I wanted to be a paleontologist. Dad would take me fossil hunting on Joggins beach where we'd methodically comb stones hoping to find carbon imprints of leaves, trilobites, or fish with scales, fins and bones finely drawn like sepia watercolours. One day Dad and I spent hours, finding only common shells and petrified wood. Mom returned with the minivan, my little brother in the back, calling us in from the surging Atlantic tide. She glanced down and found a perfect fern tip fossil, no bigger than her thumb. "Good eye," said my dad, as we crowded around, admiring her needle-in-a-haystack discovery.

Violet doesn't look up from her book, annotated with purple sticky notes. Bailey is unfurled. Absorbing sunlight as if vitamin D could replace food. I can see Ramsey Lake stretching to fill its earthen container. Except for a powerboat and fancy cottages on the opposite shore, the scene is prehistoric. I look skyward and imagine I'm staring through the blue ice of the glaciers that raked themselves across this landscape 15,000 years ago.

★ ★ ★

Bailey and I make it to Club Goldmine in time for her first day shift. We hang out with Keesha, who summarizes her week of double shifts as "not bad." She's optimistic, though, saying, "Tonight and Saturday have the most potential. Never count your money by the day," she suggests. "Wait to see the total at the end of the week, then the bad days disappear."

For an experienced veteran, a stage show without clients becomes an exercise in expending as little energy as possible. The girl forced to go onstage kills time with her back to the non-existent crowd. A butterfly tattoo, one wing per butt cheek, flaps as she claps her ass. Instead of removing her tube dress, she pulls the fabric down until her breasts pop out. Large and natural, they seem to have their own personality, which at this moment is extremely unimpressed.

Shop talk out of the way, the three of us move on to listing the phrases men use to talk about vulvas.

"My favourite is the wizard's sleeve," I say. "That one I can really picture."

"Meat curtains," Bailey adds.

"A canoe full of moose meat," says Keesha.

"No one actually says that!" I exclaim.

"Swear to God, I have heard that one multiple times," Keesha insists. "I even have a couple friends who've gone for the surgery."

"What surgery?" Bailey asks.

"You know. The one where they cut off the dangly bits that hang down." I quickly cross my legs against the psychic scalpel. "Your faces." Keesha laughs. "Looks like you seen a ghost. Obviously they freeze it for the procedure."

"But why?" I ask.

"It makes it look smaller. Everyone wants a tiny, pretty pussy. I thought about it, but I'd get my tits done first."

"Bailey?" An acne-scarred client hesitantly approaches our table. He was part of a duo who'd beaten us at pool a previous evening around dinnertime, before the rush. Bailey suggested he come back and teach her on her day shift. He leads her away, gazing sweetly up at her.

"Your girl got a regular already?" Keesha asks. "I thought you said she was new."

★ ★ ★

Good to his word, Fish Shorts shows up to look at my car. I slip a sundress over my outfit, replace heels with sandals, and push outside, blinking like I've been in hibernation. Fish Shorts and his friend are on their way to a lake. They have two twenty-four cases of Bud in a pickup, which is towing a powerboat. He flips through my owner's manual wearing a black muscle shirt emblazoned with a skeletal fish head. With pliers he plucks a fuse from under the steering wheel and examines it. "It's perfectly new. This is not your issue."

"That would have been too easy. Well, thanks for trying."

As a hard rule I don't go on dates with the guys I meet at the club. I never attend their parties unless I'm getting paid. But I have to fight myself not to accept Fish Short's invitation to ditch this place and head to water.

★ ★ ★

"Dancers make terrible mothers," Donny tells me. He has dated a lot of strippers, even married one and had a kid, then divorced her.

I met Donny earlier in the week, and even though he only took me for two dances, I enjoyed his company. He came on strong with a cutting sense of humour and a kicked-puppy neediness, but it was day shift, so I didn't mind spending a few hours with him. Plus, he tipped in Percocets. But this time he's brought a rowdy crew of leather-clad, cigarette-smelling bikers, including his best friend, Mikey.

"After my bitch of an ex-wife left me, Mikey and I shared a bed for two months," Donny says. "Never fought with him like I fight with women, unless we were arguing over who got to be the big spoon."

"I was the big spoon," Mikey says.

"You were the little spoon—look at the size of me!" Mikey and Donny are equally large men with round shoulders and guts, fists that swallow beer bottles.

"Never slept better. This guy's a world-class cuddler." Donny cuts his sweetness by groping his friend's chest. "Plus, he's got better titties than any woman. Bigger than my ex's, that's for sure." They play-wrestle, remaining in constant contact. Their homoeroticism is intriguing, but I've already been tucked into this corner for an hour, even though the bar has filled with better options.

"Careful." Donny punches Mikey hard in the chest. "Don't want me to think you're a fag. Me and the boys would have to take you hunting, maybe you'd fall on my gun." I cringe at the violence at odds with his jovial tone.

I took an extra pill from Donny an hour ago, doubling what I'd normally take because I was so drained and the hours left stretched before me, insurmountable. I'd wanted the pick-me-up rush of energy it reliably delivered, but instead I was slowing down.

Bailey winds her way among the gang. "Violet just got here. Do you want to hit some tables with us?"

I need more time before stuffing my blistered feet into my heels and regaining composure. While my slow-motion thoughts try to coalesce, a red-bearded member of the crew grabs Bailey's hips from behind and crudely gives her a few thrusts before letting go.

She spins to face him. "What the hell?"

He's wasted and cackling. He tries to toast her, even though she has no drink, and almost sloshes his pint of beer onto her. The patch on his jacket is a horned skull decorated with red and yellow wings.

Bailey tries again. "Michelle, you want to come?"

It sounds like she is shouting to me across a busy highway. I don't think I can make my voice loud enough so she'll be able to hear me, but I say, "I'll just be another minute."

"I'll come back," Bailey says.

Donny wants my full attention. "Do you even know how many guns I have?" he says.

"How would I know that?"

"Wow, you're acting like a bitch today, aren't you?" He and Mikey laugh.

Was my answer rude? I feel confused.

Donny continues, "Four. I keep two in my truck, one at the cottage, and I sleep with one under my pillow."

"That's cool?" I don't know how he wants me to react. Goosebumps ripple up my arms.

He leans in. "I bet you thought I was kidding when I called you a bitch." My river is shallow and I'm slipping on the rocks. "I wasn't," he hisses, then throws his head back and lets out a deep belly laugh. "We'll be back. The boys and me are going to get some steaks, you'll wait for me." He presses an extra pill into my hand.

The bikers roll out, but I can't move from the empty table. I swallow the pill. Bailey comes to collect me and touches my arm. "You're cold."

"I'm exhausted," I say, but the word isn't strong enough.

"Let's try selling a double dance. I'll do most of the work, and you can warm up."

She walks us to a table with a man picking at the label of a beer. As soon as we sit down he says, "You girls are too pretty to be working here."

"Aw, thanks," Bailey says.

"Meaning what, exactly?" Anger rushes in to save me from total collapse. "Do you think strippers are usually ugly? Or that girls who work here are low class? Or that I'm pretty enough to be a waitress, or like a trophy wife? Our whole job is to be pretty. If we aren't pretty, we can't work, so I'm not sure what you mean by that comment."

"I guess I meant that you're both very attractive girls."

I sip the Caesar I'm still holding, so laden with Tabasco it's like the waitress was cautioning me to slow down.

"So," he tries to change the subject, "do your parents know you do this?"

Bailey brushes her hair off her shoulder. "Oh no, it's my little secret." He turns to me. I try to make up a similar line but instead hear myself say, "That's a very personal question, sir. Let's talk about your wife instead. Does she know you're here?" I cock my head.

He laughs uncomfortably. "Can I buy you girls a drink?"

"Nope," I say. "Can you not see I'm literally holding a full drink? I only want dances. Are you buying?"

"Well, maybe if you sit here and talk to me while I finish my beer."

I hold up my index finger to stop him. "That means you want to talk to every girl in here first." Bailey touches my arm, but I can't stop. "You want to know about our relationships to our fathers and ask if we do extras and see who will give you her phone number before choosing which one of us is most deserving of your twenty fucking dollars."

"I don't know who you think I am," he bristles. "I'm a normal guy, not like the creepy old men you must get all the time. I don't even come to these places often. I'm just here to relax and talk to some pretty girls."

"For free." I want to slap his face. Make him rub the coarse stubble that will leave red scratches, like steel wool, when he buries his face in someone's tits later.

"Excuse me?" he responds.

"You want to talk to girls for free. This is our *job*. You understand that, right?"

"We have to go." Bailey pulls me up.

"You have a great night, sweetheart." I knock my chair over backward as I stand, its upturned legs like bull's horns.

"So, you're in a bad mood," Bailey says, following me as I storm into the bathroom.

"I just hate them all." I pace in front of the row of red stalls. "Why do they feel entitled to such personal information? My parents were awesome, no complaints. But imagine I was sexually assaulted as a child, like everyone assumes we all were ... Can't I keep one goddamn thing to myself?"

Bailey and I agree that I should take a break, so I sit, arms crossed, on a couch watching the stage. The dancer drops into the splits so hard the crack of her heels can be heard above the music. She spins down the catwalk like a drunk salsa dancer. Her momentum could hurl her off the stage, and in this mood I wouldn't even help her. I'd stay right here and let others take care of the madness.

A voice behind makes me jump. "I came back to apologize for earlier." Donny drops onto my couch, his weight throwing me off balance as I tumble into him. "We can work this out if you'll admit you're a liar."

When we left the dorms this morning, security had posted a warning about black bear sightings on campus. Remain calm, do not run, do not play dead.

"What have I lied about?" I try to push away from his chest, but he pulls me back.

"Everything. For starters, you won't even tell me your real name. Why do you have to treat me this way? You're exactly like my ex."

I am no longer capable of parsing what is bullshit, what is a game, and whether my fear is justified. I just need to get away from him.

"I thought we had a real connection, but you're just like every other whore, aren't you?"

I shove off the couch and bolt. Burst into the changing room where, miraculously, Bailey is fixing her makeup. I'm crying in panicked sobs. "Are you sober? Can you drive me home? I need to go home."

"Babe, of course. What happened?" She takes the combination lock from my shaking hands, twirls in the numbers, and gathers my things as I fall onto a chair.

"I don't know. Nothing happened. I'm confused. Am I a terrible person?"

"No, honey, you're the very best." She slips my feet out of my heels.

If Bailey had asked for permission, management would have told her to throw me in a cab. Instead, she sneaks us out and drives me home. Supports me into our apartment and locks the door before returning to finish her shift.

My sobs are wretched in the concrete echo chamber, so I close myself in the bathroom and run the shower.

I am so grateful I am no one's bitch.

Too weak to stand, I sit beneath the spray. It washes off makeup and hairspray, my curls unravelling like twists of yarn.

★ ★ ★

SATURDAY

When I get up Bailey is at the table selecting pills from her broad assortment of vitamin supplements. She arranges them on the table like a fistful of precious stones. "What happened last night?" she asks.

"I got head-fucked by that biker," I say, massaging my tense jaw.

Bailey frowns and shakes her head. "I didn't like him when I first met him, and that was before all his friends showed up."

"I couldn't figure out a way to get you away from there," Violet says. "I'm sorry I didn't try harder." She is lacing up running shoes.

"Honestly, I'd already lost it long before you came in, Violet," I say. "These day shifts are killing me. I know it can't be all money, all the time, but six hours of no clients and only making minimum wage for shift pay is insulting. It burns me out."

Violet applies a cloud of sunscreen. "Next time you could refuse to be on schedule. You can freelance and only come in at night. It sounds like you'd be willing to lose the shift pay in order to get more rest." She's so calculated. Why haven't the endless days affected her like they do me?

"Can we not talk about how bad day shifts are?" Bailey says. "I have to be there in two hours."

"Don't all the pills make you sick on an empty stomach?" I ask as she shakes out a gel cap containing Rhodiola, ashwagandha, and Schisandra.

"They basically are food." She chokes them down with a glass of water thick with green superfood powder.

I pour boiling water onto a black tea bag and let it steep ruby brown before stirring in cream with a plastic spoon. I miss my favourite porcelain cup. The perfect grip of the handle. The greens, browns, and reds in the potter's glaze like earth and moss. How Luke is always so pleased when he says good morning to me, as if it's the first time we've woken up together.

"Are you actually going for a run?" I ask Violet.

"There are trails in the woods around campus," she says.

Bailey is incredulous. "You know it's still a heat wave, right?"

"I'm only doing ten K today."

"I promise I will never run ten kilometres in my life," Bailey vows as Violet leaves.

I follow Bailey to the gazebo so she can smoke. "How was the rest of your night?" I ask.

"It was good. I made a lot."

"Donny ruined my night," I say. "I don't know why I let him get to me like that." His eyes, while he swore at me, were brimming with tears, as if I was hurting him.

"In general you seem to know exactly when to leave," Bailey says. "But you were so worn out, and we all know it can be a shit show."

"It felt like he wasn't even talking to me." I shiver.

"He was talking to every girl who called him fat or gay, his mother, his ex-wife. You don't even exist for him."

"You're so wise," I say. "Honestly, you're the most empathetic person I know."

"Oh, stop." She smiles.

What I don't admit is that I've been indulging, taking more Percocet than I need, getting high before my shifts and higher still at work. I swallowed Donny's offering, praying for the revival it usually gives me, unsure if I could make it through on my usual amount. But, like being caught in the undertow, my high crashed into the frustration of needing to pass out and not being able to.

The first time I snorted an opiate, I felt an immediate kinship—oh, *this* is my drug. Compared to cocaine's slap in the face, or the terrifying hallucinations of pot or MDMA, the opiate was transcendent. I became aware that every muscle in my body was tense and I was able to completely relax. Relief spread through my limbs and chest. My brain stopped its incessant worried chatter. Inside myself, I sank into a warm saltwater pool and floated effortlessly.

Swallowing a lump in my throat, I say to Bailey, "I'm sorry about Sheldon." She gives me a tender smile, and I continue, "I'm sorry that I never know what to say. I get so caught up about saying the wrong thing that I end up saying nothing. But that shouldn't have happened to you. Men are horrible ..." I trail off.

Bailey doesn't need to hate men like I do. She pities them, holds their fragile egos with compassion. "He didn't ruin it for me," Bailey says. "I've had a really good trip. I'm very grateful to you for bringing me here."

"Do not tell me you are grateful. I cannot hear that."

Bailey points out of the gazebo. "Look at that crazy bitch," she says with respect. I lean up on an elbow to see Violet running in the distance, her form obscured by waves of heat shimmering over the yellow grass. Even the ravens are silent today.

Bailey checks her phone when it beeps, sighs, and turns it over.

"Still texting that Matt guy?" I ask.

"He's texting me, but I'm over it."

★ ★ ★

When I show up at work that night, the atmosphere is completely different, and it's not just because I spent the day resting. People talk about a golden age of stripping, something that no longer exists, but on nights like this I catch a glimpse of what it might have been like in the 1980s and '90s. Club Goldmine is packed with a friendly crowd, here to have fun and be entertained. When it's my turn onstage, I have butterflies, but from the first beat, the 200-person crowd is stamping and cheering. The bigger I smile and the more I blow kisses or drop into a squat to twerk in front of perverts' row, the more wildly the crowd responds, throwing bills, whistling, even pounding the stage. When I take out my tits, the bar erupts like I've scored a touchdown. Their energy feels like an acknowledgment that being the centre of attention for three songs, naked, dancing in seven-inch heels is a miraculous feat.

The crowd worships us all equally, validating whoever is onstage as the pinnacle of sexy, offering us the respect we deserve. A drunk guy in the front row earnestly yells, "You go, girl!" after every song. When I get offstage, exhilarated, a man tells me he would never be brave enough to do what we do.

Maybe in the old days it was always like this. Not only are men approaching *us* to go to the VIP, but they are keeping us so busy we don't get a moment's rest. It's harvest time, don't slow down, don't take breaks. Money anesthetizes my swollen ankles and sore muscles. Push, keep smiling. Dry lips, tangled hair, my panties on and off again, damp with sweat. My clutch, tied to my wrist, bloated with bills.

I order bottles of water when I'm offered drinks as I tilt-a-whirl between weekenders, men fleeing the city to boat, fish, and camp, golfers, miners, locals who come here every Saturday, hunters, bikers, construction workers, and dads.

Violet, Bailey, and I finish on such a high of success that we decide to pack up the apartment and drive through the night, home to our beds, our pets, our people.

CHAPTER 8:
THE ROUNDUP

FOXXDEN
OTTAWA, ONTARIO

This DJ is desperate for attention. "It was Kennedy's birthday a week ago and she's still hungover. Don't trip, don't fall," he teases the girl onstage over the loudspeaker. He'd push her if he could get away with it.

A few months after returning from Sudbury, Violet and I drove six hours to get here in time to prep and make it to the start of the night shift on a Friday at Foxxden.

The DJ is responsible for hiring. His table is in everyone's way, on a landing halfway up the staircase. The club is split-level: stage and bar on the first floor, VIP upstairs. Already patrons are clogging the stairs. Bossy girls push through, clearing paths for themselves.

"You've both got too many tattoos," the DJ says. "But we're short tonight, so go get changed. Oh, and none of that hardcore gangster rap—hip hop only."

We tail a girl with a duffle bag into an upstairs changing room, a tight ring of space surrounding an island of lockers. Violet and I share an open locker with an oval sticker with the name Missy. The holographic pink letters have been scratched off with a key, engraving the metal beneath.

I avoid making eye contact with the girls occupying the mirrors, menacingly rattling the ice cubes in their iced coffees.

"Am I getting old or is the music really loud?" Violet yells when we get back downstairs.

Adjusting to the crush of clients three deep at the bar, I stake out the central stage. It is raised a foot from the ground, a horizontal barre across the mirrored back wall as if we're ballerinas. I take in the other strippers, and as always in a new club, I am stunned by their brilliance, the sharp peak and taper of painted eyebrows, the don't-fuck-with-me energy, and the agility with which they criss-cross the bar as if, like men say, they were born in heels. Flawlessness requires hours of effort and tons of money. I feel like an amateur.

Violet and I split up, try a few tables, and are quickly rejected. Regrouping, we reassess. "They work in teams here, in packs," I say. Nearby, two girls descend on a table, demanding Hennessy and pitching a double table dance. One girl bends the other over, showcasing the hypnotizing ripple effect of gentle slaps on her partner's bubble butt. Both brim with self-confident assertiveness—I can see why people assume all sex workers are amazing at sex.

"I see now what the stripper message board meant about this club having 'a party vibe.' This place is fast paced," Violet says.

"It's like the men want to be taken, not talked to. It's going to be a problem for me," I say. "Being nice is my whole shtick."

★ ★ ★

The spooky VIP has triangular booths like cake wedges, containing a chair with a blue light that turns colours to dried blood. I finally find a client willing to stay for more than a few songs, when the loudspeaker announces, "All girls report to the stage. All girls. Get out of the VIP and get up from your tables and report to the stage immediately." The club's not allowed to tell us to stop making money, but I see girls in the booths beside me getting dressed and rushing downstairs like recalled spirits.

"Now, girls! Not next song. Right now, let's go."

"I guess I'll find you later?" I say as the confused client hurriedly pays me and disappears.

Downstairs a line forms. The music switches to honky-tonk. "Saddle up, boys, it's time for the Roundup!" says the DJ like a caller at a square dance. Violet is near the front as the line lurches forward and girls begin to shuffle across the stage.

"Is this a joke?" I ask the girl ahead of me.

"Don't even," she snaps. "I just lost a good client."

The girl behind me is searching the crowd, hoping her client will wait for her. "They do it twice a night to showcase us. It means all the guys get to see you," she says, like the club is doing us a favour.

Patrons are laughing and clapping along to the barnyard song. The DJ provides a running commentary about girls he knows when they are spotlighted under the silver disco ball at centre stage: "It's Paris. Watch out, boys, she'll grab you right where it hurts—your wallet. Nikki, she's a butter-face. Just kidding, she's pretty, if you like that sort of thing. Ariel—this little mermaid's always wet. And Tatianna, her special skill is having absolutely zero gag reflex, you know what I'm saying, boys?"

Some girls do a little curtsy or a shake, while others keep their heads down. Some, chin up, stare out at the crowd impassively, highlighting the absurdity. I want to dig in my heels and step out of line, but I'm on a conveyor belt. At centre stage, the blinding spotlight slaps me with a humiliation that leaves my skin tingling, ears ringing.

When the parade is over girls continue to stand around. "We're not through yet, boys. The best is yet to come," The DJ says. "For this next song all these beautiful ladies will perform a free table dance. Who wants a free table dance?" Cheers from the crowd. The DJ switches to rap and girls grab whatever guy is nearest and begin a lacklustre dance. The girl who was behind me in line pushes me onto the guy sitting beside her and says, "Hurry up! Don't let them see you standing still."

The guy raises his hands. "No really, you don't have to."

"Apparently I do." I turn my back to him, move with as little effort as possible. Table dances are no contact, so there's a small shard left of my fragmented dignity.

The DJ continues to police us: "Don't be stingy, girls, tops off." The song playing is "Rack City," but no one is racking up cash right now. I turn to face my guy and scrunch the triangles of green fabric of my bikini top, move it off my nipples, but refuse to untie and remove the whole thing. He is staring at the floor, but most of the men are stoked, fixated on the flesh closest to them. The dancers grind, faces granite. I try to leave as soon as the song finishes, but the guy stuffs a bill into my hand and says, "I'm sorry."

Following the roundup, most girls let the tension dissolve and return to work, but I seek out Violet, fuming. "That was exploitation. I've never felt that way in this job before. That was—"

"Unbelievable," Violet says. "Like cows at auction. How dare they force us to pay to be here, then work for free? It's—"

"Insulting! It's not even like this club is full of money. It's not worth it."

"And every client here is a fucking lawyer." Violet's voice is shrill. "I can't help fighting with them because they're so arrogant, wanting to talk about how rich they are and then tell me I have to 'earn' a dance from them, but it just wastes my time."

The rare moments when Violet shows me her rage, I feel like she's letting me in.

"Lawyers are the worst," I agree. "We should go to San Francisco—I heard strippers unionized there once."

"Or Portland. Apparently there are queer-friendly clubs where you can work with armpit hair and different body types and no one cares how many tattoos you have."

"The promised land," I sigh.

The pace in the club quickens as girls push to make up for lost time. We stand in a whirlpool of bodies and noise, trying to catch our breath.

"I hate this club," Violet says.

"Being new here doesn't help because the regular girls are so hot. And there's so many of them," I add.

"Sixty girls per shift," Violet says.

"Plus, I need to work on my stage show. It's embarrassing."

Violet shakes her head. "The stage is so low to the ground and open here, I don't think it matters. After my set I went directly to a table where they seemed to be watching me and they asked if I was going up soon."

We burn the last of our energy by returning to work with pep and insistence. At the end of the night my voice is hoarse and I've made significantly less money than at my home club.

★ ★ ★

We spend the next day dealing with my car's power steering, which on this road trip reached an undrivable low. The mechanic insists I leave it overnight for a full fluids evaluation.

"I'm pretty sure if we top up the power steering fluid, it will get us home to my regular garage," I whisper to Violet. "But can we buy a single bottle?"

The mechanic hovers. "Watch your pretty little shoes," he says, nodding to a puddle of motor oil.

I shudder because I have become a sexual empath with men. Any sweet naïveté I had about sex has been obliterated, and now, whether I want to or not, I can intuit how men like to fuck, how exactly they would fuck me if they could. It's a sixth sense that I read like an aura. I imagine the mechanic's hands, spiderwebbed with grease, extra dry from orange pumice soap, abrading my breasts. I'd rather not be invaded by the knowledge that my dentist eats pussy like he's snorkelling, that fathers of friends would jackhammer unrepentantly, or that the soft boy I thought was cute for a minute would cry if I said no.

Violet breaks our huddle. She's small without her heels, but she steps up to the mechanic, orders a single jug of power steering fluid, ignores his dire warnings about ending up stranded on the side of the road. In the parking lot we double-check the owner's manual, cautiously turn hot greasy knobs, and pour glugs of viscous liquid into the engine.

★★★

Even though Violet and I brainstormed selling strategies, that night at Foxxden we are being frustrated by politician clients who pity us, lawyers who think they're smarter than us, and broke, bewildered partiers who wander in off the street.

I end up doing doubles with another girl on a long white couch. Ottawa's entire design aesthetic seems to be based on lumberjacks, beavers, and assorted early-settler fantasies. The bachelor party section of the VIP has birch branches planted in a vase of blue rocks.

"Why is this couch white?" I ask the girl after the men leave. "I kept worrying I was bleeding all over it." I dip a finger between my legs to check for leakage.

"I always make more money on my period," she says, untangling her outfit. "It's the hormones—the men can smell them." She would have made a great flapper, with her small breasts and short hair. "One time I forgot to change my tampon, and you know when it gets so heavy it starts falling out? I didn't wanna stop the dance, so I told him to close his eyes for a second, like I was gonna do something sexy, and I flung it out of the VIP. I wiped the blood onto the back leg of his jeans."

"You are a legend." I laugh. "Where did you throw it?"

"Toward the DJ booth. I hope it landed on his head."

★★★

"Hey, boys! Who's the lucky bachelor?" I ask a table of ten before realizing that every single one of them is from my high school graduating class.

Equally surprised, they greet me by my legal name, the one I stopped using after high school. Hearing it reanimates my fifteen-year-old self. Panicked, she demands to know how we grew up to be a failure. In my mind I throw a blanket around her shoulders, hold her tightly. Leave the present for Michelle to handle.

"Well, this is awkward." I sit down. Why? We should run. But if we stay five minutes, they might feel as compromised by the interaction as I do. I'm not ashamed of my job, but there are people I don't want to do it for, and these guys go to the same grocery store as some of my extended family. They could easily out me. This encounter feels like I've been shoved dangerously close to the edge of a cliff. God, I don't want to have to tell my mother what I do.

The bachelor is a farm boy, a man now. He looks the same, a freckled redhead with a few more wrinkles. He's marrying a girl who was in grade nine when we were in grade twelve. He asks if I remember her and I say no, because I can only picture her as a thirteen-year-old bride.

"What are you doing with your life?" one of the others asks me. He used to wear skateboarding shoes but didn't know how to skateboard.

I'm flooded with teenage memories. The sound of gravel under the wheels of the school bus before I turned on Rise Against so loud it hurt inside my headphones, accompanied by the smell of hay, manured fields, and Axe deodorant. My rural high school experience was four years of boredom and unbelonging, but sharp words cut through the haze. The popular boys, some of the ones sitting at this table, used to call my friends faggots. They used to call me a goth, punk, freak, and, most vehemently, a slut. Seeing me here probably makes them think they were right.

I break into a cold sweat. Familiar faces stare expectantly at me from around the table. What *am* I doing with my life? The only thing that floats to mind is that I'm waiting to see if I got into creative writing school in Vancouver. It's such a tender and hopeful dream that I instinctively hide it. I'm so focused on acting calm that I forget I could lie. "I'm just doing this right now." Their reaction registers as pity.

I didn't have sex with of them in high school. I didn't have sex with anyone except a long-term boyfriend. He was a sweet guy and our relationship kept me protected from other boys. He was convinced I'd "make it" as a writer one day. It's sad that he'll think I've ruined my life when one of these guys tells him this juicy gossip. Desperate to turn the focus away from me, I ask them how they're doing. While they talk about taking over industrial family farms and getting married I completely leave my body. It's life-saving, this skill of detachment.

My former classmates have reached the stage of goading each other, asking how the rules work at Foxxden, if they're allowed to touch. Even though I know now that expressing my sexuality doesn't debase me, the fifteen-year-old inside is in emotional agony. We never wanted to give these high school jocks any piece of us. I'm trapped in a collision of continents as separate worlds smash together. The teenager can't be pacified any longer; dissociation isn't strong enough.

"I'll be right back. I'm going to go get a drink." I escape and scan the bar for Violet. She's easy to find, a grim sentinel by the stairs.

Deadpan, I tell her, "I just ran into every guy from my high school."

"No."

"Yes. I can't avoid them, and I can't go onstage with them watching, and if I don't go onstage I'll get fired, so I think I'm going to leave."

To my surprise Violet says, "I hate this place. I'm coming with you."

We slip upstairs and into the changing room. Girls aren't allowed to take breaks, so the fact that we're getting dressed means, to anyone watching the cameras, that we're making a break for it. In two minutes we are hurrying down a back staircase to the exit. The walls are tiled with mirrors. Distorted, funhouse, smashed panes. At the top of the stairs behind us the door bangs open and a bouncer shouts, "Run, bitches! Never come back."

We break out onto the street. Fresh air. Market stalls closed for the night. Merry crowds milling between bars. Even outside, the smell of spilled beer.

"Well, that was a total writeoff," Violet says as we walk away. "Should we go back to the Airbnb?"

"Let's go out." I'm too shot with adrenalin to settle down. "There's a lesbian bar down the street."

We maintain our work personas for talking to strangers. A pretty vet technician buys us tequila shots and says, "I can't believe you're strippers. Is it a hard job?"

I bite down on the lime wedge, sucking out the sour. "It's great. I get to party at work. Hang out with naked women all the time. It's the best job." My belly is full of salt and fire. I skim the surface, offering her only the cream.

CHAPTER 9:
NO CONTACT

THE DISTRICT
VANCOUVER, BC

When I apply at the District I am surprised to be met by a lady manager. Intimidatingly sexy and augmented in every way, older than me yet ageless. She brings me into a VIP stall with leather benches and surprisingly bright lights. Tells me to strip, and then steps outside, closing the burgundy curtain for my privacy. Like a doctor, she knocks on the doorframe, asks if she can come in to examine me. When my body passes the test, she asks, "Are you a stage girl or a VIP girl?"

"I just moved here from Ontario, we don't have those distinctions."

"Don't tell anyone you're from Ontario," she warns. "It's all extras clubs out there." Untrue. "And we don't allow that in Vancouver." Also untrue. "This club is completely no contact. I don't judge you for your past, but the other girls might."

The hierarchy of shame between no-contact, contact, and extras clubs would be laughable if it weren't so divisive. One night I tried Moxy's, a no-contact club in Ontario, but the girls acted grossly superior, making it clear they were exotic dancers, not dirty strippers. I never went back.

"Contact" is an ill-defined concept. Whether clubs allow it depends mostly on zoning laws. I might have reconsidered working at the District had I known it was no contact, but I like the swanky nightclub vibe. It's a strip club that doesn't feel like it's stuck in the eighties.

"VIP girls here give air dances," Boss Lady says. "And you will need to audition if you want to perform onstage. Our stage girls are true entertainers. They do spectacular shows and are paid by the club." Her ponytail is so tight it pulls up the sides of her face. "Do you spin fire?" she asks. "Or have some other talent like sword swallowing or contortion?" I tell her I'll stick with VIP, hoping that avoiding the stage will leave me more opportunity to focus on my hustle.

Boss Lady directs me to a shoebox changing room, with mirrors, magenta walls, and the floor and counter strewn with girl stuff that can't fit into the inadequate lockers. She fusses over a collection of empty glasses, lemon wedges, straws. "I told you all to bring these back to the bar when you finish—this isn't your mother's house."

A girl in a white corset says, "You can be my mommy any day, Crissy."

"Phoenix, I told you not to call me that." I presume Boss Lady prefers her more majestic full name. She introduces me, absolving herself of responsibility by saying, "Take care of our new girl," and leaves.

Phoenix kisses at me. "Hey, baby." Sex appeal oozes off her. I feel like I owe her money just for standing beside her.

My new co-workers are chill and friendly. They clear a patch of counter space and ask me pleasant questions about my life.

How long have I been in Vancouver? A couple weeks.

Why did I come? A creative writing college program.

Did I move here alone? Yes.

Luke stayed behind. He encouraged me to stop treating writing as a hobby and make it a pillar of my life. He is doing that at home with music, composing classical pieces on a piano inherited from his father. We've planned visits at three-month intervals, and I have to stop myself from breaking the time into hours, minutes, nights alone.

Phoenix watches me undress. "Cute butt," she pronounces.

The outfit style here is different—glitzier, bejewelled. I've been getting bored of my brightly coloured bikinis and knee-high socks anyway. I feel most comfortable, most powerful, in all black. If I want to fit in here, I'll have to buy new lingerie. Some girls are wearing bold, theatrical makeup. I wonder if they're the ones who perform onstage.

Fifteen minutes after arriving unannounced at this new club, I'm on the floor. I try to observe who talks to whom and whether there are cliques. But everyone—strippers, bartenders, bouncers, and Boss Lady—mingles and hangs out together waiting for the night to pick up. The big central stage has a two-storey pole and I'm glad I get to avoid it. The music is loud enough that I can slink into the new space, a caiman with only her eyes above the lily pads.

I do a lap of the bar. Even though I've become good at walking in heels, I need to tread carefully on this first pass; any unseen obstacle could lead to a fall. Out of the corner of my eye I catch a glimpse of a girl's body in a dark mirror: slim waist, curvy hips and butt. She's hot, I register immediately. And then I realize—it's me. The voices in my head freak out. They remind me that we hate ourselves. That one day it won't be as easy to pass as conventionally attractive, as young, and this job will only get harder. I push back—maybe I am hot. I must be, to consistently get hired at new clubs. I take a moment to enjoy how I look as I pose subtly in the mirror.

What would I lose if I believed I was hot more often?

★ ★ ★

Raven is the star of the District. She has won pole championships; she is a competitor, an acrobat. Men say mean things about her bodybuilder physique, but I don't think she cares. She doesn't need to sell lap dances because she makes her money from the bar for headlining onstage. Nudity is an afterthought. Between sets, she hangs out in the separate changing room reserved for the stage girls, wrapped in a silk robe like a boxer. She ends the night by spinning flaming poi and spitting fire across the stage. Afterwards, a hush falls in the crowded bar. Lighter fluid is the incense in her temple.

★ ★ ★

My co-workers are downright welcoming and Boss Lady makes sure to call us her employees, instead of just "girls." However, after a few shifts, I realize the no-contact hustle and competing with feature girls is really hard, but I stay rather than bounce around trying to find a better club.

When I first moved to Vancouver, I subletted a room in a rad queer collective with an elderly cat and people who shared a record player and worked nine to five. After my month was up, I faced the housing crunch and ended up in a student boarding house managed by a slumlord. I needed a key to get into my bedroom and would routinely come home to find someone had left the front door unlocked and ajar. At three a.m. on my first night, a drunk housemate knocked on my door asking if I wanted to share some frozen pizza with him. I put a chair under the doorknob. Stayed awake until dawn. Gentrification had boarded up windows and fenced off modest bungalows along Cambie Street to make way for condos. The landlord casually mentioned our house was to be demolished in two months, so I stuffed my things into garbage bags and absconded.

I moved into the two-bedroom apartment of a school friend near Broadway and Commercial. SkyTrains and Starbucks. Sidewalks alive with either the very rich or very poor. Spring overflowed the gutters with pink cherry petals. Someone spray-painted crescent moons along my alleyway with the tag line, *Look Up*. Mountains, skyscrapers.

Tonight, I'm lost in my own head. Thinking through a story for a speculative fiction class about stripper convicts, imprisoned on the moon, who instigate an insurrection after the earth is destroyed. Is the desire for total freedom a strong enough character motivation?

The District is busy, but not for me. Patrons are drinking, partying, dancing together like at a regular nightclub, encouraged by the hotshot DJ who thinks he's performing in Ibiza. Between incredible stage sets, when I should be able to sell dances, there are go-go dancers who hop up on smaller poles around the club. They booty-pop and vibrate in a jarring style that reminds me of dance classes. This club has a lot going on and doesn't want to pick a niche. Like an old dog, I'm having trouble adapting my tricks.

Standing at the base of an ornate staircase leading to the second level, I watch Veronica onstage. Her themed sets are extraordinary. Sometimes she wears a Pikachu costume. Other times a Mario outfit complete with a cardboard box full of coins the size of dinner plates. Today she is writhing in an inflatable pool, pouring buckets of ice on herself.

I startle when a man yells at the side of my head, "This club reminds me of New Orleans, with all the lights and girls in cages and stuff." His crookedly held drink threatens to spill. "What made you get into this type of work?"

"I really like to party. This job is so much fun."

"You party with the other girls?"

"All the time. After work we get wasted and have sex with each other."

"No way! You're lying. Really? Do your parents know what you do?"

This is the first time I could honestly say yes to that question. I finally told my mom this summer. I was back home, sitting on a boulder in a small park sandwiched between a block of townhouses and a polluted stream. Mom was three provinces away, sipping a glass of wine after a day in her garden picking bags of string beans for the freezer.

Across the street from the park a woman was screaming at her man. When he went inside their house she threw something at the front window, something too soft to break the glass, a child's toy perhaps. She followed him inside.

I wrapped my arms around my knees. A strong wind picked up debris and herded it down the street, threw dust in my eyes. Mom was telling me about a friend of hers, who met another woman at a farmers' market. Over peach preserves and strawberry jam, the two of them got to talking about the fact that they shared an uncommon last name. Which led to the discovery that they also shared a husband. Two marriages marked by frequent, long business trips, a hardworking husband who regularly sacrificed evenings and weekends to overtime at the office. He had maintained two families for years, lived his life like an avalanche. I understood it, how the lies could get away from a person.

"Mom, I've been a stripper for five years."

I'd hoped we could skip all the shock and pain and jump right to laughing about the absurdity of life. But she said, "I could have given you money," and it sounded like I had punched her. "I thought you were on welfare. And the job at the shelter—was that real?"

"I've worked a few other jobs during this time, but stripping has been the best job by far. It—"

"What about Luke? How could he possibly love you?"

The woman across the street from the park ran back outside, a kitchen knife in her hand. She stabbed the blade into the cherry tree in her front yard, wiggled it back out, and then stabbed again. Three times, at heart height. I was floating, the boulder under me a boat surrounded by an ocean of dandelions, yellow heads nodding righteously.

"Luke loves me very much, Mom. I started before I met him. It's not an uncomplicated issue but—"

"I thought you were a feminist. You're telling me you participate in the abuse, the torture of women?"

"Torture? No, of course I don't support the torture of women. I think our feminism comes from different places. Stripping lets me subvert the patriarchal system. I believe my body is my own—"

"To sell to men!" She was sobbing. "I've failed you. I thought I was a good mother, but I obviously fucked up somehow."

"You are a great mother. Always encouraging me to be creative and independent. Strong."

"So it's my fault? You're saying this is my fault. What could I have done differently? Your father and I tried so hard." She was spinning out, devastated that her child had chosen what to her was an incomprehensible, dangerous, humiliating life.

Cheeks hot, shame like vomit in my throat, I said, "I'm not broken. You don't need to fix me."

I realized her reaction was not something I could control. Mom was panicking and the woman across the street had noticed me staring. It was time to move. The path out of the park followed the polluted stream, with banks where I had picked springtime violets. I tinctured some in a mason jar of purple flowers and vodka. It would be ready in three months, a medicinal distillation to ease grief.

"Well, I guess that explains a lot then, doesn't it?" Mom was saying to herself. "It shows what you really think of me, the amount of respect you must have." Anger was rushing in to clot the bleed of hurt.

"I want you to talk to someone else before we talk again," I said.

"Who the hell would I want to talk to about this? I don't want anyone to know my daughter is a stripper."

A shredded garbage bag caught in a stand of sumac snapped in the wind like a ruined flag.

"Talk to a therapist, talk to anyone, but I can't be the person who processes this with you." Guilt wanted me to stick around and accept her words like lashes. Love wanted to preserve our long-term relationship.

"How dare you—" she started, but I hung up.

In the silence I felt incredibly light. That went okay, I told myself. And then I laughed because I'd just shut down the parts of myself that wanted to apologize, that wanted to weep with shame.

I don't understand why clients ask about families. Is that really the story they want to hear? So I ask him, "Do you want to go for a dance or what?"

"It's no contact here, right?"

I already know he's not going, but I have to try. "No contact, but it's still really sexy."

"Me and the guys are heading over to Sapphire Palace after this. It's full contact. You should come with us."

"Like, leave my job and go party with you guys for free? Thanks, I'm good."

The locals know the District isn't worth it for lap dances. The only way I can make money is from tourists, or rich execs who want to show off to their out-of-town business partners, boys who've flown in from the oil fields. Or from Charles.

Charles is that extremely rare client who actually spends good money, regularly. I was hesitant to approach him at first because big spenders often come with demanding egos, but he was genuinely friendly, said I was always welcome at his table. His private booth is an extra by-the-hour expense he pays so he doesn't have to sit too close to strangers. I'm one more drunk-party-bro rejection away from giving up, so I join him. Defeat shows in my posture. After paying my fees, I will have to put the cab ride home on my debit card.

"Not going so well tonight? The crowd seems tough." Charles squeezes my knee. "You look absolutely stunning. I can't understand why you're not busy."

I find his proper language, loaded with flattery, endearing.

"You can sit with me for the rest of your shift if you like. Oh look, that's for me." He claps his hands as the bottle service he ordered, held aloft by a waitress, makes its way across the club. A sparkler glimmers atop a blue-lit bottle of vodka. The flashy light and pyrotechnics let others know the recipient is willing to pay twenty-five times the retail price for alcohol.

"Planning to drink that all by yourself?" I joke.

"Oh no, I rarely have more than three drinks. I'm just trying to keep everyone happy."

Like hummingbirds, girls flit in and out of Charles's booth, serving themselves. Even pretty waitresses in tight black dresses stop to talk. Everyone says money tonight is especially bad. One girl with a Posh Spice wig says she should have known better than to come in on a full moon, a month before Christmas, when the Canucks lost their hockey game last night.

"Regular people are staying home," I say. "Trump's election was so polarizing, everyone is waiting to see what's going to happen."

"We live in Can-na-duh," Posh Spice mocks. "He's not our president."

"That's so ignorant," I hiss. I've learned time and again not to talk about politics at work, but I can't help myself.

"Trump wants to make people like me richer," Charles interjects. I freeze, waiting to lose any respect I have for him if he offers a trickle-down, devil's advocate response. "But he can't call swaths of people rapists and terrorists and close the borders. It's not right," he concludes.

"Exactly." I'm shocked to be in agreement.

Posh Spice leaves the booth with an exaggerated eye roll, and Charles covertly hands me a solid roll of bills.

"Wow, thank you." I try to be cool, but it's a lot of money. "Do you want dances? It's almost the end of the night."

He waves it off like it's nothing. "No. It's rare that I find someone I can really talk to. I want to know more about you. The real you."

★ ★ ★

It is my third semester at writing school and it has been more than a year since I first moved to Vancouver. Living out of suitcases and flying back and forth across the country makes me feel like I'm always getting ready to leave, but today is a rare sunny October day and I feel comfortably settled. I sip a matcha latte at a café and reread my journal, reflecting on this chaotic period.

I spent the summer in Ontario with Luke, relieved to realize that we were becoming stronger as a couple by supporting each other's growth.

Luke and Mira were the best parts of being back, but it no longer felt like home. I missed the bigness and excitement of Vancouver, but I couldn't convince Luke to move back with me. I worried that after I finished my final semester I would have to return to Ontario permanently to be with him.

I started working at the Royal again. It's faded small-town charm felt bleak and sleazy compared to the District. I'd grown accustomed to no-contact dances, and to Charles bankrolling me. It felt more difficult than ever to let dudes grab my tits for twenties. In fact, some nights it had started to physically hurt. It was like an allergic reaction that left my breasts swollen and hypersensitive. I asked Luke to stop touching my chest when we had sex because my body couldn't tell who was touching me, just that it was increasingly uncomfortable.

Then suddenly, the week the elderflowers began to bloom, I stopped wanting to be alive. The solstice made me feel complete, like I was finished and had somewhere else to be. Distinctly, I felt done. I sat at the kitchen table with a razor blade. All the feelings that had been strangling me as they tried to crawl out of my body, stopped. The only thing that existed was the shrill sting of the blade as it sowed the fields of my wrists and forearms. Heads of blood grew from the furrows, then burst, spilled red tears down to my elbows and congealed on the pinky sides of my hands. Mesmerizing pools formed on the table. I could have stared into my own blood forever.

Luke came home from work sometime after I'd cleaned up and joined me on the porch. The sky was pink and blue cotton candy. "Why are you wearing a sweater?" he asked.

"I did something stupid." I gingerly pulled up my sleeves.

"Take it off," Luke said. "Fresh air is the best thing for cuts."

He pulled me onto his lap, securing me while he thought about what to do. I watched a hundred crows commute overhead, from the dump where they forage daily to the flat factory roofs where they sleep.

"Were you trying to kill yourself?" Luke asked.

"I'm not sure."

A small wind chime tinkled. I felt almost nothing, and it was such a great relief. Luke brought me inside, sat me at the kitchen table, and dialed a crisis hotline. I talked to a nice, older lady while Luke collected every sharp object and hid them. He called his sisters and mom, rallied our friends, and for the following week I was never allowed to be alone.

I'd thought about wanting to die for as long as I could remember. It came as a self-soothing theoretical solution to periods of stress, boredom, or sadness. And it came in moments of extreme beauty. Looking at the stars often brought it on. Pinprick glimpses of other galaxies, maybe long dead, make me ache to turn myself back into pure starlight. But I'd never wanted to kill myself so strongly before. So blood-and-flesh viscerally. Cutting my wrists dominated my thoughts, became a fixation.

A week in, I collapsed in tall park grass, Luke by my side. It was the golden hour, timeless summer. I was a child, in a similar light, floating down the shallow Miramichi River. Slippery green algae, snails, and crayfish, water tannin rich as tea. I was one of the frogs, damselflies, minnows. I was the cracked mud bank and the flat warm rocks. In that same light, I was an adult begging Luke, "Please. I can't do this anymore. It's done, it's over, just let me go on a walk by myself."

"No." Luke was drained from waking up multiple times a night to check on me and tracking me all day. He was extra tired because he used to do similar things trying to keep his dad alive. "Maybe cancer or a car accident if it has to be violent and too soon. But not this way, babe. I know you feel like you need my permission, but I'm not going to give it to you."

"It's selfish of you," I sobbed.

"It is, but I need you here with me." He was crying, too.

In my brain, this constant loop: I am so sorry and hateful and guilty. I am so tired.

I didn't say, "You'd be better off without me," because it sounded so much like a cliché that it reminded me I was probably sick, that the feelings I was having, which felt like the truest feelings I'd ever had, were probably not original, and even my death wish wasn't really mine.

Butterflies and bees collected dandelion nectar. The light kept me bound to the world, stuck in its honey.

Later that week, when Luke brought me along to his mom's house so he could play piano, I stole a razor from her bathroom. Put it in my bra like a teenage shoplifter. When we got home I said I needed a nap. "Will you be safe if I walk Mira to the hardware store and back?" Luke asked. "Fifteen minutes." I looked him in the eye and said yes. When I heard the front door close, I laid one of our sheets in a patch of sunshine on our bedroom floor. Hoped it would soak up the blood so he wouldn't have to see it dripping, horror movie–style, down the stairs.

Slicing the tips of my fingers, I fought the plastic surrounding the razor. Finally, getting a sharp corner free, I couldn't press the millimetres of blade deep enough to open a vein. I kept trying. Slashing over previous scabs, stacking frantic thin lines from wrist to forearm. I was terrified, but so tired of being held back.

Luke came home in a rush, ran upstairs, and found me curled in a ball. Blood like bright poppies on a sheet patterned in wildflowers.

"I had a feeling I shouldn't have left," he said quietly. He took the razor away, put a trembling hand on my back. "We need to take you to the hospital."

Institutionalization lasted a week. I remember only pieces. Luke was there every day, bringing me chocolate and tea. He sat beside me in meetings with a doctor and a social worker to decide whether I could go home. I said the hospital felt like a punishment for being sick. It pained Luke to say that he needed a few more days, that he didn't yet trust me not to try again. The doctor spoke so softly, in such a low register, it was almost as if he didn't want me to hear what he was saying. I couldn't pay attention anyway, focused instead on how the doctor constantly fingered a ring of keys, clink, clink, a brass-rattle.

Mom flew in to see me during visiting hours. Although the issue of me being a sex worker was far from settled between us, we didn't talk about that as we sat in the ward's cafeteria. I could tell she didn't know what to do with her hands. There were no lists to make, nothing to do. "I've never had depression myself," she said.

"I don't have depression." I was ferociously inking a picture of a tiger in a colouring book. "I mean, I do—I always have—but that's not why I want to die."

She winced at my bluntness. "Whatever it is, it doesn't really matter. I don't understand it, but I talked to my sisters, they say it's like a hole in the ground. Sometimes you just fall in and there's no reason."

That metaphor is tired, I said, unsure if it was out loud or inside my head.

"You have to keep finding your way back out and it gets easier every time," she concluded.

I wanted to tell my mother I that hate this place. That I can't eat. That the sleeping pills and mood stabilizers make everything taste like metal, even my own saliva. That the doctor and his borderline personality disorder diagnosis are bullshit. BPD is the new hysteria and nymphomania— it's what they call women who don't conform. It means I'll always be written off as attention-seeking and lying, labelled untreatable. I wanted to tell her that the book I'm reading is horribly written, that I can't focus on the letters and the plot doesn't make sense and the act of reading makes me nauseated, but I couldn't remember what I'd already said.

A patient wandered over, carrying his radio, tuned as always to static. He asked if we had cigarettes, said they told him if he was good, he'd get his smoking privileges back any day now. Another patient in the corner was eating packets of peanut butter, peeling one open after the other, cleaning each plastic tub with a finger.

"It's not like falling," I said. "It's active. It's more like starting a race car, zero to a hundred." I could see myself in her concerned expression. It was disconcerting, being half of someone else.

Colouring book pages of snowmen and cartoon dinosaurs decorated the cafeteria windows. A mandala with bright pinks and yellows was titled, *Wednesday—full of woe.* Outside was a small courtyard, a patch of grass, a circular cement path surrounded on four sides by brick hospital walls. I wanted Mom to leave so I could go lie in the courtyard grass, sharp and dry, with a blanket over my head, like I did the first day until a nurse told me I couldn't cover my face. Instead, I agreed with Mom that everyone wanted me to get better. My forearms were covered in itchy red scabs like the peeled-back pink skin of a birch tree.

I was discharged angry: I'll be good, I'm good now, just leave me alone. In September I returned to the West Coast. Even though my family worried that it might be too soon, Luke advocated for my freedom, arguing that finishing my degree would give me purpose.

In Vancouver, suicidal urges break and recede like the tide, leaving me stranded on a beach of physical depression. Most days I struggle with pointlessness and exhaustion, but right now I feel grounded by this milky green tea. I put down my journal. Through the steamy windows of the bright café I watch people enjoying the sun in Grandview Park.

There is a fig tree in the backyard of our house just down the street. Leaves wider than dinner plates, clutches of unripe fruit, green globes. When I'm having an extra bad day, my roommate and old friend Kay feeds me healthy meals. Venison stew, chock full of reishi and turkey tail mushrooms. On her days off, she peels me away from the cops and murderers in my television void and drives me over the Ironworkers Bridge to Lynn Canyon. Straight into the prehistoric magic of redwoods, ferns, waterfalls. Moss drinking moisture from the air. White salmon flesh, the corpses of ecosystems.

★ ★ ★

A well-dressed waiter seats Charles and me at a large slab of glazed wood. We've been seeing each other occasionally in and out of the club for more than a year. Charles shakes off his Gore-Tex raincoat and adjusts his James Bond–branded Rolex. I order the most expensive drink on the menu, a sangria cocktail, and ask him, "How's work been?"

"Busy. You know how it is." He launches into a story about his work nemesis, whom I know a lot about by now. I like being able to glimpse worlds I'll never be a part of.

It's difficult to read the menu under these romantic low lights. Our waiter says most people order the signature pan-seared salmon and we follow suit. I can't tell if I'm hungry. When I'm not at school or forcing myself on forest walks, I'm lying in bed watching dizzying quantities of TV, blood pooling on one side of my body, heart rate slow. The only thing I can do, other than lie still, is eat. So I sneak out of my bedroom when Kay isn't home to consume cashews dipped in honey, chocolate bars, cheese, anything fatty, salty, or sweet. My body imagines I will be satiated by rich foods, but instead I end up bloated, self-hating, watching another episode.

I force myself to pick daintily at the food. The first bite of salmon melts like butter. In the classy restaurant kitchen, I imagine the trash filled with tails, spiky fins, and ancient hooked faces with sharp teeth.

"Tell me about your family." I want to hide through listening. When we met outside Charles said I looked sad. Even in the nighttime rain he read my sullen face, watery eyes.

"Well, you already know my sister is sick," he says. "She's doing as well as can be expected. Calls me early morning or late night to make up the time difference. It's difficult. I can send money, but it is not the same as being there. I guess we're alike, you and I, we like it here but still miss home."

It's hard to hate someone who, perhaps foolishly, leaves his heart so open. Yet I wonder what Charles thinks this is. Does he imagine he's helping a friend by giving her a free meal, or does he know we're playing a delicate game, that I would not have come to dinner if he didn't routinely give me money?

★ ★ ★

"I can't hear you! It's really loud in here." He is shielding his eyes from a strobe-light attack.

"Where are you from?" I try again.

"I just got off a plane from Fort McMurray. I've been out in the bush camps for the last month, but I've got this whole week off." His flannel shirt is shabby next to the well-dressed partiers pushing us to the sidelines, but I guarantee he has more money.

"The VIP is much quieter," I say.

★ ★ ★

"You'd make better money if you smiled more," a man says.

★ ★ ★

Scarlet and I are standing on Granville Street waiting for her boyfriend to pick us up. We live outside downtown and finding a cab on the weekend can take thirty minutes. The entire blocked-off party strip is filled with wasted people stumbling out of bars after last call. Some puke into overflowing trash cans; others line up to order pizza by the slice. I drop pocket change into a paper cup on the end of a fishing rod held by a panhandler who sits in a boat made from cardboard boxes.

Scarlet's phone rings. "What? ... Where?" She struggles to hear. "Okay, we're on our way." She hangs up and turns to me. "Apparently there's a crazy guy with a knife running around here. There's a warning on the radio. Raff wants us to meet him somewhere else. He's a Black guy driving a Bimmer, so he can't get down here anyway—too many cops."

We weave between groups of girls hunched on wet sidewalks with waterlogged satin heels. "Where're you pretty girls going?" a man slurs at us, trying to block our way. "Bitches!" he yells at our backs. A fight breaks out between two packs of men orbited by screaming women. Pinks, yellows, greens reflect off puddles like a garden of neon lilies.

We turn off the main strip, rain bouncing on our umbrellas. I watch the bushes and the corners of buildings and keep checking over my shoulder. Police cars shriek past and headlights slice through the rain as Scarlet's boyfriend pulls up.

★ ★ ★

"They don't pay me to smile," Akira says. Her stage show is full of technically difficult acrobatics, and she remains poised as a show pony. She never shakes her ass, never lets her hair down, and despite her diminutive height, she's capable of looking down on any man.

★ ★ ★

"Sorry, honey, this is a no-contact lap dance." I remove his hand from my hip and make a show of wagging my finger so that the ceiling camera will record me saying no.

"So I can't touch you at all? Even if I pay extra?"

"It's a bylaw. I'll get as close as I can. Believe me, you get to see everything." I snap the strap of my black thong. Out on the floor, people are allowed to touch the parts of me that don't matter—my calf or shoulder—but once we're in private, a total purity barrier must be maintained. It's difficult to get men to pay to just look at a steak, so the hungry ones go elsewhere.

A minute later, I'm awkwardly straddling him without touching his legs, and he strokes my back. "You really can't do that," I say.

As I stand up, a bouncer throws open the curtain, yelling, "No touching! Do it again and you're out."

The client crosses his arms.

"I feel bad for you guys," I coo, trying to restore a sensual ambience. "It must be so hard to keep your hands to yourselves."

"What's the point of this?" He pouts. "I can watch porn at home for free."

★ ★ ★

From my bed in the basement apartment I watch fat raindrops fall on the stone walkway that divides my house from my neighbour's. Morning sunlight is trapped in the atmosphere. I am a fallen tree, spongy, splintered, covered in moss. If I stay still long enough, I'll be digested by mushrooms and ants, returned to the soil. I check my phone and my stomach clenches. A text from Charles: *Hey beautiful lady. Can I take you shopping today?* It's too early to be Michelle.

Hours later, I meet Charles at Starbucks. I arrive first and buy him a coffee, a small gesture of reciprocity. I'm wearing big sunglasses in the futile hope of concealing my identity should any dancers or managers see us together. There's a good chance I'd be fired for poaching from the club. I feel like a mistress.

"What do you want to shop for?" Charles excitedly flicks through a catalogue of items he's starred from an upscale department store.

"A leather jacket." I have decided on my terms. It's not a $2,000 Gucci bag, but it's also not a trinket. It's a staple item, practical for Vancouver's too-cold-for-just-a-sweater winter.

Charles leads us through a store I wouldn't dare enter on my own. Other strippers would act entitled, but I'm too intimidated by the price tags to touch anything, worried I might leave the stain of my class on imported silks and hand-sewn leather.

"Let's get you some lingerie." Charles chooses a collection he thinks will suit me. I am skeptical about the difference between designer and mass-produced underwear, but the pink lace hugs my body and plumps up my chest. It makes me look rich, and the richer you look, the more money people give you. I take selfies and send them to Charles as part of an unspoken agreement. I look so good that I also send them to Luke, with a text about what I'm doing. Luke writes back, *I wish I had enough money to take you shopping like that.*

I don't want you to be my sugar daddy, I respond. Luke is at work hanging drywall. This outfit costs more than he'll make today.

Once the lingerie is wrapped and boxed, Charles and I return to the main floor. Surprisingly quickly, I find a timeless, well-cut, fitted black leather jacket. I hate the stark contrast between its Italian perfection and my grown-out roots and mud-speckled running shoes. Charles looks like a happy baby. "You look so good in everything," he fawns.

At the cash, I try not to think about Sarnia, that idiot man and his ugly purse, holding my breath until Charles's credit card beeps affirmative. I wear the jacket out of the store, and the stiff leather creaks as it adjusts to my form.

★ ★ ★

The owners of the District are throwing a staff appreciation party. Past managers emphasized my precarious position as an independent contractor, so the idea of being formally valued is appealing.

I invite Casey, Bailey's ex and my long-time friend, as my guest. He's one of my only friends in the city.

Casey is a street nurse who hates sleep and being alone, loves people, loves if not being alive at least the fact that life exists. My first weekend in Vancouver he guided me on a tour of downtown that wound up in the alleys behind Hastings Street. Long alleyways between SRO buildings, broken up by Dumpsters. Looming telephone poles, wood and wires buzzing with orange light. We snorted coke off a cigarette pack, then climbed a metal staircase up the side of a building onto a roof overlooking the city. Saw a million points of light offset by the profound darkness of the harbour and the mountains.

The staff appreciation party coincides with Chinese New Year. The District is closed to the public and decorated with red and gold banners and hanging lanterns. There's a catered meal along the back wall, but most people congregate around the square main bar.

"Michelle." Phoenix welcomes me with the safety of my work name. "Come do shots of absinthe. Is this your boyfriend?" She slips her hand up under Casey's T-shirt, runs her sharp nails across his skin. "He looks like he'd be freaky."

"We're friends." I take a shot, green and disgusting.

She flicks her tongue at him. "I love freaks."

An hour later, the open bar has demolished any awkwardness. Casey is chatting up the cute waitress, though he tells me later during a baggie exchange that her pupils take up her whole eyes and he thinks she's on acid.

Onstage, the MC is asking which male bouncer can climb highest on the sixty-foot pole. The bouncers take off their shirts, climb using their biceps, and the winner gets a dildo. One bouncer does a striptease, lots of flexing and thrusting.

As the night progresses, multiple girls get on the pole at once, performing high, medium, and low tricks, spinning at different speeds. Lady Boss is twerking on the dance floor. She puts her hands on the ground and backs her impossibly round ass into me. I hold her hips, feeling blessed. I wish Luke were here to enjoy this lewdness, even though he doesn't like the gluttony and pomp of partying with strangers.

On the way home, Casey says, "My favourite part was when that girl's tit popped out of her dress and it was so casual. She didn't notice at first, but when she did she just tucked it back in, like no big deal. Don't get me wrong, I'm known to lose a couple nights' sleep, pass out, then wake up and eat old pizza crusts with ketchup on them." I laugh, barely able to follow his logic. "But that was pretty wild. Things got intense there for a minute."

"Do you want to make out?" I ask.

"I'm flattered. I'm honoured," Casey says. "But I don't know if it's a good idea."

We find the next bar, get the next drink. As the party high wears off and I sag around a fancy glass of grenadine and crushed ice, I'm glad I

didn't intensify my loneliness by complicating one of my only friendships here.

★ ★ ★

"Did you know that most reports of rape are fake? In the morning,
women get embarrassed that they acted like a slut so they cry rape."
This pretty boy university student is testing me.

"That sounds like some men's rights bullshit to me, sweetie." I wonder how many women he has coerced or manipulated into sex, or if he's
here to practise these pickup-artist tactics on strippers before he uses
them on "real women."

"You must be one of those extremist feminists," he responds. "It's a
shame. If you weren't such a bitch, you'd be the hottest one here."

★ ★ ★

I'm pretty sure Scarlet and her boyfriend, Raff, are trying to pick me up.
We are parked in a lot overlooking the Pacific. The car is humming, bass
turned up high. Scarlet and Raff are passing a joint. I don't want any, but
I love the way it makes the car smell. We are folded inside the stormy
weather, lost to the world.

Scarlet is one of the most attractive women I've ever seen. She has
a smouldering-soft, whisper-in-your-ear kind of sexiness. And her boyfriend is cute, too. I can imagine them fucking each other extra hard
because I'm watching. Letting out all their pent-up, mainly monogamous, energy.

"We've got vodka at our house." Scarlet tucks her hair behind her ear.
Her smile seems innocent, but there's something I don't trust. As fun
as the night could be, it could also go terribly wrong. I worry she might
have a jealous meltdown. Or, a week afterwards, tell our co-workers that
I fucked her man, without context. Vancouver is an extremely expensive
city. I need this job more than I need a threesome.

★ ★ ★

Every client chokes upon walking into the VIP. I want to make it clear that the sour reek isn't emanating from me, but I stay silent because I don't know how to explain it. They all leave after one song. Each hour Boss Lady pulls back the curtains and crop-dusts the rooms with Febreze. For a few minutes it smells like funeral flowers, grand chrysanthemums wilting, caving in on themselves, but nothing can erase the stench, which a co-worker informs me is a dead rat rotting inside the wall.

"It happened in my apartment once and the landlord wouldn't do anything," the girl says. "Doesn't matter how hard you clean unless you break through the drywall and find it. There's no way they'd bother doing that for us here. They'll just wait until it's done decomposing— the dry ones don't smell as bad."

I wonder if the whole city, from SROs to multimillion-dollar mansions, have their walls insulated with mummified rats.

★ ★ ★

Priscilla approaches me at the base of the stairs. "You shouldn't stand with your arms crossed. It makes you look defensive and unattractive. It's all about body posture. Also, I've been meaning to tell you, you should do your makeup darker, outline the whole eye with black liner, like mine. It's like you've never heard of a smoky eye. I could do your makeup for you one night if you want."

Priscilla, with her off-kilter blond wig and makeup you could peel off like a rubber mask, is odder than most of the girls here, many of whom are also actresses or fitness instructors. I remind myself that she's trying to befriend me. I wonder if she is perplexed when the "helpful" criticisms that she gives to all the girls continually go unheeded, or if she's heard the rumour that she's allowed to work here only because she sleeps with the owner.

I used to care about club dynamics like this, wanting to know how the power trickled down and played out. It used to feel fun to eavesdrop on drama that wasn't mine. But now it feels a little sad and boring. Either way, it's not like Priscilla has a ton of social power here.

★ ★ ★

"I'll pay you to sit this song out," a client in the VIP says frantically. "It's my wedding song."

★ ★ ★

Ginger is heavy into weed. While we get ready for work in her apartment she records herself blowing a cloud of smoke at her phone, adds a filter of a sexy alien, and posts it for her followers to like.

She adjusts herself on her bed and gasps in pain. "After I had cancer I got this degenerative spine thing and chronic pain." She waits for the spike to pass. "It's why I can't keep a real job. I know it sounds like an excuse, but I get tired like you wouldn't believe. Some days I can't even open my eyes."

Her bedroom has a rose-beaded bedside lamp, a white iron headboard looped like cursive letters.

"A night wearing heels must be really hard," I say.

"It kills me the next day. That's why I get so frustrated when it's dead. Girls who work every day can balance it out, but sometimes I can only work one night a week. I love our job, though." Ginger straightens her spine. "It lets me live."

★ ★ ★

Are you working tonight? I'd really like to see you ... naked. Charles punctuates his text with a kissy face emoji.

I'm already in pyjamas, fetal position, Netflix. *No,* I respond. *I can't handle the lights and noise of the club. It's too overwhelming.* Being honest about the magnitude of my depression was easier than thinking up a fresh reason for why I look so devastated every time Charles sees me, which is most days I work. He texts back, *It's been too long, I need to see you, how about you come to my house instead?*

My bones protest. It takes all my effort to tear myself away from the television. I sit up, rub my dry eyes, focus. The obstacles between me and my money seem immense, but I say, *That's a perfect idea! I'll be over in an hour.*

Instead of the full glitz required by the club, I apply only an electric-pink lipstick. I try brushing out my hair, long and blond, but humidity has made it bushy, so it goes back up in a bun.

I'm going to Charles's house, I text Luke.

Be safe, he responds, unusually short.

My belly squirms as I justify, *I need to make rent. I haven't made it to work all week. I can't be in the club with all the flashing lights and noise. This will be easier in some ways.*

Are you sure you don't want me to transfer some money?

No. I don't want that kind of relationship with you. Everything is so expensive here. I need to be able to afford it myself or else I should give up and come home. Besides, Charles is chill.

Fine, he says. No heart emojis, no *my love*.

Wearing the jacket Charles bought me, I get out of a taxi in front of his brick apartment building. Orange floodlights illuminate five crows fighting over a scrap on the lawn. There is a chicken manufacturing plant nearby, Casey told me, with a Dumpster where seagulls and crows scavenge for beaks and entrails. They carry the pieces across the neighbourhood and you wake up with a severed chicken foot on your doorstep like a curse.

Charles buzzes me into a building that fifty years ago was a church: taupe carpet and walls, stained glass outlining the windows. I trudge up a wide set of stairs, knock on his apartment door. I feel like a shell of a person and wonder how I'm going to get through this.

"I've missed you, luv." Charles sweeps me into a rocking hug. Squishy and warm, it's good to be held. Charles hangs my coat, brushing off droplets of water so they don't stain the leather.

"I'm so glad you could come, Michelle. Can I make you a drink?"

Summoned by her name, Michelle takes the reins. She is me, after all. We share this body. To say she is only a persona would diminish her strength, wit, charm, and survival instincts. Charles and Michelle slip into an intimate rapport, blurring the boundaries between friends, lovers, employee/boss.

Charles removes ice and a bottle of vodka from a freezer now empty except for a frozen salmon in plastic wrap. "It was a gift when I bought this condo," he says. "With some lemon, butter, and thyme it will make quite a meal. You'll have to let me cook it for you one day." He's too sentimental to throw out the salmon, though he never cooks.

We tour his apartment. There's ornate woodwork around the dining room ceiling and dusty unpacked boxes on a twelve-person table. His tidy bedroom looks like it came straight from the showroom: mirrors on the closet doors reflect an oak headboard, large bed, and neat navy sheets with an extraordinary thread count. Showing me the spare bedroom, Charles says, "I had Savannah staying with me for a few months while she got stuff sorted with her mom and her—what did she call him?—baby daddy." I have no idea who Savannah is—it's impossible to keep track of all the girls that Charles helps. "She moved all her stuff out when I was away, stole a bunch of cash, and left the front door unlocked. I hope she's all right."

French doors open into a living room the length of my apartment. Like a movie theatre, tube lights run in the corners of the room, pulsing blue to purple-pink mood lighting. Outside the window the world is black. Constant rain makes night feel like the bottom of an ocean trench.

Searching for something light to say, I ask him, "Remember that one night we went to the grocery store, and the cashier had absolutely no filter and asked point-blank what our plans were for the night?"

Charles laughs. "If I remember correctly, we were paying for two limes, two lemons, and a bottle of soda water."

"And I was carrying a bottle of gin. Plus, you're old enough to be my father." Charles frowns and I quickly redirect. "I didn't know you had dogs." I point to two shih tzu gargoyles curled on a sectional. Ugly and ancient, the creatures are at odds with everything Charles likes to present. "My ex didn't want them in the divorce," he says. They raise their heads, jingle the cat bells on their collars, return to sleep. Charles is right; it's much quieter here than in the club.

After a few drinks I start playing on a pole that he has set up in the centre of the room. A permanent fixture attesting to the profession of the majority of his guests.

"Pole is an art form," he says. "I hate that they force you to take your panties off. It cheapens it."

I climb using shins and biceps. Brace myself while clamping the pole tightly between my thighs. Release a hand and extend my legs, leaning into a horizontal extension. "I don't know. I'm grateful that I get to take off my clothes onstage. Not at this club, but where I danced before. Since I don't have the talent of the other girls, getting naked is the point."

"You could improve, if you wanted," he says. "Lots of the girls offer one-on-one classes. It's a skill like anything else." This would be the moment to ask him to pay for private lessons. That way he'd get to support one of his other girls and I'd benefit. But my baseline energy isn't there. I'd flake and waste the opportunity.

A disco ball shoots stars across the floor, walls, ceiling. We're alone on his private dance floor. Charles reaches for my hand, formally spins me, pulls me against him. My feet trip over his. His breath is bad. This makes me sad. I wish he had someone who loved him enough to be honest, which I can't afford to be. His tongue darts into my mouth. Even Michelle recedes from reality. She and I take a break inside me. Recline on an antique red velvet daybed, waiting for it to be over.

Charles waltzes us to the sectional. The gargoyles don't even stir. I keep my legs firmly closed and he doesn't try too hard to open them. I unbutton his jeans and pull out his penis. It's cool to the touch, fluttering between flaccidity and alertness. Maybe it knows something is missing. I press my face into his neck, needing the kissing to stop. He worms inside my shirt and up under my bra to fondle me. It's so like high school I have to swallow nausea.

No sex act for money is morally better or worse, yet I don't let clients touch or lick my pussy or fuck me. On the few occasions I did I wasn't able to dissociate from the physical discomfort of it, and I felt distressed by arousal and disgust. Sex workers I've talked to exist on a spectrum from hating every second of sex with clients to truly enjoying it and feeling like it allows them to explore new things or be in touch with their pleasure. But I was not able to maintain my work persona in those encounters and became simply myself, which felt emotionally unsafe. Even though I consented to be paid for those exchanges, some of them settled into my body as trauma. There are so many sex workers who are not in a position to have boundaries around certain sex acts. I am grateful, and I am acutely aware, that it is privilege that lets me enforce my personal limits.

Even though I know sex work isn't morally wrong, sometimes I still experience shame. I've had to confront this directly since I told my mom. Her initial anger didn't last long. She took three days of silence before asking if we could talk and came to the phone conversation with concerns and questions based on deep reflection. I was prepared to be defensive, knowing my capacity to feel shame is expansive, but she shared her fears instead of judgments and confessed her worries about the potential for men to be violent. We agreed to disagree about what feminism means, and she told me my dad said, "Well, it is the oldest profession in the world." This showed me he accepts that I am an adult and can make my own choices. I never want to talk to him about it directly.

"For years there was always this distance between us. I couldn't get close to you," Mom said. "But I feel the wall between us has been knocked down. Maybe now we can have a real relationship."

"Michelle." Charles repeatedly whispers my name while wetly kissing my ear. The cloying, muddy sound makes me want to bolt.

I think about Luke. He once said, "You tell me that any extras you do are different from what you do for pleasure or fun. I trust you." When I pushed him on it he said, "I do struggle with my masculinity more when you do extras. But I believe that choosing to have sex, whether for money or not, doesn't morally degrade women. It doesn't tarnish your soul or make you less worthy of love. It's always your choice what you do with your body."

Luke works hard to separate what he truly feels from what society tells him he should feel about loving a sex worker. Closer to the beginning of our relationship Luke told me about a time he mentioned to a co-worker that his partner was a stripper. The co-worker laughed and said, "That's fun for now, but those aren't the type you want to marry." I cried when I heard this, as it reminded me that "normal" people think sex workers don't deserve love and family. Luke no longer asks me to help him work through the stigma he has to deal with. When he does express concern it's usually about risk, and my time with Charles isn't risky. It's very tidy and safe. In this "relationship" format, the work is sheltered from the criminalization and targeted violence faced by other types of sex workers.

Charles's penis grows in my hand, straining for the climax that, once he's hard, comes quickly. One of the gargoyles follows me into the kitchen and stares while I wash my hands, lathering them twice with dishwashing soap. While Charles cleans up in the bathroom, I make another drink. The vodka is high end, but all I can say about it is that it's cold.

Charles wants to cuddle, suggests we watch a movie by his favourite director. I ask him to call me a cab.

"But you've only been here a few hours. If you're tired, you know you can always sleep here. No funny stuff, I promise. That's the part that I miss the most since my wife left, having someone to sleep beside."

"Maybe next time." Despite the genuine care I have for Charles, friendly feelings that return quickly after the act, I will never let my dreams transpire so close to him. I'm incapable of psychic boundaries while I sleep.

He holds my jacket for me. "I wish you'd stay." He hands me a roll of money.

His spit has dried on my lips. I want to go home and brush my teeth.

I miss you, I text Luke on the drive home. The cab windows are streaming with rain, tributaries that catch the lights of the city and wash them out into the Pacific. *When are you coming to visit?* I ask, knowing he's four hours ahead and sleeping. Maybe it's late enough that mourning doves are weeping outside the attic bedroom we used to share.

★ ★ ★

When Luke finally walks through the Vancouver arrivals gate and sees me waiting, he grins, revealing the lightning-shaped crack in the veneer of his front tooth. We embrace and the smell of his shampoo is comfortingly familiar. I pluck a few of Mira's white hairs from his felt coat, the one he wears when he wants to look fancy. It feels like the awkward first date we never had. Should we kiss now or wait until it feels more natural?

"Your hands are freezing," I say. "Have you eaten today?"

He has to think about it. "No, I was too nervous about seeing you. Is that the jacket?" he asks. "You look like a rock star."

"You look pretty good yourself." I run my hands through his black curls flecked with white. "You'll be a silver fox soon."

On our afternoon walk, I eagerly show Luke the flora that has been bringing me joy. "It's wild to have spent my whole life in one climate and then move to another. There are so many species I've never met before. Look at this one." I point out *Gunnera*, a giant rhubarb.

"It looks like a dinosaur," he says.

Crouching, I peer under its continental foliage and spiky stems to the red seed pods shooting up from the ground like alien eggs. The path around Trout Lake is filled with people. Dogs chase sticks into water, joggers puff by in groups, and children play on a sandy beach.

I stop at a monkey puzzle tree with wavy branches covered in interlocking triangular plates. "This one looks like a spiny anteater."

"I'm ready to be done living apart," Luke declares.

I kiss his cheek. His close-cropped beard against my lips reminds me of that morning, how he kissed down my arched core, my legs falling open, welcoming pleasure.

"School is over after this semester, so I guess I'll move back after that."

"You don't sound very excited."

"It's not you, it's our city. There's no energy, no potential. Are you sure you don't want to move to Vancouver?" I had hoped his multiple visits would change his mind. "You haven't even seen the cherry trees in bloom." The gusts of pink petals in springtime had felt like city magic, a reason to stay.

"I wouldn't be as depressed if you were here," I admit. His arrival led to an immediate lifting of my sadness, but I try not to overthink it. I'd rather feel happy than worry about how dependent my mental health is on him.

Luke swings our hands. "Vancouver is too far away. We'd have to completely start over. It's too far from family, and we'd be giving up on our anarchist friends. Besides," he says, "it goes against our values to spend this much on rent." I love that he sees our shared life together as a forgone conclusion, one where we just have to work out the details.

Storks wade among lily pads on the lake. Smoky blue mountains, like the backs of whales, breach the horizon.

"Are you sure you don't want to stay here because of Charles?" Luke says with a note of uncertainty.

"I need that relationship to end," I say. "He wants to see me multiple nights a week and I'm always making excuses."

"I'm glad to hear you call it a relationship," Luke says. "He seems to have become something more than a sugar daddy."

"Yes and no," I say. "I used to think having a sugar daddy would be like role-playing. That we'd act out a fantasy of him being a rich man and play with fetishes around money and power. But in reality it's a lot of emotional labour. It's more like I'm dating a nice guy I really don't want to be dating, and because there's money involved I feel like I owe him."

We walk beneath a curtain of willows. "He always wants more, and he knows too much about me. And I know it's crazy, but I care about him. Not romantically, but I like him as a person. The whole thing feels ... icky."

"It seems like it's pushing your boundaries," Luke says. "I know you like to keep work separate."

"I can't go back home," I say. "I need to live in a bigger city."

"On the East Coast that leaves Halifax, Toronto, and Montreal." Luke offers to leave the place where he has lived his whole life, if I can let go of Vancouver.

"Halifax is too isolated."

"And I hate Toronto."

Only one choice left.

PART 4:
SELL THE FANTASY

CHAPTER 10:
KILLED IT

DIAMONDS
BURLINGTON, ONTARIO

I'm going to spend all summer in Ontario, in limbo, until Luke and I move to Montreal in the fall," I complain. "I need little trips like this to have something to do. Plus, it's so much nicer working with you guys."

"I'm so happy to be with my besties for bonding time," Gigi sings.

"And party time." Bailey swallows a Percocet with a mouthful of vodka and grapefruit juice.

"When was the last time we worked together?" I ask Bailey. "Sudbury?"

"I can't remember. That feels like forever ago."

We've rented a ground-floor hotel room. Glass doors covered by a pleated brown curtain open onto a parking lot. I can hear the air brakes of nearby trucks, slowing into snarled traffic on the QEW. Inside, it is as if a stripper bomb exploded: floor littered with heels and luggage, makeup and body products on all available surfaces. I pick through our collective outfits, dumped across the beds, looking to try a different style.

"I'm a bit nervous," I admit, as I shimmy into a one-size-fits-all fish-net dress. "I've gotten so comfortable at the Royal. Even though it's not as busy as it used to be, and they started charging that extra fee on weekends every time a guy wants to go to the VIP."

"I hate that fee!" Gigi yells from the bathroom.

"It's such a desperate money grab by the club," I say. "Maybe they're almost bankrupt. I end up having to give a free dance just so clients will pay to come to the VIP."

"That sucks," says Bailey, her voice flat.

"At least the Royal feels safe and predictable, though. I'm nervous about tonight and having to compete with Toronto girls. They're all going to be so hot. Hey, what's wrong with this dress?" My boobs poke like bread dough through holes in the fishnet.

Bailey says, "Those dresses look better on girls with fake tits, babe."

Gigi emerges, an amazon. Luminous fake tan, bronzer, and sharp cheekbone contour, big spiralled hair.

"You look perfect," I say. "I can't believe you only started stripping this past year."

"Already being in the industry made it an easy transition." Gigi thrives on intensity. "Stripping is more fun than escorting, even though I still do both. And they're both more fun than working on my master's. Social work stuff is so boring sometimes," she moans. "Anyway, stripping lets me justify all these dumb products. Why would I need this fifty-dollar highlighting palette to escort? Tricks don't notice stuff like that. I wear it to impress other girls."

"I don't know," Bailey says. "I think escorting is easier. I only have to entertain one client at a time. I know exactly what they expect of me because they're paying for a specific service. Stripping is scarier. You have to make them believe something, create a whole reality, make them fall in love with you ..."

"Okay, baby girl, slow down," Gigi says. "You're getting ahead of yourself." She and Bailey escort together regularly, sharing the costs of hotels and promotion on pay-by-the-ad websites.

"Why don't you pick an outfit?" I suggest.

Bailey refocuses with effort. "I got these online. Do you think I can pull it off?" She holds up a mermaid-themed set with a shell bra and holographic scales on the bottoms.

"I think you might feel overdressed," Gigi says tactfully. "This club isn't costume friendly."

"Good," I say, packing my favourite all-black outfit: a black G-string—the stripper's equivalent of a little black dress—a black bikini bra, leather ankle-wallet, and matte heels. "I never need an excuse to wear black."

In the cab Gigi warns us about the manager of Diamonds. "I've seen him scream at a girl for being five minutes late. He forced her to give him cash on the spot or he'd fire her. There's a lot of rules, too. You'll see them tacked up everywhere. I can't tell if girls follow them or not." She is trying to apply glitter to her eyelids, but the driver is racing between lights and braking hard, so the gold sparkles fall onto her cheeks like stardust. She started working at the Royal but soon after branched out into the GTA solo.

We arrive in the last few hours of the day shift while the music is still soft. Bored strippers are ignoring the few clients who have already been picked over, carcasses cleaned to the bone. We wait to meet the manager, who is leaning over and whisper-talking at a girl sitting straight spined on a high stool. She's wearing street clothes, so maybe he's told her she needs to endure a lecture before getting dressed or agree to the terms of a punishment or a fine. Choosing her moment, the girl bursts off her stool and takes a swing at him. We scramble out of the way as the manager, helped by a bouncer, wrestles the girl into a headlock and throws her into the street, locking the door behind her. I wish she'd been able to land the punch.

"We could leave in solidarity," Gigi whispers. I'm flustered with the shame of replacing that girl, normalizing the violence that just happened.

The manager approaches, dusting his hands. "New ones, let me see your arms." Confused, Bailey and I pull up the sleeves of our sweaters.

"I don't want any addicts in my club." He twists my forearm to catch the waning sunlight coming through the glass front door where the pissed-off girl is pacing, yelling into her phone.

When we get into the changing room there is a hush, as though every girl expects him to storm in and choose a new target.

With the bar off to one side, the stage is the main focus of the club. "It's actually pretty," I say, as a dancer descends elegantly from a staircase decorated with blue-and-white-lit mirrors.

Performing onstage is still Bailey's main fear. "It's big," she says.

Two catwalks split from the mainstage in opposite directions, leading out into the crowd, a pole at each end.

When it starts to get busy, Gigi branches off, saying she'd rather work alone. Another effective tactic is for girls who look alike to hustle together. As slim blondes, Bailey and I use our sameness as a selling point. Men give up their seats for us, buy us shots with names like banana hammock and ice queen, ask us to start a table dance at the next song. I push our team hard, tease men with stories of how Bailey and I fucked in real life—wouldn't they like a taste, a little preview, in the VIP?

It's midnight and Bailey is almost too drunk. Instead of worrying about how to pull her back, I join her. We shut ourselves in a bathroom stall, bite a Percocet in half, the jagged edges scratching our throats. Tinashe is playing, the bass cranked so high the deep vibrations create a sense of safety.

In the bathroom mirror I pout to reapply lipstick. My makeup skills are on point, blended yet dramatic, but my favourite feature is my hair. It's long and thick with ashy roots that melt into a blond balayage. It will hold this wavy style for days. I spin it in my hands to smooth strays, tighten the curl, then let it bounce.

On the way out I notice a management sign perfect for the found poetry I'm collecting. I take a picture: *Stimulate his eyes 20$, stimulate his body 100$, stimulate his brain, priceless. Remember girls ... this is his fantasy world and has nothing to do with you. The better you sell the fantasy the* *more money you make. If you make sure he enjoys his visit today, he will be back with friends tomorrow.* The best part is that someone has drawn a large ejaculating penis over the entire thing.

"How's your night?" I ask Gigi. It's late. I'm trying to focus on her, but I can't stop scanning the bar, keeping tabs on who's moving and which tables have freed up. Oh, that man who has taken every girl is back from a dance, I should try to get him.

"Good, not great," she responds.

"Bailey and I are having a really good night," I gush. "She's in the VIP."

"Did you know Bailey was sober last week? She made it seven days."

"That's really good for her. It's difficult, though, because she wouldn't have made any money if she stayed sober tonight."

"You're right, she wouldn't have. You know how she has a hard time saying no."

"But Bailey needs money," I protest. "She was saying she can't pay rent, that her phone is going to get cut off."

"Those are all true things."

"Our friend is escorting to meet her basic needs. I'm happy she came to strip tonight, to take a break. It's so much easier."

"Maybe for you," Gigi counters.

"Either way, don't we have a responsibility to help her get the money she needs, so she can decide how to get healthier on her own, if that's what she chooses to do? Doesn't the harm reduction approach say we are supposed to"—I put it in frustrated air quotes—"'meet people where they're at'?"

Gigi crosses her arms. "I'm worried about her." As if I'm not.

"I told you what happened last time I tried to talk to Bailey about her addictions," I say.

It blew up when Bailey came to visit Casey and me for a trip to Vancouver Island. The three of us sat on the ferry deck in rare sunshine, observing the sea and rugged coast and keeping an eye out for seals. Loud ocean winds allowed us to share space without talking about

Bailey's transition to daily use of painkillers and alcohol. But as soon as we got into our hotel room, Casey and Bailey started bickering, something they had gotten good at when they'd been a couple many years before. "I see people strung out on pills every day," Casey said. "You're no different, no better, than anyone else."

"Don't you see how intense it makes you?" I jumped in. "You're always doing that weird thing with your jaw and I can't even understand what you're talking about half the time."

"The drugs do change my behaviour, but in a good way," Bailey insisted. I'm not depressed anymore. I have energy. I'm able to get out of bed and do the things I have to do. They let me organize my life and I'm more present at work."

Casey threw up his hands. "Okay, so now you get high at your regular job? You don't think that's a red flag?"

"Casey, you can back off," Bailey snapped. "An alcoholic who goes on coke benders every weekend can't tell me shit."

"What exactly is your daily use?" I asked.

Bailey emptied a bottle with a variety of pills onto the bed. Vitamins, herbal supplements, Percocets. She separated her treasures into piles, explained how she'd stop if it became a real problem.

"Come on, Bailey." I took a swig of whisky. "Stop the bullshit. You need help."

"I'm sick of this moralizing, patronizing garbage from you, Michelle. You think you're better than me. Remember how you dealt with the night of Trump's election? Scoring heroin and getting drug-sick for days—days!—isn't exactly model behaviour."

"That was one time. And this isn't about me!" I yelled.

"But it's not like you don't have a problem, is it?"

The bed on which we all sat took up most of the small room, leaving no space to walk away or breathe. I take Percocets every time I strip and often when I party, or if I have to go to a social event. It works out to around three days a week. Is that a problem? Outside the open window the party strip lit up and crowds began to form outside bars. Bailey stormed out to chain-smoke and I opened her bottle of pills. "She thinks she's not addicted. I guess we'll see what happens when she doesn't have as many pills as she rationed for this trip."

"Are you sure you want to do that?" Casey asked. "It could send her into withdrawal."

I swallowed one anyway and when Bailey came back I told her what I'd done in a bratty, fight-me-about-it way. Instead of meeting my anger, she packed her things and left to sleep in a shelter.

The next day we regrouped for breakfast at a family restaurant decorated with dusty plastic lobsters in cages. Casey ordered round after round of oysters and breakfast Caesars, determined to have a vacation. Bailey, her luggage at her side, cried openly the entire time. I drank lemon water, extra bitter.

"Our friendship is still so fragile after that," I say. "There's no way she'd want to hear from me about her use tonight."

"I just think we could be doing better." Classic Gigi, aware that we need to act differently, even if she's not sure how.

Bailey joins us. "A girl told me Club Goldmine in Sudbury went under. I heard the one in Hamilton is closing, but I didn't know that Goldmine closed, too. When did that happen?"

"A while ago," I say.

"This place is closing, too," Gigi says. "Within the next couple years it's going to become a condo tower. Strip clubs are dying."

We watch a girl onstage who doesn't even have to dance. She walks between the poles, constantly bouncing. Her huge butt jiggles, hips like shelves jutting out from a sculpted waist. Occasionally she drops into the splits to cheers from the audience. Every part of her is sexual, her whole body a sex organ.

"How much do you think it costs to look that way?" Gigi wonders.

"I'm sure she paid off her boob job long ago," I say.

"She has so much more work done than that," Gigi says. "Liposuction, BBL or butt implants, Botox ..." The words drop out of the sky like cold rain.

"What's BBL?" Bailey asks.

"Brazilian butt lift. It's where they take all the fat out of your stomach and thighs and inject it into your ass."

"I need it!" My hand flies to the soft cushion of fat that protects my viscera. "I wish I could unhear that." I will always know it's a surgical possibility, one I will never be able to afford, to have the kind of flat stomach that my eating disorder still demands.

"I've been thinking about getting Botox for my wrinkles and crow's feet," Gigi says.

"You don't even have those," I argue automatically.

"Girl, shut up. You got all the hairs lasered off your vagina, and you get tattoos. That stuff is way more permanent than Botox."

The girl onstage has injected, prodded, acidified, inflated, cut, inserted, reduced, carved, sculpted, and perfected her vessel. Under the pressure of extreme beauty standards, she's become a diamond. Every single man in here wants her, and every single girl is jealous.

"The time is coming when we'll have to decide if we're going to age gracefully or not," Gigi says.

"Fuck aging gracefully," I say. "I'm going to fight it as long as I possibly can."

"Face it," Gigi says. "We probably have another five years of being reasonably hot. After that, it's surgeries and stuff, or we're out."

"Nadia's getting her boobs done," I gossip.

"Her boobs are perfect already, aren't they?" Bailey asks.

"I thought so," I say. "You know, girls used to work to buy condos or cars, things they could keep once they retire. Now it seems like everyone has to invest so much money to alter their bodies that they can't possibly have savings. It's like everyone's working so they can keep working."

★ ★ ★

This young Russian meathead smells so good. He's grinning because he knows he's hot. I shove him onto a couch in a mirrored corner of the vip where the glass is smudged with a hundred handprints. I skip the beginning of my routine and straddle him. Run my nails up his stomach, and he twitches under my touch. I twist his shirt and pull him closer. He whispers to me in his language and I don't even care what the words mean; he can call me any name. The syllables charge my blood and ache like foreplay. Powerfully, I pin him to the couch.

He seems like a truly bad man, rude at his table, posturing, obviously cruising for a fight. Probably I hate him, but it doesn't matter now. We grip wrists, interlock fingers. I explore the prickly ridge where his shaved skull meets spine. Hold back from biting the exposed cords in his neck when his head lolls back from the pressure I put on his erection beneath his jeans. He drags his fingers over my forearms, pushes back my shoulders as if opening my rib cage. He has a scar on his cheek that I only notice because we are so close. I want to hear him moan, I want to make him cum, but exactly three minutes later, the song ends. I turn away from him while putting my bra on, embarrassed.

Back on the floor I assume whatever created that flash of chemistry has ceased to exist, that it simply blinked out of existence, but a scent of it must have lingered. I have to laugh at the pang of jealousy that hits when I see him take the next girl.

★ ★ ★

On the cab ride to the hotel Gigi is furiously tapping at her phone.

"Who are you texting?" Bailey asks.

"Just some man who didn't pay me," she answers. "He said he was going to the ATM after we did extra dances and he never came back."

"But he gave you his number first?"

"Yeah, before we even went for dances. He really wanted to take me on a date." She rolls her eyes. "I'm letting him know that I looked up his construction company online and found his home address. I'm telling him that if he doesn't want a crazy ho showing up at his doorstep while he's getting his kiddies ready for school, he'd better e-transfer me my money ASAP." She blows a kiss at her phone and drops it into her over-stuffed purse.

★ ★ ★

"We were a slutty blond whirlwind," I exclaim as we get back to the hotel room.

"Yes, babe, we killed it." Bailey kisses me. Her skin feels like stars. She cranks the heat all the way up and we discard our clothes, roll around on one of the beds. The money flowed effortlessly. It should be over now, but neither of us can stop.

Gigi crawls under her covers with her back to us. "I'm really tired and you guys are both annoying me. Can you seriously be quiet? Go hang out in the bathroom or something."

Bailey runs a deep bath, grinds her teeth. She empties a bottle of bubble bath, antifreeze blue, into the steaming water. Lights two autumn-scented candles she brought from home and turns off the overhead light and whirring fan, plunging us into moody, flickering darkness. The scalding water brings sensation back to the places where numbness had taken hold. Wet tips of hair slick to Bailey's rib cage. Foggy remnants of makeup smudged by client's thumbprints and palms. She smiles, but her lips are pressed thin. As I come down, guilt whispers that *I* will not wake up needing to get high again. Quiet between us leaves space for the gentle lap of water against porcelain. I wish I knew how to hold her better. Our knees are the tips of icebergs. Smooth legs connect beneath the water; at least there is softness in this.

★ ★ ★

Sometime before dawn I stumble into the bathroom. Limbs tingling. Stomach cramping. Heart revving like an overworked engine. On the toilet I rest forehead on knees, trying to steady the high-voltage ringing. When I stand, sound crescendos into unconsciousness.

I wake up on a pile of wet towels. Pain above my left eyebrow. It must have hit the countertop. No blood, but it's swelling. Could have been worse: eyes, teeth. The bathroom is a moonless night. Press cheek against cool tiles. Wait for the rodeo of substances to wear themselves out. Crawl up the rim of the bowl. Stomach surges and empties water into water.

CHAPTER 11:
THE BEST STRIP CLUB
IN CANADA

MOONLIGHTER & SIRENS
NIAGARA, ONTARIO

FRIDAY

Using the sunblind mirror I apply lipstick and try to psych us up after hours of driving. "We are both super hot, total babes. They will definitely hire us," I tell Gigi.

"Will you work here if they only want you?" She pokes her fear of being turned away for being judged too fat.

"Of course not. We're a package deal. If they don't want either of us, for whatever reason, we'll turn around and go back to the Royal."

"Tail between our legs ... Oh God, I don't want to go back there tonight. It's so dead and every bitch keeps talking about Niagara like it's the holy grail."

"I know. Are you ready?"

It's a relief to see Moonlighter is no nicer than any other club when the lights are on. Shoddy tables and ripped carpeting. Horseshoes on either side of a runway stage. A daytime manager who looks like someone's scruffy uncle says, "Sure you girls can work here. As long as you don't have boyfriends. No boyfriends in the club."

We return to the car triumphant.

"Stage one complete." I say. "Now we just need to get our licences from the city, find a hotel, get groceries, get ready, and then come back to work for eight hours."

It feels like a bad idea, voluntarily walking into a police station to register as an exotic dancer, but Niagara clubs require licences. The receptionist's counter is so high I feel childlike handing up my identification cards through the slot in bulletproof glass. Gigi does the same and we wait nervously for criminal background checks and paperwork to come through.

Under the umbrella of sex work, strippers have the most societal acceptance and legal safety, but I'm still not excited to have my occupation entered into the public record. Some municipalities enforce dancing licences—another way that institutions line up to take a cut. Gigi and I spend hours getting ours, including a frenzied trip to a local tax office and government services centre and calls to past employers. It costs us $600 each for a one-year licence on a wallet-sized card.

Before looking for a hotel we go to a health food store. I fill a red basket with coconut water, chocolate paleo tarts, premade salad, and a bottle of probiotic brine-fermented gut bacteria. "Luke would be disappointed in me for buying a ten-dollar bottle of pickle juice without any pickles in it." I laugh.

Gigi doesn't share my guilt. "I put my body through hell while I'm working." She picks up vitamin powder that promises to improve everything. "Knowing I have bougie snacks to come home to at the end of a shift is self-care."

As we settle into our expensive hotel room, Gigi says, "This better be worth it."

"The stripper tax here is steep," I agree. We're deeply in debt before getting started.

"If we end up coming here every weekend, we could rent an apartment for the summer. With everything priced to gouge tourists, I bet it'd be cheaper," she schemes.

"I'm tired from running around and you're planning world domination."

She crinkles her face, cute and kissy, but she is dead serious when she says, "I've got goals."

Gigi performs the backward calculations for how much time two femmes need to shower and complete hair and makeup. "We have to start getting ready in an hour to make it in for nine."

"Then I'm watching one hour of television." I huddle under cool covers and cycle through limited cable options until I stumble upon familiar characters. "Yes! *Special Victims Unit*! I love this show. Is it too much, though? Should we watch something with less sexualized violence?"

Gigi is sprawled on her parallel bed. "Don't change it. It's a guilty pleasure for me, too. It reminds me that I'm not wrong to think the world is hella messed up." We watch as two female detectives shake down a brutal pimp.

"Sometimes I feel like I'm studying it so I can know what I'm supposed to do when a bad thing happens to me." I snuggle back into a wall of pillows.

"In real life I know cops don't give a fuck about solving the murders of sex workers," Gigi says, "but man, do I ever love Sergeant Benson."

I've seen this episode before. They let the pimp go and he kills the girl.

★ ★ ★

The parking lot is packed when we arrive. Bass seeps out of the building like heat. We bypass the lineup and bouncers roughly check our work bags for drugs and alcohol without looking at our faces. I'm nervous they'll discover the couple of pills I have stashed in my wallet, but they're not looking that hard.

When two glorious dancers in full glam tramp down the narrow staircase from the changing room, I flatten myself against the wall to get out of their way. They pass without acknowledgment.

The entire top floor is for dancers and it's full. Multiple rooms with lockers and mirrors. Girls curling their hair and eyelashes, playing songs from their phones, swapping stories about what unbelievably stupid thing their man did this week. Gigi and I wedge ourselves into the back of a cramped row of skinny lockers. Girls navigate the tight spaces, stepping over bags and bodies, their legs elongated by heels. Being constantly in someone's way, it's impossible not to feel too big.

"Is it my imagination or is every girl here insanely gorgeous?" Gigi voices our shared concern.

"I look like a basic bitch." I pick nervously at my pink department store one-piece. "I literally just bought this and thought it was so cute, but everyone here is wearing custom designs."

"The outfit lady will be here tonight," interjects a girl crouching in front of her locker, spritzing herself all over with body spray. "Her name is Mary. She'll be set up in the bathroom after ten."

"Thanks. It's our first time here."

The girl gives me a half smile. "You have to go sign in with Viktor before you can work. The office is downstairs."

A lineup of girls waits to sign in with the night manager. I notice a plain white scale, like those in gyms and family bathrooms, in the corner of the office. It bolsters the rumours from other travelling girls about Moonlighter's strict body policing. I imagine a trial-by-scale, in which the boss-turned-judge decides to fire a girl but wants to humiliate her first by weighing her. I picture the nauseating surge of digits as the pounds spike and settle on a number he claims is proof her body isn't good enough. I doubt there is an actual cut-off number of "too big" and assume his decision is based on how much he dislikes a girl's skin colour, curves, attitude. I wonder if he lets us take off our shoes, unclip our hair.

Do implants count as fat? I imagine us butchering ourselves, trying to remove the parts we could work without. I hope Gigi hasn't seen it.

"How long have you been working here?" Viktor asks coldly from behind a desk when we get to the front. With a skin fade haircut and tight black T-shirt, he is much younger and cooler than whoever hired us this morning.

"We got our licences today." I hold mine out like a free pass.

Grimly, he collects an exorbitant stage fee, all the cash I have on hand, and shoves papers forward for us to sign. After I fill them out, I notice Gigi has lied about her birth year. I should have done that. Mine is now, glaringly, the only one below 1990. Viktor grinds his gum so hard his jaw flexes. He looks behind us to the wall covered by a mosaic of surveillance feeds.

"He's not excited to have us working here," I whisper to Gigi as we scurry onto the main floor. "We should avoid him as much as possible."

Shaken, we survey our situation. The girl onstage is announced as Cleo. Every mesmerizing movement slips into the next, like a cobra. I half-expect her to have fangs. Cleo is not the only one. There are about sixty girls here, and sure, every one of them is attractive, hot, but there are twenty who are drop-dead gorgeous. The most perfectly beautiful women I've ever seen.

Gigi has noticed, too. She tugs at one of her naturally frizzy curls. "Some of these girls are literal angels. I should have straightened my hair."

"We need new outfits. Now," I say.

Thank God for Mary. The entrepreneurial seamstress has transformed the women's washroom into a fantastical pop-up stripper store. Flocks of girls like starlings pick through a rack of every colour and textile. Outfits adorned with rhinestones for the princesses, chains for the baddies. Everything is straight-pinned together so it can be adjusted to individual curves and finished with a sewing machine perched between the sinks. The counter is a display table showcasing a jewellery box of sparkly chokers, diamond necklaces, and body chains. There is a stack of new bandanas for the girls who rushed to meet cut-off and forgot theirs at home. Packs of gum, travel-sized baby wipes, and individual tampons. To the right of the hand dryer is a suitcase full of knee-high socks, fishnets, and sex-shop stockings.

"This is magical." I'm overwhelmed by choice.

"This is one of the steps, I'm sure of it," Gigi responds.

"Steps to what?"

"Becoming an angel."

I sift through Lycra and mesh, drawn to the black outfits. Occasional pinpricks feel like static shocks. Mary helps us choose outfits to suit our bodies. I trust her when she says in her Eastern European accent, "You don't have the chest for that one, try this instead." She helps me in and out of things until I find a black mesh bikini trimmed with holographic gold strings that makes me feel powerful. She lets us wear her creations out of the washroom on half credit, a favour for girls like us, cash broke and underdressed.

"What a lifesaver," Gigi says, now swathed in an elegant criss-crossing lavender bodysuit. We bring our budding confidence onto the floor and split up.

Soon it's shoulder to shoulder, squeezing through cracks in crowds to make it to tables. I try to introduce myself to individual men, but they prefer girls who captivate the whole table with a little taste of the dance right there, tits in the face, rather than my prudish handshake. Men keep telling me I'm too nice. Too pale. That I have too many tattoos. That I'm too shy. After multiple rejections, I realize other girls are repeatedly circling, pushing, pressing, coming back, trying again. Standing still is being dead in the water.

"I haven't made any money yet," Gigi says when we reconnect.

"Me neither. Being 'pretty enough, naturally' isn't working for me. I feel so ugly."

"Don't talk to me about being ugly," she snaps. "You're skinnier than me."

I'm surprised by her venom. "But my tattoos are really throwing people off. They're too piecemeal and punk."

"It's not the same thing, girl." Gigi is using her bossy tone, but I'm unsure why we're not on the same page.

"We're both getting rejected, though. I totally don't fit in here."

"Keep that self-deprecating thing you do to yourself," she says. "You're closer to whatever it is we're both supposed to be. Anyway, it seems girls are working in teams, let's try that."

We approach a large table together. Yelling to sound fun over the music. Drape our arms around men's shoulders, slide onto their laps, act excited to meet the bachelors. They don't like us together. Her elegant style clashes with my glam-goth outfit and our bodies are different sizes, making her seem too big and me too small. Men ask if we know "those girls over there," if we can go get them instead. The men mean the triplets. In the pyramid of angels, the triplets are at the top. White hair, light skin, curvy-thick bodies. They step into horseshoes ringed by customers like Cerberus in stilettos. I don't even think they ask first; they just start performing and expect to be paid.

"What would it take for us to look like them?" I ask Gigi. "Could we ever?"

"Objectively, those girls are hotter than we'll ever be. We're not in our early twenties, and we don't work every night to afford those surgeries."

It's midnight before we finally start selling dances separately. As soon as I make money I pay for my outfit and buy another, a V-shaped one-piece made of artfully placed swatches of fabric. I slog on, through brambles of rejection, toward more steady clients as the evening climaxes. By the last hour the entrance to the VIP is a beehive. Men hovering, grabbing the first girl to reemerge. I catch glimpses of Gigi during the last hour but don't have time to check in. We are both hustling as hard as we can to make up for the rough start. It's hard to shake the feeling that I'm selling a substandard product. A brand-name knock-off. That men are only taking me because the hotter girls are busy. So I overcompensate. Get naked faster, grind longer, and let dudes slap my ass harder.

Back at the hotel I smear coconut oil on my face to melt off the makeup. My knees are scratched from the VIP couches and my shins are bruised from the few table dances I managed to sell. I want to sleep, but my thoughts are racing. "Every guy was with a bachelor party from another city, ready to party. There was so much money there but not for us." My throat is sore from yelling over the music, resting at a recovery octave. "There is so much potential. Way more than anywhere I've worked before. We just need to figure it out."

"I don't know," Gigi says. "Something feels off." She counts her money, calls the total mediocre.

I wash my face, moisturize, sit on the bed, and take a long drink of carrot and orange juice. Pick at a chocolate dessert, made mostly of coconut oil and dark chocolate. It melts between my fingers. "Did you see the office has a fucking scale?" I ask.

"Of course I saw, and I don't want to talk about it," Gigi says.

★ ★ ★

SATURDAY

When we sign in with Viktor on Saturday night, he says, "You both need to go over to Sirens at eleven." Sirens is Moonlighter's weekend overflow club. They share a parking lot and are owned and operated by the same people, but Moonlighter girls are supposed to be hotter while Sirens is known as an extras club, a synonym for grimy. It's not like we can say no to Viktor.

At eleven, we get dressed, leave the already busy Moonlighter, and walk across the parking lot, heads down. Sirens is barely open. They still have the house lights on, music low enough to hear the clink of bottles as bartenders stock their stations.

"This sucks. How are we supposed to make money when everyone is over at Moonlighter?" I ask Gigi as we change into our outfits for the second time.

"I prefer working here," says a girl beside us. She looks to be in her thirties, with pregnancy stretch marks on a loose tummy.

"How come?" Gigi asks her.

"It's chill over here. Less pressure. Don't worry, it'll get busy."

Within the hour, Sirens fills with men who are too horny to wait in the Moonlighter lineup, eager bachelor parties, and locals choosing a more relaxed atmosphere in which to spend their money.

Sirens has two parallel stages. They put Gigi and me up at the same time and in this situation our differences showcase variety. Men who like Gigi's body type and style gravitate to her side and men who like mine come to me, an even split. They place their five dollars on the stage, creased lengthwise like a tent, or throw American ones. We dance to songs about mean girls making money.

★ ★ ★

I luck into a near-perfect client, a nineteen-year-old unionized tool and die machinist. A recent convert to strip clubs, he is here without friends to indulge completely. He tips me a different-coloured bill every song. Big tips are a novelty and it boosts my battered confidence.

★ ★ ★

"So are you the bachelor?" I ask the next guy, whose friends push him out of his seat and pay for his dance.

This VIP has brightly lit individual cabins side by side along the walls. I like how private they are so the men and other girls can't see what I'm doing, or not doing. I have no problem with girls offering extras, but I prefer not to in this public context, and I make less money because of it. The guy I'm dancing for is sunk deep into a cushy chair with broken springs. He is unable to give more than a half smile.

"I'm not a bachelor," he says. "We're, uh, celebrating my divorce."

I pull his face into my chest. "Let's not talk about that now." He'll have to face whatever failings ended his marriage in the morning.

★ ★ ★

"I don't care if it's less classy or whatever. I like Sirens better," I tell Gigi during a moment's pause. "There are girls here with every body type, every breast size, and I like looking around and seeing cheap wigs, fake tans, and bad tattoos. It makes me feel more at home."

"Because you feel comparatively hot?"

"No. I like it because we don't all have to be perfect and the same. Plus, I don't have to spend my night watching the triplets rake it in."

"I heard the lineup for Moonlighter is forty-five minutes. Guys give up and come here because they're ready to spend."

The variety of dancers at Sirens means Gigi and I appear less mismatched. As a team, we approach guys with two horseshoe tables pushed together and climb into the middle of their miniature stadium. Shake our asses in their faces. Lie along the table, arch our backs, lift and spread our legs. They can't touch on the floor, so they crane and crowd to peer at the marvel between our thighs. After one song we press them to go to the VIP and the table sends their bachelor for double dances.

The door to the individual cabin is a diaphanous curtain. The client sets his drink beside a collection of half-drunk, forgotten others. Spreads himself on the orange and itchy armless loveseat. Gigi and I each straddle a leg, pet his chest and arms.

"Feel his shoulders," I encourage Gigi as I squeeze. "You must work out all the time to get so strong." He splits his attention frantically, trying to make memories of this culturally accepted time out of monogamy. Sure, a lap dance is not sex, but it's not not.

We don't even have our tops off yet, but the groom is so eager. "How much would you both charge to come to our hotel for an after-party?"

Gigi puts a finger to his lips. "Enjoy the moment, babe. Relax."

"But how much do you charge, though? Just blow jobs—well, I don't know what the other guys are going to want, but I just want, ya know, a small party favour."

There *are* bachelors who come to the club because their friends have forced them to. These "good sports" come to keep their friends happy and participate in tradition. They look at some titties, get one lap dance, and then head out. But about half of all bachelor parties have best men, fathers, or brothers-in-law, and in this case the groom himself, who spend their time at the club trying to recruit strippers for extras.

Gigi is the more industrious of the two of us. "What are you going to give us?" Her voice is so silky, I could listen to her forever.

"Whatever you want." He's worked up. "Champagne, steak, room service—"

"Cash." Gigi says.

"Sure, if that's what you want. My best man's the money guy, you'll have to ask him. We're all nice guys, I swear. Didn't plan on this, but you all are so hot."

Gigi and I smile at each other. He's not sober enough to make a serious offer.

Strippers aren't trying to steal husbands or ruin marriages. We're just trying to make money. On my end, it's a very straightforward interaction. But looking at this messy groom and knowing that the way that he wants to celebrate his marriage is by paying for a blow job ... It makes me feel like I don't understand straight, monogamous people at all.

Gigi and I take our tops off. Like a drowning man, the groom latches onto our flesh. He grabs our breasts, hard enough to make me wince. Gigi knows I experience more sensation and pain in my breasts than she does.

"No, sweetie." She pushes his hand off me, replaces it with her own. Her fingers hover, soft scratch of acrylics, as she trails up to my collarbones and down over my belly button, to my hip points and back to my breasts. "Gentle is sexy," she tells him.

I move close enough to kiss her. She smells of matte foundation, tropical fake tan, and floral deodorant. I recline on the client like he is a prop in our magic show while she moves down. Carefully, she removes my new underwear. The chain-link straps clink as she sets it on the side table. Her forehead touches my stomach as she pretends to lick my pussy, breath moist against my shaved skin.

I moan toward the client. Her curls fall to the side, revealing her teenage hippie tattoo: *Growth*, over two leaves of freshly germinated seed. The client is desperate to see down. She looks up at him through fluttery lashes, wipes the corners of her lips as if they're wet, and returns. Her nose occasionally brushes my clit. Cute. The client's erection pokes into my back. There's a power rush that comes with being the centre of complete and undivided attention.

★ ★ ★

"Tonight was the best money I've done in ..." I pace around the hotel, pop out fake-diamond stretched earplugs, pull off lashes. "As long as I can remember. I guess it's from stage tips and tips on top of dances, right? Because we wouldn't have made this much lap dancing."

Gigi and I made within forty dollars of each other, on the upper end of my very best nights. It's a huge relief.

Gigi sighs. "Not that I'm not grateful, I just really wanted to work at Moonlighter, you know? To be at the best club, be the hot girl."

"But the difference in money."

"I know, I know." She is trying to untangle the clasp of a rhinestone choker caught in her hair. "I started escorting around the same age you started stripping—twenty-two. I wouldn't wear makeup, I'd refuse to shave my legs. Once, I painted my nails with Wite-Out, coloured them with highlighter, like in high school, and that was totally fine back then, but we change for the job."

I remember how stubbornly I wanted to keep my pubic hair. How I cracked under the pressure of being the only one and began to shave it bald. Unhappy with the nicks and itchy ingrowns, I switched to getting Brazilian waxes. Every four weeks I would endure the alarming pain that ripped little screams out with the roots of the hairs, until one wax strip ripped off a chunk of my vulva skin. Then I switched to laser hair removal, itself a painful, almost ritualistic process of erasure. Before stripping, my pubic hair was dark and glossy. Now, if I go a couple weeks between shifts, it grows in blond and patchy, with bald spots and white scars from digging out ingrown hairs with a pin.

"Stripping made me want to up my game so hard, and I did and I'm happy about it," Gigi says. "But we're not at the Royal anymore. I want to be an angel, you know?"

I fall asleep compiling lists of everything I would have to change to feel happy about my body.

★ ★ ★

SUNDAY

Gigi and I wake up at ten minutes to checkout. Across the divide between our beds we discuss staying an extra night. Money can be inspiring like that. She calls the front desk, purchases the room for an extra night, and we go back to sleep for a few hours before trying our luck on a Sunday shift.

Though much slower than the frantic Saturday, it is steady, long, and I spend the hours after midnight fixated on going home.

Our extra shift finally over, we get dressed alongside every other girl also trying to get out as quickly as possible. "I've known these guys for a while," Gigi says. "They came all the way from Burlington to see me, and they don't want the night to be over."

"I really don't want to go to their hotel," I plead.

"It's fine." Gigi reapplies lip gloss. "I'll go by myself."

There is safety in numbers—what if something bad happens to her that I could have prevented? And I have to admit, barely scraping by at Moonlighter, fumbling and flailing, has damaged my ego. I wanted to earn stupid amounts of money. Money that would mean I am beautiful, successful, worthy.

"You can't go alone," I say. *Hustle*, my ego hisses.

"I can go by myself and I will."

"Aren't you tired?"

"I'm high." Gigi is in a mood. "These guys are rich, so I'm willing to put in after-hours effort. I'm a big girl, I can do this on my own. I want you to come but not if you're going to complain or want to go home in an hour."

We are in a top suite of the Marriott: thick carpet, soft lights, and the pleasant aroma of vaporized weed. Gigi slides into the lap of her guy, a rap producer. The way she giggles at the things he says only to her, I think she might have a crush. This leaves me to entertain rich-boy handsome Jamie, who introduces himself as an "influencer."

"What does that mean?" I ask.

"I'm about the seamless integration of photography, art, and leisure. I market luxury products. Use my personal brand to make international connections, facilitate business. I'm an ambassador, really." He pops a bottle of champagne, watches me taste it.

"It's good," I say flatly.

"It better be," he scoffs. "One glass costs seventy-five dollars." I upend the flute and set the empty crystal down with a shrug. He decides to laugh, pours more.

The producer plays his protege's mix of slow, low-register beats. Gigi and I dance with each other in front of a window wall overlooking

Niagara Falls. The waterfall is floodlit red, blue, and gold, while hotel and casino lights glitter against a black sky. I am high up and beautiful, possessed by the ancient, untouchable spirit of a girl who knows her body's power.

"On the bed," the producer orders.

Gigi and I strip and tumble, touch and kiss. I arch into her, enjoying her safe touch. She has an uptick in her smile that lets me know she has this all under control. I want to wrap myself in these plush sheets and sleep for a week. Instead, we spread our legs and shake our butts. The men make it rain one-dollar bills. The sheets fill with money, the coppery smell intoxicating. Gigi rolls on top of me and bills stick to our limbs. She is elegant, despite the fake eyelash that is coming unglued.

The summer we met she would play the washboard and I the guitar, singing folk songs with our friends around the campfire.

I lift her tits and lick a nipple while she shakes her curls and bounces on an imaginary dick. When the money runs out I'm not sure what to do next, but Gigi is full of energy. "Let's get in the Jacuzzi."

Hot water from gold taps fills the pearly tub, but Gigi is off with the producer, working her own game. Jamie is going on about how he found the "authentic local vibe" in Jamaica after a recent photo shoot. The water is so hot we both have to stand, wincing while we adjust, before we can sit. My sore muscles are grateful, but I wish Jamie would stop talking. I want to slip under the surface, shut out everything with heat and pressure. My most peaceful dreams are where I can breathe underwater, float meditatively in prismatic aquamarine, silence inside and out.

Jamie paddles to my side of the bath, starts to kiss my neck. I feel uneasy now that we're alone and swirl bubbles over top of me. He starts rubbing my thigh and I feel a surge of anger. He kisses my mouth, but I keep my teeth closed and lips passive. I fight the urge to bite his lip, tear the skin, mixing blood with the water. My body is tingling, raw nerves so overstimulated every touch verges on pain. I'm running on fumes, every last drop of being fun, acting interesting or sexy, exhausted.

"I have to go." I get out of the tub and wrap myself in a fluffy towel despite Jamie's protest. I need to get out, before I start screaming or crying. Boldly, I open the closed bedroom door, shout into the dark that I'm leaving.

"Give me a minute." Gigi is exasperated.

I collect and count the one-dollar bills on the bed. "Don't you think our time together was worth more than this?" I ask Jamie.

"Look," he acts insulted, "I might have been inclined to pay for a service of some kind, which you never offered, but believe me, there are plenty of girls who want to hang out with guys like us for free."

"Gigi, Let's go!" I yell. She apologizes for my rudeness, still sweet and flirty, as I drag her out the door.

In the cab I can't contain myself. "If you had told me they weren't going to pay me, I wouldn't have gone."

"No one forced you to come, and it's not my responsibility to negotiate your money," Gigi says. "You could have worked for it like I did."

I hate her furiously. "Fuck you."

Neither of us says another word until we're in our drab, comparatively small room.

"Can we please forget about tonight?" I flop onto my bed. "I'm sorry I lost it. I'm just feeling too old to be messing around with uncertain after-hours stuff. I get so tired."

I'm jealous that she's a better hustler. That she knows how to get what she wants from men outside the rules of the strip club. She stands stiffly and I'm sure she has justifiably mean things she'd like to say, but instead she offers an olive branch. "At least we're going home tomorrow."

"I can't wait," I say, wiping away tears.

★ ★ ★

THURSDAY

We drive home for the slow days of the week off and return to Niagara in time for the next weekend. Gigi texts from the parking lot of the motel, *I'm going to stop crying in the car and come upstairs but you can't laugh at my hair.*

I'm sure it's not that bad, plus, get up here, you already left me alone for an hour and it's so creepy. I have put the dirty microwave and the lamp with a cracked shade on the orange carpet so I can spread my makeup across the folding table. Plugged my curling iron into the only electrical outlet within reach of the mirror, waiting for it to heat up.

Gigi's key in the lock startles me. "I hate it, I hate it, I hate it!" she shouts as she shoves the door with her shoulder to lock it behind her. "I look like the mom from *That '70s Show*." Her hair has been blown out and teased, perm-like. She plucks at a corkscrew curl, which coils tightly back into the poof. "I went to that same blow-dry and style place as last time where the same guy made me look so beautiful. Maybe he sabotaged me because he realized I'm a stripper. He had to know I hate it. It's costume party hair. The worst part is I still tipped him because I was too embarrassed to tell him to stop. What should I do? Do I try and comb it out? If it was any other club I'd rock it, but it's Niagara."

"Leave your shoes on!" I warn, as she starts removing them.

She pauses to look around. "This place is seriously hellish, huh?"

"Look at the pillows." I point to their yellow stained cases. "And the bathroom is grungy. We should have brought flip-flops for the shower."

"You were the one who wanted to see if we could cut our costs this time," Gigi reminds me.

"I know, I know, but I didn't factor in the cost of getting bedbugs."

"Focus," she says. "What do I do about my hair? We need to be there in two hours."

"I can fix it. Sit down." Gingerly, I comb through the mess. "Heat styling it again is really going to damage—"

"I don't care. I need to look incredible tonight. Promise me perfection." She folds her hands in her lap. I wrap sections around my curling wand. Puffs of steam escape the dark brown strands like souls. Each section falls first into my palm and I spin it around my index finger before drawing it out to its full length. "You should have let me do it from the beginning. This is turning out really nice."

She lets her shoulders drop. "Did you see how there are metal plates screwed onto the door and the frame to hold the deadbolt in place? The wood underneath it is splintered, like someone used a crowbar to get in. I'm christening this the murder motel."

"I don't know if I can stay here." I finish with a cloud of hairspray on her curls spiralled like apple peels. "I'm twenty-eight. I don't want to sleep in my clothes and be terrified all night. You're braver than me, so I'm just warning you, I don't know if I can do it."

"Do you think Viktor will send us to Sirens again?" she asks.

"Honestly, I'll volunteer to go there instead."

"Well, it's only open Friday and Saturday. We'll have to get through tonight at Moonlighter first."

★ ★ ★

Near midnight we are lost in the crowd, the music too loud to bother with conversation. We push aimlessly from one side of the bar to the other, hoping to stumble on to an opportunity. Meanwhile, the beautiful girls move with purpose, paths parting before them in the sea of men.

A guy catches us on the way by. Hands us money to take his bachelor for a double dance after an ongoing table dance has wrapped up. When the song ends, I grab the bachelor. "Hey honey, you're coming with us." I try to tug him out of his seat quickly so he won't have a chance to say, "No, not you."

The table-dance girl leans over and slaps my arm. "Excuse me, does it look like I'm fucking done?"

I drop him into his seat and shrink back while she starts a new song. Intimidatingly slowly, she poses, shifting her ass and tits with her hands. Shakes her mane like a stallion and sends blistering vibes in my direction.

"It looked like you were trying to steal her client," Gigi whispers.

"I know that now," I snap. "What a rookie mistake. Should I say sorry?"

"I don't know," Gigi says. "Girls get jumped for less, but apologizing makes you look weak." A notice in the changing room says police are looking for information about the shooting of a dancer in the parking lot. Small transgressions can have big repercussions.

When the table dancer finishes, I blurt, "I'm so sorry about that, I didn't mean—"

She turns her back to me, dresses with stone composure, leaves me nauseated in a cloud of her perfume.

★ ★ ★

I admit defeat. I can't compete with the triplets, or the party girls downing a million shots and scream-laughing. I can't pull off the "I'm so hot I don't even have to talk to you" vibe because those girls are so cool I look comparatively cutesy. So I strategize and seek out individual men who look as overwhelmed and out of place as me. This lands me an illustrator of custom coffee cups. We spend much of the dances looking at his social media portfolio influenced by manga and old-school tattoos.

Then I find a young guy who is sick of being called big boy by the dancers. Though I can't fit on his lap, I rub his chest and we rousingly debate an age-old question, eventually agreeing that Star Wars may have more cultural staying power, but the Star Trek universe is far superior.

At the end of the night, I am dancing for a doctor younger than me, across from a fireplace that overheats the largest of the VIP lounges. My veneer of cleanliness melts like icing off a warm cake. My thighs dampen his blue jeans. His palms leave wet streaks in my hair.

★ ★ ★

"This is where you're staying?" the cab driver asks as he pulls into the parking lot of our motel. "It's got a bad reputation. You sure you don't want me to take you girls somewhere nice?"

The murder motel is split-level with a blue metal gangplank that rattles as we tiptoe up to room 205. Along the way we pass an open door with an older man smoking, shirtless, on his bed. He sits up as we pass. "Hello," he calls, as if we would want to stop for a chat.

Barricaded inside our room, I stand in the space between the bed and the television. Gigi pulls the orange curtain closed, but I'm already fixated on the single pane of glass, the ease with which it could be broken, the access the night has to us.

"If that creepy guy down the hall knocks on our door because he wants to be our friend or whatever, I'm going to lose it." My legs and arms are crawling with imaginary bedbugs. "I won't sleep tonight, I can't."

"What if you take your kava kava and skullcap tincture? I think I brought valerian capsules and regular sleeping pills."

"I need to get out of here." I'm expecting footsteps on the gangplank, my heart racing. "Where can we go?"

"We could walk our bags over to the Best Western. It's a safer hotel." She is disappointed. Money is, after all, the bottom line.

I break out of freeze into flight, stuff my makeup and work bag into my suitcase. "If we're going to work, we need to be able to sleep."

The plastic wheels of our suitcases bounce over cracks in the sidewalk as we drag them down the motel strip at four in the morning. "You warned me about that place when I was booking online. I should have listened to you," I admit. "Now our expenses will more than double."

Gigi keeps it light. "Doesn't it feel like we're brides running away from our weddings?" Broken glass and dandelions in concrete are our confetti. We put the next two nights on a credit card, a safety many girls are unable to afford.

★ ★ ★

FRIDAY

"Let's get out of this hotel and go live our best lives," Gigi says. "I want to see something truly beautiful today."

"Would one of the great wonders of the world count?" I say.

Crowds of tourists don't detract from the elemental power of Niagara Falls. Every shade of blue surges over the cliff and explodes on the rocks below. Vaporized water cools our skin. Above, a rainbow glistens.

"I miss working with Bailey," I say. "I really thought we'd be able to help make stripping work for her."

"I miss her, too." Gigi nods. "But it wasn't a good fit."

"I had bad boundaries when I first started. I wasn't detached and assertive enough. It's a learned skill. I had to practise."

"I had to teach myself entitlement," Gigi says. "I'm disgusted by it in the real world, but if I don't act like a princess in the club, I don't get anything."

"I'm almost too good at boundaries now," I say. "I keep everyone at a distance. Stripping taught me I should charge for emotional labour, and now I don't want to provide that for free when I'm not at work."

The cobblestones are wet. Seagulls shriek. I'm nervous to continue. "I feel the same way about some sexual stuff now, too. Like, because I know how valuable sex is, and because it sometimes hurts or triggers me, it kind of seems like a job. Not with Luke," I say quickly when she looks at me. "But when I think about dating new people I'm like, why would I do that for free?"

"Especially with men," she says. "Being a ho, I know everything men are going to try, everything they are capable of, and I'm bored of it."

"I already explicitly don't date new cis men," I say. "But I still really love having sex with Luke. I'm scared if I keep doing this, one day it'll all blend together and fucking him will feel like ... work."

"You gotta keep the magic alive, girl," Gigi warns. "Ending up hating sex is a real potential hazard."

"I've already written off men in general. I don't care about that loss, but I don't want to hate sex as a whole. And I really don't want to hate sex with my partner."

Over the railing, far below, the *Maid of the Mist* looks like a toy boat in the churning cerulean waters.

Gigi has to raise her voice to be heard over the crashing roar of 3,000 tons of water per second. "I'm going to move away soon," she says. "The prairies are calling me. I want to start having babies, live near my family."

"It's finally time?" She's hinted at her departure before. "When are you leaving?"

"After this summer. But I'll still want to do work trips with you. Strip clubs are illegal in Saskatchewan, so I'll have to work elsewhere."

"Let's turn around," I suggest. "There's a botanical garden back there I wanted to check out."

Once in the interconnected greenhouses of the botanical garden I can't help but fret, "My hair is going to be frizzy—I'll have to wash it before work."

"Never mind that now." Gigi closes her eyes, lifts her face to the sun that filters through palms and vines.

We follow narrow paths, admire red hanging heliconias, fat cactuses, and the antics of dust-bathing house sparrows. A bride and her photographer block our way. She drifts around striking soft poses, her swan-white dress accentuated by the surrounding stone and the lattice of dense green fauna.

"I wonder if one of us danced for her fiancé last night?" Gigi whispers.

We stop to investigate a fountain where sculptures of cherubs pour water from a pitcher. "Look, it's us!" I point to the bottom of the statue where an alligator with demonic eyes, serrated scales, and overgrown claws waits for a cherub to fall into its jaws.

"River monster kin." Gigi smiles, and we exit into a grove of magnolia trees, their silver branches laden with fleshy blossoms, one warm day from unfurling.

★ ★ ★

We reach Moonlighter before dinnertime to avoid the crush of shift change. Without a hundred girls the labyrinthine changing rooms are sedate. The few early birds spread out to separate chambers, makeup and tinny phone music delineating territories.

Gigi and I set up in a mirrored corner on a counter constructed with two-by-fours and painted plywood. Years of spilled energy drinks and coffees, nail polish, and oil-based products stain the surface like a faded map. Dated washing machines, coated in layers of dust, are relics from a time when girls were allowed to show up dirty, become clean.

"Look at that poster." Gigi points with a wand of lip colour. Most signs in changing rooms are photocopied, all-caps warnings from management: a new fine, a hike in stage fees, or admonitions telling us that if we must eat, we have to do it in our cars. But the poster she pointed to is glossy and professional. It shows a crying woman with a man's hand covering her mouth. The portrait is overlaid with a red sketchy font: *I am not for sale.*

I read the fine print. "It's from the RCMP. It wants you to call the police on women who have bruises, are being controlled by threats and violence, have tattoos or brands, or who have their movements restricted."

"Oh, great," Gigi says. "Call the police and they'll respond to a fucked-up situation by making it worse."

Police involvement makes me think of arrests, incarceration, deportation, and physical violence. "They don't address the root of the problem."

Like war, sex trafficking is an experience so far removed from my own that I cannot truly understand it. For those who have been trafficked, sex work is not a job; it is enslavement. It scares me to look at, as if witnessing other people's pain on that scale might break me. Gigi and I exchange a hopeless look.

★ ★ ★

"Oh my God, you're so beautiful." A college girl grabs my arm. "How do you do this job, though? How much money do you make?"

"It varies," I say coolly.

"Are there a lot of creepy men? Have you ever been assaulted? What is the grossest thing a client has ever asked you to do?"

I roll my eyes.

"How much money do you make? I want to find a sugar daddy." She giggles. "But not one where I'd have to suck his dick or anything like that. My God, you're, like, so pretty."

She hiccups, steadies herself. "I'd make a great stripper, but my boyfriend would never let me."

★ ★ ★

"Don't do that," I say for the millionth time. "You can't touch during a table dance." It's not like he can't hear me; he just doesn't see me as a person. His friends join in, pinching me from multiple directions. "Stop it!" I yell in his face.

Then, staring straight in my eyes, he grabs and twists my nipples. White-hot pain. I yelp and slap him across the face, almost fall while extricating myself from the horseshoe table and the tangle of legs. Arm crossed over my throbbing chest, I say, "Fuck you, pay me."

"You didn't even finish one song." He smirks.

"Give me my money right now or I'll get the bouncers to kick you out." There is no way I'd ask these bouncers for help and risk being labelled a troublemaker. It's supposed to be my job to police the clients' hands and mouths. Either way, both fault and punishment are mine.

Luckily, my hollow threat works and the guy, already bored and casting around for the next girl to hurt, tosses a twenty onto the ground.

In a bathroom stall I choke back tears. My nipples are always too sensitive, so it's hard to tell if they're bruised or swollen. At least they're intact. Years ago someone told me they'd worked a shift where a client bit off a girl's nipple. The storyteller said she'd seen the nipple hanging by a strip of skin off the bloodied breast.

★ ★ ★

I buy a white lace bodysuit from Mary and immediately three men in a row approach *me* for dances. I've never worn a white outfit before—it stands out, virginal under these red and black lights.

These two come to me and make it easy. Usually, I find couples to be more trouble than they're worth, with the woman glaring at you, or the husband constantly asking if you'll go down on his wife. We're in a VIP booth on a couch facing a mirror. I crawl between them, using my knees as wedges to separate them or push them together. The woman is writhing as her boyfriend whispers in her ear, kisses her neck. She's pulled her shirt up over a plain beige bra, begging me to touch her. I run my hands over her pillowy body. She is belly breathing, almost panting with desire. I can smell her arousal like a thunderstorm.

★ ★ ★

"Be very careful how you talk about your money," Gigi warns me the second we return to the hotel room. I sink onto my bed and rub my jaw, trying to release the tension from hours of forced smiling. "Can we both admit that you are objectively hotter than me?"

I don't want to talk and definitely don't want to fight. "You're so beautiful," I say, but it doesn't address the fact that I kept coming out of the VIP to see her statuesque, in the middle of a crowd of men all trying to grab someone else.

"You are the worst work wife I've ever had," she says. "You don't know how to work with me and how to sell our bodies together. I'm sure you didn't even notice, but one table we went up to tonight said no to me because they only wanted my 'hot friend.'"

"That's horrible." I barely know how to sell myself at this club, let alone a package deal. I scratch at my knees, translucent as oily paper.

"Your blond hair, your skinniness, your literal fucking bone structure ... You get to capitalize on those things while I can't."

"You're right. It's unfair."

"Damn right it's unfair. I barely made my stage fee today and I need you to see the difference. Count your money."

"I know it looks like I was super busy, but a lot of it was one or two dances. Half the time in the VIP I was waiting for a new song to start or getting dressed."

"Count it," she commands.

Maybe the discrepancy isn't as wide as she thinks. So I open my wallet and begin counting. A completely unique feeling of revulsion builds as I stack the bills into neat piles of hundreds. From across the room she fumes.

"See?" she hisses. "Admit that this is easier for you than it is for me. I work harder than you and make less. Admit it."

No. Not true. I want to tell her I am worked ragged and nothing feels easy, but my money is a brick in my mouth. The girls at the club, the management, most of the men, and now my only friend in this alternate reality all hate me. I don't tell her what she both wants and doesn't want to hear. I slink past her and lock myself in the bathroom. Shower until the hot water runs out, and when I emerge she ignores me on her phone while the television attempts to sell us hair transplants.

★ ★ ★

SATURDAY

When we wake up in the afternoon Gigi and I give each other a wide berth. She leaves to get Jamaican takeout from a food truck down the street, and I call Luke from bed. "She was mean," I say, "but the pressure here is wild. These girls are so perfect."

"Do you remember that Medusa poster?" Luke asks. "It says, 'Beauty must be defined as what we are, or else the concept itself is our enemy.'"

I groan. "Of course I believe that, but isn't objective beauty also real?" Outside seagulls circle the parking lot. It feels vain to talk about this but also crucial.

"Do you think Gigi is beautiful?" Luke asks. "And can you accept that other people see you as beautiful?"

"Yes, but this is work, and we're not beautiful like the other girls here."

"I'm not sure if it's worth going down the rabbit hole of objective beauty. What could you possibly gain from that?" It's a good question. "Remember that you take trips with Gigi to support each other. If you can't do that, you probably shouldn't work together."

When Gigi gets back she sits on my bed and offers me a jerk chicken wing. "I need you to stop shit-talking your body. I can't handle you complaining about being ugly when I see you making more money than me. I've got my own insecurities to manage. I can't hold us both up."

Allspice and Scotch bonnet seasoning warm me from the inside. "I'll work on that. Being here is like my whole life of not fitting in with pretty girls, men telling me I'm too strange or weird or gay. Being an outcast and not knowing why."

"That might be true, babe, but I'm not the right person to talk to about it with."

We both have purple under our eyes. Too tired to smile, I say, "I'm sorry you didn't make money last night, that's trash. At least we get to work at Sirens tonight."

★ ★ ★

We have to sign in at Moonlighter at nine and stay there for an obligatory wasted hour before Sirens opens. We've barely paid our fees and gotten onto the floor before the DJ, on the loudspeaker, shouts, "All girls report to the Gentlemen's Lounge. All girls! Everyone in the VIP, at tables, wherever you are, report to the downstairs lounge now." Gigi and I are standing by the staircase, so we go down and find seats on a couch against the wall. The room is saturated with deep-sea blue light. For a full five minutes girls flow non-stop down the stairs. They fill every seat until it's standing room only.

Gigi bounces her crossed leg nervously. I feel sick.

Viktor hops up on a low centre stage. The music is turned down in this room, but it still thumps from the main floor where patrons must be wondering why there are no girls.

"Listen up!" Viktor shouts. "Some of you are getting too old and too fat to work here. It's disgusting. You know who you are and you know you've let yourselves go."

Wow, I mouth. The littlest hairs on the back of my neck bristle.

Gigi finishes off her energy drink, rattles the straw in the empty can, and snaps, "Michelle, you have nothing to worry about."

"Some of you have been running up tabs. Cleo! Where's Cleo?" Viktor asks the room of dead-silent girls. One of the angels raises her hand.

"You ran up hundreds of dollars in tabs and tried to get the bouncers to collect for you. You're supposed to be collecting after every hundred." He leaves space, as if she's allowed to explain herself, but when she tries he cuts her off. "I'm sorry, we don't need that kind of drama here. It's unprofessional. You're fired. Get out." She sits resistant for ten painful seconds, but realizing he's not going to let her finish the night, she gets up and weaves through the crowded room. Girls press themselves together to get out of her way. She slams her feet as she stalks upstairs. If Cleo is expendable, we are doomed.

"I have no problem going out and recruiting from Toronto and Vancouver. We are the best strip club in Canada. Don't come to me bitching and complaining about who can work here and who can't. We don't need ugly fat girls. The rest of you, put in some goddamn effort. I'm going to pick out who has to stay down here. The rest of you, get out of my sight."

We are swept into a line trying to make it back up the narrow staircase. Viktor picks girls off like salmon. One out of ten are kept behind.

"Wait for me, okay?" Gigi is convinced I'm going to make it upstairs and she won't, but Viktor sinks his claws into us both.

"Michelle, you stay. You too, Gigi." I'm surprised he even remembers our names. He must have a list.

When the ones who passed his test have ascended, there are fifteen of us left. A couple of older Russian ladies, a few chubbier white girls with tattoos, and a young country-styled girl I know from the Royal.

Viktor resumes his place on the stage, two feet above us. "Honestly, I'm disappointed in your quality. You should be ashamed of yourselves. Listen, you get a gym membership, you work out and lose weight, maybe you can come back, but for now, no working nights. You're all day girls. Or you can work at Sirens only. If you come to Moonlighter, I don't want you here just for long weekends or when it's good. Be here at least three days a week for day shift—Monday, Tuesday, Wednesday—but get off the floor by ten."

Zoning out, I stare at the stomach of the country girl. She has visible abs, which requires less than ten percent body fat, and I happen to know she's twenty-one.

"You can go over to Sirens, but get off my floor," Viktor finishes and leaves. No one says anything. We shuffle directly to the changing room, put on clothes, and pack our bags. I'm grateful they chose us both.

In a daze, Gigi and I trail our cohort of rejects outside. Unprotected in the open air, we're hollered at and catcalled by men as we head across the parking lot toward the neon stars of Sirens.

Inside it's quiet, house lights still on. The bartender with holographic nails is pouring shots for the two older Russian ladies. The DJ has stopped collecting names for the set list to comfort a girl who is crying in frustration. I hear him tell her she doesn't have to tip him and she doesn't have to dance onstage if she doesn't want to. In the changing room Gigi sits in a chair and I lean against the island countertop and mirror in the centre of the room.

"Well, that was fucked up," I say, but no one is outraged. No one is threatening to slash the manager's tires or wait for him after closing.

"Is it my nose?" one girl asks, squishing it down. Another lists off girls who are bigger than her, wondering why they were allowed to stay.

"This is exactly how they want us to feel," Gigi says. "It's a completely appropriate way to treat sex workers. That makes total sense to them. They have no qualms about that behaviour at all."

"You look perfect," I say, as I catch her staring at her face. "A literal goddess."

"You know what?" she says. "We are beautiful. You, me, all of us, we are fucking beautiful."

"Should we leave?" I ask.

"I can't imagine sitting around the hotel, watching cable, and eating. We haven't even made back our expenses for this trip yet."

"Let's work then."

We hustle constantly to keep our moods from slipping. I target guys who like my type and keep them in the VIP as long as possible. I tell them how much I enjoy working at the best strip club in Canada. Robotically, I make more money than I've made in Niagara any day so far. The end of the night comes quickly.

"I was planning my summer around this stupid club," I rage when we get back to our hotel room.

"It's like they were mowing the grass, picking out the weeds." Gigi empties her clutch. Lip gloss, hoop earrings, and vitamins spill onto the bed along with bills.

"It's worse than that." I tear into a Pepperette. "It's a psychological attack. Viktor picked the most broadly hurtful things to say to us, knowing we wouldn't argue because we're already so insecure about not being hot or young enough."

"Whatever we had to do to look like angels, I guess we didn't do it fast enough." Gigi sighs.

"Luke texted me a smart thing."

"Of course he did. What did he say?"

"Other than saying the manager is total scum, he reminded me that I have crushes on all types of women."

She laughs. "Okay, and?"

"And I don't have those kinds of standards with the women I'm attracted to. Those standards don't correspond to my actual desires, so I shouldn't accept them for myself. It's not real."

Gigi points to her pile of bills. "But the money is so good. Maybe we could come to Sirens on the weekend, like Viktor said."

"And be forced to work day shifts during the worst days of the week? You saw how quiet it was until late. No. Niagara needs to be dead to us. It is dehumanizing to be treated that way. We can't come back."

"I hope he dies in a fire!" Gigi yells. It's so specific and vicious that we cackle.

CHAPTER 12:
LAST CALL

**THE ROYAL
SOUTHERN ONTARIO**

D J Tony and I exchange a friendly hug. "Long time no see, stranger. I thought you quit."

"Hell no, I'm going to do this as long as I can," I say, and casually add, "I've been working in the Falls." Tony raises his thick eyebrows, a cheers to my new prestige. I hurry on, "I'm moving to Montreal, though, so I'm trying to make a little extra on a weekday."

"You're always on the move." Tony nods approvingly. He always manages to find the obscure house remixes I request for my set, and I like how he introduces girls simply by their names. Tony is clearly just trying to get through his shifts, working weddings on days off, raising a daughter. When I ask, he shows me a picture of her in a power pose as Wonder Woman for Halloween, proud in blue and red spandex.

There are many girls on shift, none of whom I immediately recognize, and almost no men in the club. Compared to the sheer potential of the lineups in Niagara, the Royal is a letdown but also a relief. A wave from the waitress, a hug from the bouncer, I do the rounds, saying hello to old regulars. I sit with Sean and his friends in their spot at the back bar. "I missed this place," I tell them.

"It's the goddamn Cheers of strip clubs, that's for sure," Sean says.

Harry comments, "Wasn't so cheerful when you had your little accident the other week."

Sean tries to wave him off, but Harry persists. "This old fucker can't hold his liquor if he's not high as a kite. He passed out in the bathroom, smashed his head on the floor. We had to drag him out—mind you, this bastard's like three hundred pounds."

Sean objects, "I'm two fifty, max."

"Had to call an ambulance and everything. Thought he'd had an aneurysm and died like Elvis." Retelling the story is cracking Harry up. I can tell it was the highlight of his month.

"Where's Bruce?" I ask.

"You really haven't been around in a while." Sean's alcoholic rosacea is bright red across his nose and cheeks. "There was a power struggle and they fired Bruce. Someone will have to wrestle control of this place from the decrepit hands of the owner once he finally kicks the bucket, but it won't happen a moment sooner." He slaps me on the back. "You're the old guard now."

★ ★ ★

Eyes closed, I dance on this stage in my dreams. My favourite third song, by Kiiara, is about changing from a ghost into a holy spirit. The intermittent wash of red, black, and white lights is an ultraviolet cleansing. Like a spider at the centre of her web, I'm connected to every table, horseshoe, missed step, shot glass, statue.

★ ★ ★

There is a girl in an elegant gold gown. Her body has grown and shrunk around pregnancies, but her hair is exactly the same, so fragile it can't grow beyond her shoulders. She catches me staring and does a double take.

"Jersey!" I throw my arms around her before remembering maybe I shouldn't. We stopped speaking after the incident with her man, and it wasn't long before she moved on from the Royal, but she hugs me back warmly. Forgets my name but calls me baby girl, which I love. Holding her hands, I ask, "How have you been? You look incredible!"

"Good, working in the States mostly. They make you wear these—" She curtsies in her Jessica Rabbit dress. "I forgot no one does that up here."

"How's your son?"

"Girl, you're sweet. He's in grade two. I got him a little sister a year ago. We're all good."

★ ★ ★

The old barfly hobbles up. "You still got that same boyfriend, Michelle?"

"Yup, still the same one."

"It's been years now! When are y'all gonna get hitched?" I refuse to make eye contact so I can continue to scan the empty room, willing something to change. He never gives me any money, and if I let him, he will talk forever.

"How about your parents? They still live in that little town?"

"Still there." I wish I hadn't told him that. I used to be so forthcoming that the ones who've known me for years know too much.

This club is depressing. How does this place even afford to pay its wait staff and bouncers? Oh yeah, strippers keep this place running with our house fees, extra penalty charges, and buying our own drinks. When I texted a friend to see if she was still working here she said no, because they told her she would have to pay triple the regular stage fee because she'd gotten fat. It sours my warm welcome, reminds me these places can be ugly.

The barfly says, "I took a drive out east, must be five years ago now. It's a pretty little town your parents live in. A river runs through it, if I remember right. Boy, all you Maritimers are so friendly. That must be why you're such a sweetheart."

I try to give him a smile, but it's more of a grimace. Performing niceness, even for a senior starved for human contact, is difficult on a dead night.

The worst part is it is half-price night. The Royal now offers two days a week where guys can get a contact lap dance for ten instead of twenty dollars. I used to like half-price nights because it was easier to sell dances. No time wasted flirting and convincing, the transactional nature was clearer, faster, made easier with a dose of shame directed at hesitant men—why are you at a strip club if you can't afford a ten-dollar dance? Let's go to the VIP. But half-price nights often result in disappointment. As the industry wilts around us, we work harder for less.

Making bad money on a ten-dollar night because there are no clients feels extra insulting, so it's with relief that I notice a friendly face walk in. I rush over to Gerry, my first regular, knowing my night won't be a total writeoff.

Gerry smells like aftershave, and he holds my hands like I'm royalty. "You look better every time I see you."

Gerry buys us waters. We sit at the bar facing bottles of liquor like trophies, and I relax into our casual flirtatiousness. The Venn diagram between Michelle and me is closer to a circle in the way I perform for Gerry. I don't watch my language, hide my politics, or pretend I don't have a partner. This near wholeness is more awkward since Gerry wants to date *me*, cook me dinner, make love to me, and find me a secretary position in his office building. At least I'm not the only stripper he's low-key in love with. Gerry is a sweet man, cautious, understanding. I believe he would be a generous partner. He could go to a normal bar, get a hobby, sign up for a dating website, but he keeps coming back to strip clubs to be consistently romantically rejected and manipulated. I don't exploit his confusion the way that other, better, hustlers do. This leaves us playing a keep-the-balloon-in-the-air type of game. Redirection, flirt, contact, float, so he can ignore the seemingly obvious truth that his love will always be unrequited.

He doesn't go for dances until late, so I tell him I need to go make some money. "Work it, girl," he says, like we're friends on a sitcom. When I whisper that I want to spend the last hour of the night with him, in the VIP, he grins. "You'll have to twist my rubber arm."

★ ★ ★

"As manager I'm in charge of mixing herbicides with the spoiled ship-ments of milk so that when we pour it down the drain and out into the river, the nutrients in the milk don't make the underwater plants grow like crazy and clog the pipes."

This client has talked me into such a stupor I am barely aware I have pulled the second half of my Percocet out of my wallet.

"Hold on, what are you doing?" he asks.

"Oh, it's just a Tylenol. The music is extra loud tonight and I've got a bit of a headache." Normally, I would take it discreetly, but I'm worn out already and losing money by letting him talk to me at the table on a ten-dollar night. I need to get high, get focused, get on my game.

"You shouldn't take painkillers while you're drinking," he says with as much disgust as concern. "It's very bad for your liver."

"Oh really? I didn't know that." I chase the pill with a gulp of gin and tonic. I've had this guy before—how dare he tell me I should endure his kneading of my breasts and his stale cream breath sober?

He is offended I didn't listen to him. "You should take better care of yourself," he says, trying to flag down the waitress.

I bought this round of Percocets from a middle-aged man with a spinal injury who lives in the suburbs. I stood awkwardly in his beige bedroom, clothes and empty pop bottles on the floor, blinds closed, assailed by the most aggressive laundry soap, while he counted out 100 pills. Each pill represented two possible nights of being high enough to work, or one night of partying.

Luke was not impressed when I told him how much I was going to buy. He doesn't do drugs, as his mental health is too easily compromised. It's a gift to those who love him.

Though Luke wouldn't say it, I bet he thinks I should find another job if I can't work without drugs. I argued it was better to buy a lot at once than to go back every few weeks, but Luke cautioned, "If you get caught in a traffic stop on your way home with that much, you could be prosecuted as a dealer."

I began to sweat when the guy handed over the zip-lock bag and I felt the combined weight of usually weightless individual pills. Yet I was also reassured, as it meant I could renew my contract with stripping.

★ ★ ★

There is a half-hour left and I'm letting Gerry massage my back in the VIP. The fact that he enjoys giving massages and leaves whole songs where we just talk is part of the reason I bother keeping a regular who only comes in on half-price nights. He reaches around from behind and squeezes. Face buried in my hair, he says, "I love your boobies."

I despise the reach-around move. I hate hands that slither, touches that are too soft or too rough, too sharp, and anything involving flicking or knocking. Having my tits squeezed has begun to trigger panic. My chest wants to crush in on itself or explode.

Words evoke a similar revulsion. I hate "boobies" and "stimulate" and "perky." I prefer "pressure," the heaviness of "tits," the pushiness of "pussy," but this place has very little to do with what I like.

I lean back into Gerry. "That feels so good."

"I can't believe you're leaving us."

"I always come back," I say, uncertain.

PART 5: SURFACING

CHAPTER 13: BURNOUT

PARADIS
MONTREAL, QUEBEC

A t 2:58 in the afternoon I am on the floor of Paradis with an extra-large tea and the Wi-Fi password to the Italian restaurant next door. The club is frigid. They leave the air conditioner on high all day so that when the night girls arrive and things finally start getting busy, it's cool enough.

My social life, filled with new and old friends, dance parties and protests, makes up for the disappointment of being restricted to day shift until I "earn" the privilege of working nights at one of Montreal's most prestigious clubs. Shivering, I settle onto a stool away from the main bar where a handful of girls and staff catch up on life and drama. Other girls are spread out, one reading a book and nursing a glass of wine while another practises tricks and stretches on the silver stage. The DJ lowers the house lights and begins with one sad country song before switching to normal strip club fare.

Regulars dip in to see their girl then immediately leave. It's only after dinner that things get steadily busy, but they force us day girls to leave at nine. It's like being punished, to have to walk out after a seven-hour shift when the lineup is just starting to form, knowing any night girl will make more in her first hour than I made all day.

It's not all bad, though. Day shifts are kept afloat by bachelor parties coming straight from the plane, as well as lonely businessmen. The music is quieter, the vibe calmer, even friendly between the girls. If only they would turn up the heat. I wear a silk housecoat to keep off the chill, but it doesn't keep me warm.

★ ★ ★

The client asks in a Bostonian accent, "How do you like working here?"

"I just started," I tell him. "It's classy, but it also seems strict."

As if on cue, a bouncer doing rounds like a prison guard leers inside the curtain of our VIP booth, checking that I'm not breaking any of the many rules. The rules are hard to miss, stuck to the mirror behind the client's head. The most unnerving one is "no grinding," an impossibly slippery distinction in a contact lap dance. It seems like an excuse to fire any girl at any time.

"It's worse in America," Boston says. "They don't even let you drink at nude clubs, and half the time you have to physically sit on your hands. Don't worry about the bouncers, though, they're here to protect you."

★ ★ ★

"Do you know you have moles on your back?" a client asks.

"They're beauty marks," I correct him, using my mom's old-fashioned term.

As a kid lounging on the red sands of Prince Edward Island, I noticed the same dark freckles animating my mother's skin. She and I are cut from the same pale, freckled cloth.

"Well, I'm a doctor," he says. "You should really get those checked out."

★ ★ ★

When I confide my worries about turning thirty, Lulu says, "It's no big deal. I'm thirty-six and I only started dancing last year to pay off my student debts. I was going to quit once I'd paid them off, but now I'm like, maybe I could use a new washing machine, a nice mattress, and a vacation in Bali." She smiles at my relief. "Don't worry about it, you've got a baby face."

★ ★ ★

"Don't tell anyone, but I 'ave my quitting day all picked out," Desiree says. She pets her golden extensions the way I imagine society ladies used to stroke their minks.

"You make good money here," I say. "Why would you leave?"

"I work fifty hours chaque semaine ici for the past year and it just doesn't have the same excitement for me. It's not, how you say, fun, anymore. The manager told me he'd fire me if I get any more tattoos and I have plans. Big plans, bébé. My whole leg is scheduled for Janvier."

Desiree wears a watch and glasses to work as if she's ready to switch back to studying for her degree at a moment's notice. "Besides, what's the point of paying for all this education if I don't even work in my field?"

★ ★ ★

"I've met a ton of bachelors over the years and I've never wanted to ask them this question before," I begin. "And I shouldn't ask you—it's unprofessional." But I can't help myself, so I say, "I want to know about your wedding. See, I just got engaged—not really engaged like with a ring and a proposal, but we're going to do a commitment ceremony. I know that sounds cheesy, but it'll be close friends and family, and we've already been together for six years, so it's not like anything is going to be drastically different, but it is sort of like a wedding and it's literally the only thing I can think about. But, oh my God, I'm so sorry I brought it up, you don't have to tell me anything. I'm sure this is the last place you want to talk about your wedding."

I turn away from the client and fold at the hips. Wiggle my heels so that the fat on my thighs and ass undulates. He's a quiet bachelor. Content to be away from his keyed-up entourage.

When we're done he hands me my money and says simply, "Destination. Mexico."

★ ★ ★

"You can't do this forever," a client says.

"I guess we'll see."

★ ★ ★

An American tourist wanders in, trashed. Grabs me and a French girl I've never met and steers us immediately back into the VIP. He keeps trying to bite and pinch. Not hard enough to call a bouncer but often enough that I watch his hands and mouth and keep the soft parts of myself away from him. The French girl doesn't speak much English, so he keeps saying explicit things, ordering me to translate.

"Il ne dit rien d'important," I tell her. She smiles and nods for him, adds some well-placed oohs and aahs.

A waitress keeps serving him doubles and his intoxication spikes. He stands and starts dancing, unbuttons his shirt and swings it around his head. A bouncer comes to warn us, "Keep him seated."

I ask the girl, "Pensez-vous que nous devrions arrêter? Il est très drunk."

"You want us to keep going, bébé?" she leads him.

"Yes, yes, of course, keep going."

His phone begins to ring incessantly. "It's my driver. I got a flight to catch." He pushes us off him and stumbles toward the exit.

"You need to pay us!" Topless, the girl and I get in front of him, implore him to visit the ATM first, but he isn't having it. The bouncer and the day shift manager, Dom, corral him before he gets to the door.

"How much does he owe you?" Dom asks.

"We did fourteen songs," I say.

"Il a pris une heure," the French girl says.

"Is that true? You were back there for an hour?" Dom asks me.

"I don't know. We were back there for however long fourteen songs is."

The tourist refuses to take the easy way out, even when Dom offers a discounted rate. The tourist isn't arguing over the amount owed; he would just rather not bother with the whole payment thing.

"Do you know how much the ATM fee is?" he slurs. "It's too high. If you, sir, would let me walk down the street and find one with a reasonable withdrawal fee, I give you my word that I'll come right back. I don't appreciate being ripped off. It's criminal." He is bratty, begging for discipline. Dom loses patience and calls the police.

Seeing uniformed officers, the tourist suddenly remembers how much he loves to cater to authority. He pays us in full and pulls out tips for the bouncer and the manager, even trying to tip the police as they escort him out of the building.

The next day, the bouncer tells me Dom wants to see me in his office. He waits to walk me downstairs as if I might try to run.

Dom glares at me from his reclining position in an office chair. "You told me you did an hour with the client, isn't that correct?"

"It was fourteen songs."

"I don't care how many songs." He makes me watch black and white footage of yesterday's events from the VIP security cameras. It looks like a silent slapstick movie on fast-forward. "From when you go in, to when you leave, it only takes forty-five minutes." He taps the glass showing me the time-stamps. "The other girl told me it was an hour."

"I said I didn't know how long it was exactly. I was counting the songs. Isn't that how we're supposed to calculate it?"

"I fired that other girl because she's a liar. Didn't like her anyway, but I like you, so I'm going to give you another chance."

"Okay." My cheeks flush. "I still don't understand how we're supposed to keep track."

"You sell by the song up until the third or fourth song, but if they want to keep going you switch to time sold in packages, fifteen minutes, a half-hour, an hour. I explained all this to you."

"It doesn't work like that in any other clubs, so I must have misunderstood." I force the words out.

"The rules are clearly printed on the entrance to the VIP." I have no idea what he's talking about. "You're suspended for a week. Call me on Saturday. I'll see if I can give you any more shifts."

I'm furious, recounting the story to Luke on the phone after I've left the club. "He wasted my whole day and made sure I won't make any money this week. It took two hours to get ready to be here at three, and he even let me sit on the floor doing nothing for an hour first. The makeup wasted on my face alone cost like five dollars." I pause to take a breath. "What is the point of having rules they don't even tell you about?"

"It's a power play," Luke says. "A weak management technique to keep you under control."

"It doesn't even make sense. How am I supposed to count the number of minutes?" The solution pops like a bubble and seems obvious when I remember how resourceful and adaptable strippers are. "Of course, they must use their phone alarms. If someone had told me that I would have done it." I stop pacing the side streets off Sainte-Catherine to lean against the warm stone of a building. Across the street, storefront mannequins all wear the same white nylon wigs. "I bet he suspends all the new girls so that if he lets them come back, they feel indebted to him."

"You've been ambivalent about these day shifts," Luke says. "Now you get to decide if you go back in a week. It's your choice. Come home and we'll walk Mira to the farm stand by Frontenac. Get some nice vegetables for dinner. Then we can sit on the porch and practise French."

"It *is* a great porch." I'm thinking of the sweet peas and lettuce in pots and the plastic decking, hot under bare feet, of our third-floor balcony. It overlooks an alley in Centre-Sud where I can watch cats exploring broken concrete and unkempt backyards and clouds crossing blue sky broken only by church steeples.

★ ★ ★

From a VIP booth, I eavesdrop on a white client with a New York accent talking to a Black dancer. "There are neo-Nazis marching in Charlottesville," he says. "Torch-wielding, Sieg-heiling Nazis! They ran a girl over with a car. Killed her. Did you Canadians hear about that up here?"

The dancer has given up trying to get him to enjoy a dance when he clearly wants to talk, so she's sitting on his knee, her posture impeccable. "Yes, we heard."

"Our cops kill Black people in America, shoot them in the back and blame them for holding a cellphone or reaching for their wallets. Kids and women, too, not just thugs, you know? America has lost its mind."

Cops shoot Black people here too, and brown and Indigenous people. Incarcerate immigrant families and children, indefinitely. It's a dangerous and common belief that state violence and racism stop at the border. But with the steady stream of American tourists we get at Paradis, I've been hearing a lot of frantic accounts of the chaos that's unfolding down south.

It's hard to imagine the dancer isn't already an expert on dealing with the daily aggressions of white supremacy. Despite, or perhaps because of that experience, she answers him with frosty professionalism. "Things are pretty awful down there. You'll just have to come visit us more." She stands, despite his protest, opens his legs with her knee and starts to dance.

★ ★ ★

Petite and young, a girl borrows my eyebrow scissors to cut the tags off her new lingerie.

"I'm Kiki." She shakes my hand. "This is my first day, ever." She parts her hair down the centre and twists the sections up into two buns. Secures them with cutesy pink scrunchies. "I'm trying to play up the Asian-fetish thing. Men already exoticize me all the time, so I thought I might as well get paid for it."

Her fearlessness tugs nostalgic heartstrings. "Girl, you're so tiny, you're also gonna get all the guys who want twelve-year-olds."

Kiki corrects me. "Actually, I identify as non-binary. I use they/them pronouns. In front of the ... what do you call them?"

"Clients?"

"Yeah, in front of the clients it's okay to call me she, but I prefer they."

The constant double attack on Kiki's racial and gender identities is going to be a struggle, but they seem tough. This is the first time I've heard another stripper outside my friend group of queer sex workers use any of the political terms Kiki just dropped. Even though issues of race and gender are central to this job, the language of anti-oppression hasn't penetrated the fiercely enforced binaries and racial stereotyping the industry relies on.

"Is there anything I should know?" Kiki asks, as they tie on a velvet choker. "Like, how should I approach clients? Are the other girls mean?"

I think Kiki would understand if I opted out by mentioning how training baby strippers is unpaid emotional labour, but that would do a disservice to all the more experienced girls who explained, reprimanded, and helped me over the years.

"There are a few things," I tell them. "Come sit with me upstairs and we'll talk about it." Besides, day shift is boring anyway.

After Kiki exhausts their laundry list of questions we take to the stage to practise tricks. The silver stage is in the centre of the bar, an island with two poles and a ceiling so low that the tall girls have to adjust their dances. Bend more deeply at the waist and knees, creating pretty accumulations of rotating angles. At the top of the poles are halos scuffed into the ceiling by spinning heels.

Without any prior training, Kiki can immediately do every trick. "It's easy for me because I did gymnastics in high school," they say, shrugging off my amazement.

Kiki touches my core and biceps, the muscle groups I should be employing to flip into an inversion. When I continue to fail, they easily demonstrate the steps I should follow. "You'll get it with practice."

I'm sweating from the effort, frustrated by my lack of grace. Maybe I should pay one of the corporate pole fitness studios to teach me tricks with names like "the firefighter" and "the butterfly." Even though those classes are mostly a trend for girls trying to look sexy for their boyfriends, #notastripper. But I don't want my style to be standardized. I want to dance like a stripper, dripping in gold.

★ ★ ★

With a chandelier, gaudy black and white wallpaper, and mandatory bottle service, the closed cabin rooms on either side of the VIP are designed for parties. On six couches facing each other, five girls and I entertain a bachelor party from Texas.

I'm dancing for the bachelor's awkward cousin who doesn't want to be here, but lucky for me, he can't be in the cabin without paying for a girl. Naomie is dancing for the bachelor's best friend who is in beast party mode, chasing shots of whisky with cans of Red Bull that he chugs, then crushes on his forehead. While we were still at the table he ripped his T-shirt in half and was forced to buy a replacement from the club.

Like good little sluts, we offer to switch men after fifteen minutes. Every guy wants to get his hands on something new except the Beast. "I'm keeping Dark Chocolate here all to myself," he says. By the time we're wrapping up the half-hour, he's trying to get Naomie's phone number. "You need to come out with us tonight. We're going to party our freaking faces off! Right boys?" I smirk as I imagine him beating his chest, then literally ripping his face off, leaving a bloody skull with lidless eyes and a skeletal smile. He lifts his shirt and forces our hands over his hard flexed abs.

"What name should I give you in my phone? Black Beauty?"

Naomie pauses, ready to reintroduce herself for the tenth time, but I snap, "Or you could try using her actual name."

"Are you calling me a racist?" he bristles. "Is that what you think I am? I'm not a fucking racist."

Naomie pulls his attention back to her, soothing him by petting his stomach. "There's no problem here, baby. I know you were trying to compliment me."

Later, in the changing room, Naomie and I are sneaking sips from her water bottle filled with what tastes like Smirnoff Ice with extra vodka.

"I'm sorry I made it worse," I stumble. "But he was being such a dick and no one else was saying anything. I didn't want you to have to deal with it on your own."

A strip club is a microcosm of the structural racism of regular society. While society sexualizes and fetishizes Black bodies, it also fears, stereotypes, and oppresses Black people. Anti-Blackness and white supremacy are fundamental to how strip clubs operate and profit. And as a white stripper I benefit from systemic racism just by working in one.

Naomie waves it off. "He was an ignorant loser for sure, but in the future I know what I'm doing. I've got this." Naomie is one of the calmest people I've ever met. Not calm like a lake, more like a summer storm before the first drop of rain.

★★★

It's fifteen minutes past nine o'clock on my first night shift at Paradis. I had to beg Dom to let me stay past the shift change in order to try and claw my way out of low-earning day shifts. Like schools of colourful fish, the girls are broken up by the influx of men, only to regroup in corners or against the walls. People move in currents as they jostle for space in the tightly packed club. It's the first time all day I've felt warm.

I'm grabbing lip gloss from my locker when the nighttime boss whistles at me from the office. "You!" He singles me out from the changing room teeming with girls. "Come here." The manager doesn't bother closing the door before saying, "I want you out right now." My stomach drops—not again. "I don't know who you are, but I wouldn't have hired you."

I don't bother reminding him that he was, in fact, the one who hired me three months ago.

"You're ugly," he says. "I can't have girls like you on my shift. Look—" He uses his fingers to count off the strikes against me. "Your hair looks like you just rolled out of bed, your tattoos are awful, your makeup is gross, and your clothes are cheap. Get some nicer outfits, cover up all your tattoos, get your makeup professionally done, then you come see me and maybe, maybe, I'll let you come back. Until then, I want you gone."

I've already worked six hours, so sure, maybe my curls are tousled, and my black lace outfit is a little plain, but I've been watching tutorials and practising, so I know my feathery eyelashes and high-gloss nude lipstick are on trend, and my foundation, highlighter, and contour combination is blended perfectly to sculpt my features, so I ask, "What exactly is wrong with my makeup?"

"It's disgusting. Get out."

On the crowded bus ride home I wear sunglasses in a futile attempt to hide my tears. I text Luke a synopsis, then send a full account to Gigi.

It's like what happened to us in Niagara except I was alone. Am I so horrible? Why does this keep happening?

Gigi calls right away. "Managers are trash. You know this. They refuse to see the spectrum of what clients actually desire because of their own narrow-minded preferences."

"I know." I wipe my nose with the back of my hand. "It's half the reason strip clubs are dying, because they only care about what shitty old white men want, I know, I know." The bus is an aquarium lit with green and blue fluorescent light. People knock into each other as it surges between stops.

"Girls even warned me that that boss hates tattoos," I say. "I didn't understand because everyone has tattoos, almost every single girl, but I guess mine aren't pretty enough." My tattoos represent a patchwork of interests over time. Some I regret, like the too-stiff pin-up down my calf, but others I would never change: my Fiji mermaid, my cat's skull, my magnolias, and the planets on my knuckles. "I should have worn thigh-high socks to cover the ones on my legs. I should have—"

"Screw that place," Gigi says. "There must be a hundred other clubs in Montreal. You need to find one that is less stuck-up."

At home Luke stands in the doorframe of the washroom while I roughly scrub off cover-up and glitter. My face is red and puffy, but my eyes are a cold periwinkle.

"I'm not bad at my job," I say. "The industry is trying to force me out, but I'm not ready to quit." He hugs me hard, and I let out a long rattling breath. "That sucked so much."

Luke reheats half a baked squash for me. "Maybe we should serve squash at our commitment ceremony." I fill the seed cavity with butter, watch it melt.

"The end of August isn't really squash season yet," I say.

★ ★ ★

I go back to working day shifts, making sure I scurry out exactly at nine so I don't run into the nighttime manager.

"Did he really say all those horrible things to you?" Valentine says. "That hypocritical nasty old man! And you didn't flip out on him? They would have had to drag me out of here after I assaulted him if he'd said that to me. No one gets to talk to us that way. You shouldn't be back here like a kicked puppy. You're young, beautiful, my baby, you deserve so much better." I love her full Botox lips, her permanent pout. "They must be getting rid of girls because it's almost winter, but you're so young."

Her mood drifts into worry about her own position, since she's ten years my senior.

"You're safe," I tell her. "I'm pretty sure it's my tattoos and you don't have any."

Anxiously, she touches where her clip-on extensions attach to her thin hair. "I'm going to go fix my makeup, girl. Thanks for the heads-up."

★ ★ ★

A client grabs my jaw in order to force me to return his stare. "I worship you. I would sacrifice myself for you, m'lady." He heaves dragon's breath across my skin. "What do you want? What is it you desire? Anything you ask of me I will do."

If I wasn't so burnt-out I could be whatever princess-maiden-khaleesi he wanted, but I peel his fingers off my face. "I want you to get your hands off me."

Fantasy ruined, he pays and leaves.

★ ★ ★

"I'm so bored. Tell me about your life." I've video-called Gigi during another infuriatingly slow shift.

"My life is simple and small right now. Mostly I hang out with my mom or babysit my sister's kids, but I like it. What's your life like?"

"Outside of work it's awesome. I got that mentorship I applied for, so I'm writing all the time. I'm so happy we moved here."

"Show me what you're wearing."

I hold out the phone to capture my body in front of the video lottery terminals in the mini casino section. The screens whirl: stacking cherries, exploding diamonds.

"You're killing it today," she compliments.

"I know. Too bad there's no one here to appreciate it. And it's so cold! Did I tell you I got a chest infection the first month because of the air conditioning? It's like they expect us to do jumping jacks to stay warm when there are no clients for hours. All the girls are lined up against the walls playing on their phones."

"I miss stripping so much!" Gigi yells. I love seeing her face on the screen, but I miss her in person. "I'm not kidding, even when it's bad there's still the potential that a lonely rich guy could walk in at any second. Plus, there's no reason for me to look as good as I do here. I'm so extra with my fake hair. I've been going to the gym every day too, but what's the point?"

"You're doing it for yourself, stupid. I promise we'll find somewhere to work in the summer together." Then I ask, "Should I quit this club?"

If I quit Paradis, I worry that, whether I want to or not, I'll quit stripping for good, and be out of the sex industry entirely. Or a term I like even less—"retired."

"Can you afford to quit?" Gigi switches into social worker mode. Behind her, sun streams in through the windows in her new apartment three provinces away.

"I always imagined if I was thinking about quitting it would be because I'd finally figured out how to get rich from stripping."

"Honey, no one's getting rich."

"I know. One of the girls I follow online called stripping a 'working-class profession.' I like that because everyone thinks we have so much money, but I don't have massive savings. I own nothing of value."

"Shut up, you have a beautiful, emotionally rich life."

"True, it's given me that." I sigh. "I started stripping because it seemed like a really simple equation. Under patriarchy women are both sexualized and oppressed. I didn't want to ignore that reality or spend my working hours fighting against it, so I chose stripping as a way to get paid well for playing into the patriarchal fantasy."

"Which makes sense because money is such a huge part of why anyone does any job," Gigi says.

"My time is really important to me and the ability to make high hourly wages and spend less overall time at work is the reason I choose stripping over and over. But for the last year, especially here," I rub the goosebumps on my cold arms, "it doesn't feel worth it. For the first time the cons outweigh the pros."

"Honestly," Gigi says, "I don't know what to tell you. Maybe that our careers are too short to waste time. I know Paradis is supposed to be the best club in your city, but it might not be right for you."

★ ★ ★

The client adjusts himself and grins. "That was the best lap dance I've ever had. You were fantastic."

The routine of it allowed me to be absent. I spent the songs worrying about how I still haven't reached the financial threshold of what would put me on track for a good shift. How I keep catching glares from a couple of beautiful mean girls while trying to avoid Dom. I've been darting between tables, striking out.

"That made my night," the guy continues, counting out what I'm owed and adding a tip of one hundred dollars.

Just like that, my shift transforms.

★ ★ ★

This is my last six hours. I'm quitting Paradis, I text Luke. *I shouldn't have come back after getting kicked off night shifts but I told myself some money is better than no job. It isn't.*

It's dead and I'm freezing, shivering in my robe. It snowed today. Flakes melted on contact, flurries ushering in the slow season.

I love you, he responds.

I hate this place. How dare they cap my earning potential? Use me as filler, then hustle me out as soon as it starts to get busy. They can't tell me my body is undesirable. It's my business. It's mine.

Taking the stage I perform for myself. The metallic floor reflects dim coloured lights as I walk confidently between two poles, upstretched fingers brushing the ceiling, one foot directly in front of the other so that my hips dip and sway. I warm up with my go-to tricks, leg-hook spins and the sideways V. Using the momentum of a spin I lift off, pull and swing my feet to the sky, hook my knee around the pole above me. This time I go further, straightening both legs parallel to the ceiling. I'm doing it. The gravity of my body settles in my shoulders, a stable burn. Pointed toes, glitter pink heels, legs taut and extended. Hold still, don't grip too hard, let yourself spin. Close your eyes to ward off dizziness. Hair brushes then shoulders touch the ground, and I roll down slowly. Each vertebra connecting. I sit up, new-trick proud.

CHAPTER 14:
TWO HEARTS

THE EAST COAST

I sit on one of the benches facing an old apple tree in the yard of my parents' farm. Mom and I have spiralled white tulle from the trunk out along an arch-like branch, leaving trails of fabric hanging that will frame Luke and me tomorrow, when we say our vows and light a candle inside an ornate white lantern, to symbolize spirit, family, and commitment.

Mom and I have been having weekly planning calls for the past ten months to discuss details of the do-it-ourselves commitment ceremony, down to what flower seeds she should order to grow for the bouquets. She has been texting me pictures of tablecloths amassed from bargain stores, wineglasses and plates borrowed from neighbours, and she was with me when I found the perfect dress. Though the plunging neckline and black fabric weren't what she would have picked, she was supportive.

Dad built benches and repainted his antique tractor, which now gleams a proud red. Both my parents spent the summer landscaping the farm, and everything, even the green grass beneath my bare feet, is vibrant.

Luke and I arrived a week ago to help with final preparations. Family and friends have started arriving, most from far away. The decorations are in place, flowers picked, and a table set to honour our ancestors with fresh fruit, candles, and pictures. Beauty seems to be flowing from everything into everything else.

Luke sits beside me. "You look overwhelmed."

"Everything is so perfect, better than I could have hoped." The apple tree has a hollow split in the trunk that twists the living branches in opposite directions. It's producing tiny fruit, hard and sour, hidden under the leaves. "But I feel like I don't deserve happiness because of how hard the last six months have been between us."

I'm referring to my springtime emotional breakdown when Luke began seeing someone new, someone he said he had real feelings for. All of my deepest relationship fears and repressed sexual trauma came for me all at once. It spiralled into an existential crisis where I could no longer understand the meaning of love.

The truth was, I needed therapy. I needed to look at my scattered values, pick up the pieces I was choosing to believe in, and reassemble myself. Slowly, I let go of the need to understand and conquer love and focused on feeling and expressing it.

Luke puts his arm around me. "Our good times have vastly outweighed the bad, and the rest of our lives will reinforce that." A family man at heart, he is in his element entertaining and introducing our people to each other, basking in close relationships. He twirls a glass of white wine; through it, the barn and the sheep grazing in the field appear upside down and golden.

I've been into voicing affirmations lately. "We will grow and change, and that is healthy and good. We are committing to share a horizon."

"I can't wait to read you my vows," Luke says.

"Me too. Pretty sure I'm going to sob the whole time."

A breeze is cooling the summer heat. Someone has made a campfire and smoke blows through columns of tulle.

Mom's dog's ears perk up and he sprints, barking, toward the driveway. A pack of dogs follow, including Mira, nimble despite her years. The last guests arrive, a little late and very fashionable. I hold the train of my white cotton dress above the freshly mown lawn and greet my friends.

Bailey and Gigi tumble out of a rental car, fully coiffed, and we envelop each other in a shrieky, tear-filled three-way embrace. A reunion overshadowed by the presence of a nascent fourth person.

"Hello!" I crouch, unsure how to relate to Gigi's body at six months into her first pregnancy. "So excited to meet you," I say and touch the fabric of her tight, short dress stretched over taut skin.

"Biiitch, you're getting married." Bailey rocks me when I stand. "Right, we're not supposed to say 'married,' so 'committed' or whatever. You're still a bride to us." She points to the knee-high socks they're both wearing which, in pink script, read *Team Bride*.

"You look beautiful, girl," Gigi says.

Bailey touches my hair. "Is she not a vision? An angel?"

"Wait 'til you see my ceremony dress, and Mom made me a flower crown. She watched tutorials and made it out of roses and baby's breath. I'm going to look like a fucking witch priestess, just wait." This is the first time the three of us have been together in over a year. "With both of you here, it's really real."

They teeter in impractical heels as we approach the circle gathered for the day-before barbecue. I have a moment of worry about how my friends will be received, but Bailey's and Gigi's extra-high-femmeness pays tribute to a deep part of me and to a true expression of themselves. They honour us with their presence. I cry as they are warmly welcomed.

As the sun sets, the solar fairy lights on porches and trees flicker on. A case of wine is carried up from the cellar where two fridges are packed with ham, homemade salads, and cheesecakes for tomorrow's big meal at a community hall in the village nearby. Guests change into jeans, cover themselves in bug spray, and settle in around the fire.

My little brother, an academic currently running around like a con-cierge topping up aunties' drinks, tells my friends about his plans for his toast tomorrow. He is going to say, "My sister is a lion. I guess this makes Luke something of a lion tamer."

Bailey and Gigi stifle yawns. They are drained after multiple flights and a two-hour drive, all for a stay shorter than forty-eight hours.

"We need our beauty sleep," Bailey says, and invites me to join them at their hotel.

Gigi swipes the room key. "It's weird to check into a hotel and not be doing a single sketchy thing."

"I still feel guilty," Bailey says.

It's a standard three-star chain room: beige walls, outdated appli-ances, comfy beds. The August moon shines a stunning rose gold over the parking lot next door. Tomorrow's full moon is the reason Luke and I chose this date, and I'm pleased our most exalted guest has shown up so brilliantly.

"Your tits are huge," Bailey remarks as Gigi undresses and sprawls on the bed.

"I know." Gigi dons a plastic *Wife* tiara they bought for me. "The baby stole my curls. Look how straight my hair is."

"Are you nervous?" Bailey asks me. "Like are we going to have to do a whole runaway-bride thing where your besties smuggle you out of the province? No offence to Luke—I love the guy—but I'll do it if you ask."

I've started filing my nails into points, readying them for a faded cherry-blossom polish. "I'm nervous my mom is going to be so busy she won't enjoy herself, or that it will rain, but in terms of Luke, I'm one hundred percent sure." Then I say, "What if he bails on me, though?" I feel the smallest pinch of exquisite heartbreak. Would I move back to Southern Ontario? Start working at the Royal again? It feels impossibly distant yet dangerously close. "I don't know what I'd do."

"That's what love is about, isn't it?" Gigi says. "Loving despite how much you could get hurt?"

Bailey digs through her overpacked bags. "Also, Luke loves you forever forever." Finding makeup remover wipes she says, "Michelle is getting married and Gigi's freaking pregnant and I feel like a teenager again except I'm too old to have so little direction. Not to be a downer, but seriously, what is the point of being alive?"

"Okay, first of all," Gigi counters, "you have a job that you love."

"Yeah, I'm basically a veterinarian," Bailey says sarcastically.

"But you're taking science credits so you can go to vet tech school," I say. "It seems like a good fit." I picture her at the animal shelter, being dragged around by unruly dogs and talking to lonely caged cats. "Doing something new is hard work." I touch my sternum. "There were times this spring when I thought I was literally going to die from not being able to regulate grief, rage, and fear."

"Thank God for therapy," Gigi says.

"Amen," says Bailey. "No wonder you haven't been able to do sex work," she says to me.

I blow on my wet nails, careful not to smudge them. It's a good thing Luke and I planned a low-budget ceremony because with all my savings spent, I've been relying on him. Although he insists he's happy to finance our lives until I figure out how I'm going to earn money, I am deeply uncomfortable with my loss of financial independence. But when I try to pump myself up, even to try one shift at a random club, I'm paralyzed by fear that I'll be unable to maintain healthy boundaries with clients, that I'll be hurt, or that I'll crumble under criticism and stress. Worse is the fear that I wouldn't be able to push down the rage that interacting with most men produces in me these days.

"Sometimes I panic when I think about how I might not be able to go back to sex work," I tell my friends. "It's given me so much and I'm terrified it's over."

"Working through your own trauma is a Pandora's box," Bailey says. "It's gonna take time."

"It's taking forever," I say. "And I miss some aspects of the work so much."

"I miss the money," says Gigi, rubbing her belly. It's hard not to stare at the way her body is changing, prioritizing. "I'm worried my body won't bounce back after I give birth and I'll need to get surgeries to keep working. I don't want it to be done, either. I love the ability it gives me to live life on my own terms, and I love the upkeep, all the high-femme things it lets me justify. Quitting sex work means giving up on a certain kind of desirability, but I trust the universe. If it's over, it's over."

"Well, mama," Bailey says, "whether you want to or not, that baby's gonna force you to overhaul your life."

"Really? I'm having a baby? And you think that will be difficult on my own?" Gigi throws a pillow in Bailey's direction, then reaches for a cream to prevent stretch marks.

Bailey jumps up. "Let baby daddy do that." She snuggles in behind Gigi on the bed, reaching around to rub cream on her belly.

"And you," I say to Bailey. "You've been escorting sober? You're so tough, I can't even imagine. What's it like?"

"Well, in June I got my one-year chip." Gigi and I clap. "Working sober isn't that bad. I mean, it's hard as fuck but only slightly harder than working high."

"Oh!" Gigi flinches. "He kicked."

"I felt it." Bailey is amazed.

"You want to feel?" Gigi asks.

I join them, Gigi in the middle. My chin rests on her shoulder, and she smells like country rose. She presses my hand to her belly. It's warm and dense.

Bailey turns off the light and moonlight fills the room. We hold still, as if to convince the baby to break the silence with movement.

"It's hard to believe there will be a time in the future when I won't have two hearts beating inside me," Gigi says.

Bailey yawns. "Change, man, it's big."

"Can you feel him?" Gigi asks.

I shake my head but remain alert and present. Ready to feel whatever comes next.

CHAPTER 15: SLOW SEASON

SALLY'S
MONTREAL, QUEBEC

In the winter following the commitment ceremony I tried to go back to stripping, but it felt like I'd been knocked off my stride and the game had changed without me. Or maybe I'd changed. Either way, I was hesitant to commit to another club, so I made trips outside Montreal, a week at Harlow's in Quebec City, another at Babylon in the suburbs of Ottawa.

I hated those trips. From the nice-but-tough posturing I had to do with co-workers to meeting new bosses and learning their stupid rules. To approaching tables only to be jerked around and told:

"It will get busy later."

"You look tired."

"You'd be prettier if you smiled more."

I began to feel dread when a client agreed to a VIP dance and anger when he declined.

I borrowed tactics from poisonous butterflies by loading my chest with body glitter and spraying perfume directly on my nipples. I hoped clients would refrain from touching and licking my delicate scales, destroying my wings. I combined this with a wicked bad mood. One so sharp-tongued and rude that I was becoming the angry stripper who treats clients like the scum of the earth.

My mood was made worse by physical pain. Despite warning clients that they needed to be soft with my tits, after a few VIP dances my breasts would begin to swell. By the end of the night they would throb, nipples puffed up and raw. Back at the hotel after my shift, droplets from the shower, even the friction of bedsheets, caused pain. Nothing could protect me from the fact that, at its core, stripping is about consenting to being touched. Every shift feels like throwing my body to wolves.

I kept fighting my way through short work trips until I found Sally's in downtown Montreal. I applied because I heard that Sally's was chill and hired alternative-looking dancers. I started working there in February, one of the slowest months of the year, but the atmosphere was welcoming. My co-workers had a variety of ages, body shapes, sizes, and styles. Maybe the club's management trusted us to know how to be sexy in our own bodies, or they just didn't care enough to try to enforce unattainable beauty standards. Either way, I was able to work three shifts a week without wanting to burn the place down.

On any given night, girls fought the cold snaking through the drafty club by wearing cozy sweaters with our G-strings and heels, our naked legs goosebumped. One regular who called himself the stripper whisperer offered girls dessert instead of drinks or dances. I would drop in on him for bites of chocolate cheesecake and dip out as soon as he began telling me how I could do my job better.

When I'd get too cold or bored of sitting, I would wobble on tiles laid like cobblestones down the back hallway to the changing room, where a space heater churned out hot, dry air. Sounds from the adjoining kitchen, clanging pots, cutlery being sorted, the whoosh of an industrial dishwasher, mixed with the ever-present club tracks. Warming up beside the heater, girls gossiped and shared candy from the depanneur, sweet peaches and sour cherries.

Sally's required we commit to a weekly schedule of at least three nights a week, so in order to work Friday and Saturday, dancers also had to take the hit of a slow night, which during the winter was any other weeknight. There were many nights when I made nothing, or less than nothing because I still had to pay house fees and cabs.

A young dancer named Pepper didn't understand why I'd get so pissed off during the dead nights. "Most of the time it evens out over the course of the week," she said.

I picked at a tear in the couch, splitting the seam. "But it doesn't, not like it used to. We're just getting used to making less. The standard price of a lap dance has been twenty dollars since I started nearly ten years ago, and it's been that way forever. There's never been any adjustment for inflation or the cost of living. And now clubs are forcing us to charge even less per dance." I bitterly recalled the Royal's half-price nights and Sally's own policy of fifteen dollars per song.

Pepper was unfazed. She called herself a luxury companion and had social media profiles designed to attract sugar daddies. When it was dead she worked her phone, negotiating trips and shopping dates.

★ ★ ★

Shorty is complaining about her hip implants. "I can't sleep on my side anymore," she says. "They're like concrete."

She lets me touch one of the dramatic asymmetrical bulges on her thighs. Her skin, stretched over the hard curved object, is cold.

"I'm flying to LA to get them removed in June." She cups her equally extra-large breasts and she says, "But my tits turned out fine. I'm never getting rid of them."

★ ★ ★

I introduce myself and the guy mishears me. "Michael? Pleased to meet you."

"It's Michelle, but it's nice that you'd be fine if I had a boy's name."

"Things are changing these days," he says. "People have all sorts of names and genders. It doesn't bother me. I just wanted to get your name right."

★ ★ ★

Sally's mainstage has a pole so close to the edge of the platform that dancers have to tread carefully. Since the main thoroughfare and tables are packed so close, clients and waitresses are routinely hit during a dancer's spin. A mirror along the back of the stage is held together by duct tape that, according to a client, has been there for ten years. Two giant speakers on either side and a low ceiling enclose the stage, creating a protective cave.

Frantic from touching and being touched, flirting, cajoling, and grinding, I find being called onstage gives me fifteen minutes to myself. The bass drops on the dark Lithuanian house music I've chosen, buzzing in my rib cage. I dance, movement following movement, and I am beautiful. My seductive flux, now effortless.

★ ★ ★

I like Sally's top-floor VIP. It is sultry and spacious. Large cabins, red velvet or black leather couches, a private bar, and a stage. In winter, only this main VIP section is open, like a warm heart beating inside a chest. But as the club gets busier in April, they open an overflow VIP along the exterior walls of the building where I can see the potential of summer, the influx of tourist cash building up to the climactic Grand Prix weekend. But I can't get excited, even though I'm high.

Taking painkillers at work has been mandatory for a long time. In fact, I take opiates three days a week, whether I work or not, in a notably stable pattern of use. But at work, it no longer feels like a pick-me-up that adds sparkle and fun to the job. It is a baseline necessity. I have to get high to convince myself to take even the first step of getting ready. Alone in my bathroom before a shift, I drink coffee and take the first pill while I layer on makeup. Even makeup, which used to feel gender affirming, now feels like I'm trying to conceal an aging, less feminine face I barely recognize. At least I can style my hair into voluptuous blond curls, wrap myself in their youthfulness and shine. But on shift the drugs never feel strong enough. No matter how high I get, nothing feels numb.

The overflow VIP could be remodelled into something modern and classy. Instead, it contains broken furniture, a scrapped bar, buckets to catch ceiling leaks, and decades of phased-out props: a plastic palm, a djembe, and a sixties-style pod chair. I feel like I'm leading my client through an abandoned house in order to get to creepy unlit stalls with chains of hippie beads for curtains. I sit him on a hard plastic folding chair, radiant heaters glowing menacingly above, like robot overlords.

Before I start dancing I joke, "This is the last thing you're going to remember until tomorrow when you wake up in an ice-filled bathtub missing a kidney."

★ ★ ★

I take a pretty girl and her douchebag boyfriend to the main VIP. On the way upstairs, she giggles and says, "He can be a bit rough, just so you know."

Hardening myself, I reply, "Not with me he won't be."

I sit them on a couch in the cabin whose walls are black particle-boards, pull the sheer red curtain closed, and push an ugly lips-shaped ottoman out of my way. I am clearing space on an end table littered with used shot glasses so that I can put my purse down, when, without warning, the boyfriend slaps my ass really hard.

"Don't fucking do that again," I say. No nice face. No, haha, sweet-heart, please don't.

The boyfriend grins, excited, perhaps turned on, that his drunken aggression is being met with anger. The girlfriend intervenes. "Don't worry, I won't let him."

The boyfriend pulls out a twenty and throws it at me. "Dance, bitch."

I begin moving cautiously. The girlfriend touches my tits lightly, but when he tries to touch me, she catches his hands, nervous.

"Lucky I don't bite you," he tells me.

"He's kidding. He gets like this sometimes," the girlfriend says.

"I hope you don't let him bite *you*," I tell her. I'm smiling but not joking.

"Oh, it doesn't bother me. I know he doesn't mean it."

I tell him, "If you bite me, I will punch you in the face."

He lunges forward, grips my ass and crushes, bruises. Pain stops my breath. I struggle to get away, but he holds me tighter, squeezing me to his chest. I can't breathe; I am afraid.

He lets go, leans back, puts his arms casually behind his head. I brace myself against the wall to regain my footing. I have choices: I could calmly step out of the cabin and go get the bouncer. But instead, I slap him hard across the face. He bolts up, knocking me back but not down.

"Fucking cunt!" he bellows.

The girlfriend tries to hold his biceps, but he knocks her off. She hits the couch and falls onto the ground.

My heart is racing. "Give me my money and get the fuck out." I want him to push me so that I can crush his dick with my knee or ram my pointy acrylic nails into his eyes.

He rips open the curtain and stumbles into the hall, where he rages about me to the bouncer. I'm a bitch, a liar, a cunt who's trying to rip him off. The bouncer grabs his arm and twists. "I've had too many girls complain about you tonight, you're gone."

The girlfriend gives me money from her pretty pink wallet. "I'm so sorry, he's never like this."

I taste anger like vomit in my throat. "Do you want me to call you a cab? Do you have anywhere else you can go other than with him?"

Without meeting my eyes, she says, "He would never do that to me."

★ ★ ★

Girls put on sweatpants and comfy fluffy boots, talk about getting something to eat. One wants to go across the street for late-night falafel; another is ordering takeout to her apartment.

"I feel sick," I say. My night included an energy drink, vodka, tequila, a shot of Crown Royal, and a slice of cheesecake. Usually, I'll have two vodka sodas, then switch to bubbly water, but tonight was messy. Like the old days, I drank whatever was offered.

"I eat sleep," says another girl, poetic in her fatigue.

I look around the changing room craving a familiar face. I miss Nadia. She's levelled up, flying into the States to work at some of the biggest and best clubs. And I miss Violet. She's so private, I'm not sure if she strips anymore. I always find it more surprising when dancers actually quit.

★ ★ ★

"I just want to make it until after Labour Day weekend," I tell Helena, my therapist, one rainy day in early April. Sometimes it's hard to meet her eyes, so I watch the maple outside her Westmount window. It has finally grown leaves after a slow, cold start to spring.

"But why?" Helena asks. "What's the significance of Labour Day?"

"Because it will mean I made it through the summer. I've been working all these dead nights, trying to hold on until it's good again. I just want one more busy season where it's easy money so I can save up enough ..."

"Enough for what?" Helena looks like a soft biker chick: black eyeliner, black hair. She holds a yellow pad and pen but rarely writes things down.

I avoid the question. "When I burn out of social work type jobs, the ones I've been doing on and off, everyone assumes I'll find another job in the same field. But because I'm a sex worker people assume I want to quit forever. It gets tied up with virtue, like a twelve-step program where I'm supposed to stay clean. And it complicates the struggles I have with working right now because it *is* hard, but every job can be hard."

"And that perspective is frustrating to you because you want people to recognize that sex work is work," Helena says.

"Yes." I twist a damp tissue and briefly wonder why I care so much what people think of me.

"I just feel like if I actually forced myself to take enough time off, maybe I could enjoy stripping again. Or in the future maybe I could find a job in the industry that better matches my skills and energy levels. I know some people quit entirely, move on to different things but that feels like losing my identity."

"There's a lot of grief there," Helena points out. "Plus, you'd be losing access to youth, a way of living, financial comfort and stability." She reiterates the things I've loved about stripping, which we've been over many times. "Also freedom and the ability to make your own schedule."

I worry she is getting bored of hearing me talk in circles.

"Those are all still true. That's why I let the burnout get so bad because there's so much I still love about it."

"I've seen you work really hard on yourself during this last year. I know you want to figure this all out," Helena says. "But maybe you need to give yourself the time and space to grow and integrate changes."

It feels like I'm being asked to abandon Michelle, after all she's given me.

I must look particularly moody. Helena softly shifts the focus. "How is your physical pain?"

"Not good." I look down at my traitorous chest. Since I started working regularly again at Sally's I'd been having waves of symptoms. My breasts are swollen, nipples doubled in size and pinky red, outlined by purple bruises. "I got hormone test results and an ultrasound back and they're all clear, so it has to be psychosomatic. It obviously gets triggered by work," I say. "And it doesn't calm down when I'm at home. I wake up in the middle of the night in stabbing pain and even wearing a bra makes me want to puke."

Helena purses her lips, as if there is really nothing else to say.

★ ★ ★

We close in five minutes, and even though I'm exhausted, I agree to take a drunk guy who is finally ready to pay for a last-minute dance. The stairway walls to the VIP are mirror-panelled, one cracked like a spider's web. The steps are marble, or made to look that way, very dangerous to fall down. While he watches my ass, I rely on the railing.

"Is Michelle your real name?"

"Yes."

Before he has settled into the booth, the waiter arrives to demand the cabin fee and remind him it's last call. The client has a full beer, but the waiter pushes him. "Aren't you going to buy a drink for the lady?"

"Fine," says the client, searching through his wallet for cash to cover the extra fees.

I start to dance. "How are you doing?"

"Fantastic," he says. "Me and the boys are here from Calgary." Or maybe he says Toronto or Boston, New York or Vancouver.

Too tired to do a seductive reveal, I take my tits out right away. "Be gentle," I warn.

It is Pepper's set downstairs—I know every beat and lyric by heart, the way other girls must now know mine.

"I like this song," I say. It gives me a boost of energy to shake my ass, then drop onto his lap. He touches my stomach, my long hair, fondles my tits, and even though he doesn't grab hard, it still makes me cringe. I stand to get away, turn to face him. I dip between his legs, then come up and climb onto his lap, knees digging into his hips, my shins across his thighs, bare skin on denim. Leaning my chest into his face, I slap his cheeks with my tits. He grins, hands up in surrender.

The song ends and I automatically ask if he wants another. We're already up here, I can grind through another three minutes.

"No thanks, darling. Gotta get back to the boys."

Relieved, I take his money, hug him goodbye. As I'm tucking my tits back into my bra the waiter arrives to deliver my sparkling water.

"Good night, Michelle?"

"Yeah, it was busy," I say. "But I'm ready to go home."

★ ★ ★

It's near midnight on May 1 and I'm staring into the bathroom mirror with a pair of scissors in my hand. My blond hair, long enough to reach to the centre of my back, is pulled into a tight ponytail at the top of my head. My face looks tired, or maybe I just look my age.

Luke wakes up and shuffles into the brightly lit bathroom. "What are you doing?" he asks.

We had had a fight earlier. After I texted my boss saying I needed the night off "for health reasons," and he didn't reply, Luke sat with me on the couch.

"He's going to fire me for calling in sick last minute. Or make me pay a huge fee. Maybe I can't go back there," I cried. "Why can't I make myself go?"

"You should take some time off," Luke suggested.

"I just did that. I've barely started again."

"I could help you find a different job."

"No."

"Just for a while, until your pain goes away and you actually want to go back."

"No! You don't get it. You'll never understand what stripping means to me."

Luke went into our bedroom and though he was careful not to slam the door, I knew he needed space. I stayed in the living room with my thoughts spinning and repeating, until they stopped.

"I'm going to shave my head," I say now to Luke's reflection in the mirror.

After a few hours apart, he's no longer upset. "Are you sure you don't want to wait until the morning, maybe sleep on it?" He strokes my ponytail affectionately.

Looking into my mirrored eyes, I say, "I keep crying over not wanting to lose this part of myself. The young, sexy, risk-taking, money-making persona. I don't want to let her go. But the thing is she's already gone. It's already been over. I need my outside to reflect my inside." My toes are at the edge of a cliff and I am peering down into a dark river.

"Even if I never go back to another strip club, I don't have any regrets."

Luke hugs me. "Do you want help?" His skin is extra warm from sleep.

"I need to do it on my own."

"You're going to look beautiful bald. Wake me up when you're ready to come to bed so I can see the new you."

I shut myself into the bathroom and light a white candle. Offer a silent prayer to ancient goddesses of sex work, and to all the sex worker ancestors who have come before me. *Please guide me.*

I prop my phone up on the sink and cue a nostalgic playlist from when I first started stripping. In "The Zone," Drake calls pole dancers artists—it used to make me feel singular, powerful, and beautiful.

I hold my ponytail just above the elastic. *I love my hair*, I think as I use dull kitchen scissors to sever the strands. It is so dense it's difficult to cut. But soon, jagged layers fall around my face and I hold my detached ponytail in my hand. Ten years to grow it, ten seconds to cut it off. Feeling faint, I steady myself against the porcelain sink. I plug in Luke's clippers with shaking hands, afraid to lose my nerve.

The shaver vibrates, metal warm and electric loud as I mow back and forth across my skull. I've never seen the skin on top of my head before. As layers of hair fall, I'm left with a pale scalp and a centimetre of dark roots. I run my hands over the fresh cut, a totally new touch.

Unceremoniously, I place the ponytail in the bathroom trash. I keep a small twist to give to a river, or burn in a fire, or bury beside a tree.

I sweep up the clippings, rinse little hairs from the sink, make everything clean before stepping into a hot shower. The bathroom window, opened a crack, offers a cool breeze. I picture myself surfacing after a deep dive, body shocked and accomplished.

Shampooing my scalp, I am fascinated by the coarse, prickly short hairs and by the shape of my skull. Water carries the remnants down the drain.

We didn't make it to Labour Day, Michelle says.

I'm sorry, I tell her. And I am sorry. The grief that had hardened like amber in my throat is melting. Like honey, it flows through me.

It's okay. We will figure it out.

Out of the shower, I look at myself squarely. Eyes puffy from crying, the word "femme" tattooed on my collarbone. A shocking absence of hair, but I recognize myself. It's my face with nothing to hide behind.

ACKNOWLEDGMENTS

Merrily Weisbord, my mentor and first editor, thank you for choosing my work through the Quebec Writers' Federation mentorship program. You gave me the skills and confidence to develop my voice. Your generosity of time and spirit have been a true gift.

Thank you to the team at Arsenal Pulp Press: Brian Lam, Cynara Geissler, and Jaiden Dembo. Arsenal was my first choice of publisher—thank you for believing in me as an emerging author.

To my wonderful editor, Shirarose Wilensky, your work has made this book so much better.

To all the creative writing teachers I've had over the years, especially Shashi Bhat and Amber Dawn, thank you for teaching me to love reading and how to write.

Thank you to my friends who were kind enough to let me chronicle our adventures. It gives me so much joy that you are out there living your best lives. You are angels.

Luke, my heart. Thank you for being a good man. Our love means the world to me.

Thank you to my parents, who always encouraged me to make art. I'm sorry I chose memoir. And to my chosen family and friends, your support has made me believe in myself—thank you.

★ ★ ★

I have a lot of fear in publishing this book that I'll be asked to make broad or definitive statements about sex work or to speak on behalf of others. As a slim, white, able-bodied stripper, I have many privileges that other sex workers do not have access to. My story can't stand in for anyone else's experience or be generalized. It is so important to listen to sex workers as individuals and to uplift voices more marginalized than my own.

I wish I had been more involved in sex work activism while I was working in the clubs. Thank you so much to the sex workers who run organizations like these that support sex workers. You can look up the following organizations to learn more about sex work in Canada:

- Advocacy Normalizing Sex Work through Education and Resources Society (ANSWERS)
- Butterfly: Asian and Migrant Sex Worker Support Network
- Canadian Alliance for Sex Work Law Reform
- Maggie's Toronto Sex Workers Action Project
- Migrant Sex Workers Project
- PACE Society
- Peers Victoria Resources Society
- Prostitutes Involved, Empowered, Cogent Edmonton (PIECE)
- Prostitutes of Ottawa-Gatineau, Work, Educate and Resist (POWER)
- Safe Harbour Outreach Project (SHOP)
- Sex Professionals of Canada (SPOC)
- Sex Workers of Winnipeg Action Coalition (SWWAC)
- Sex Workers United against Violence
- Sex Workers' Action Network of Waterloo Region (SWAN Waterloo)

▸ Sex Workers' Action Program Hamilton
▸ Stella Montreal
▸ SWAN Vancouver

Thank you to the sex work ancestors, for your bravery, tenacity, and heart. In the "world's oldest profession" so many have come before me. Blessings to the ones who come after.

I am not a cheerleader, a spokesperson, or a politician. I am not encouraging anybody to do sex work, and I'm not saying anybody should quit. Sex work is, and will continue to be, work, and because of that it's always going to be a complex subject.

Three years have passed since the ending of this story, and whether I go back to stripping or move on to different things, the work taught me so much about myself and the world, and I will always be grateful for it.

CID V BRUNET spent their twenties stripping in clubs across Canada. They received a degree in creative writing from Douglas College and participated in the Quebec Writers' Federation mentorship program. They currently live in Montreal.

IG: cidvbrunetwrites
Twitter: cidbrunetwrites